HANNAH M

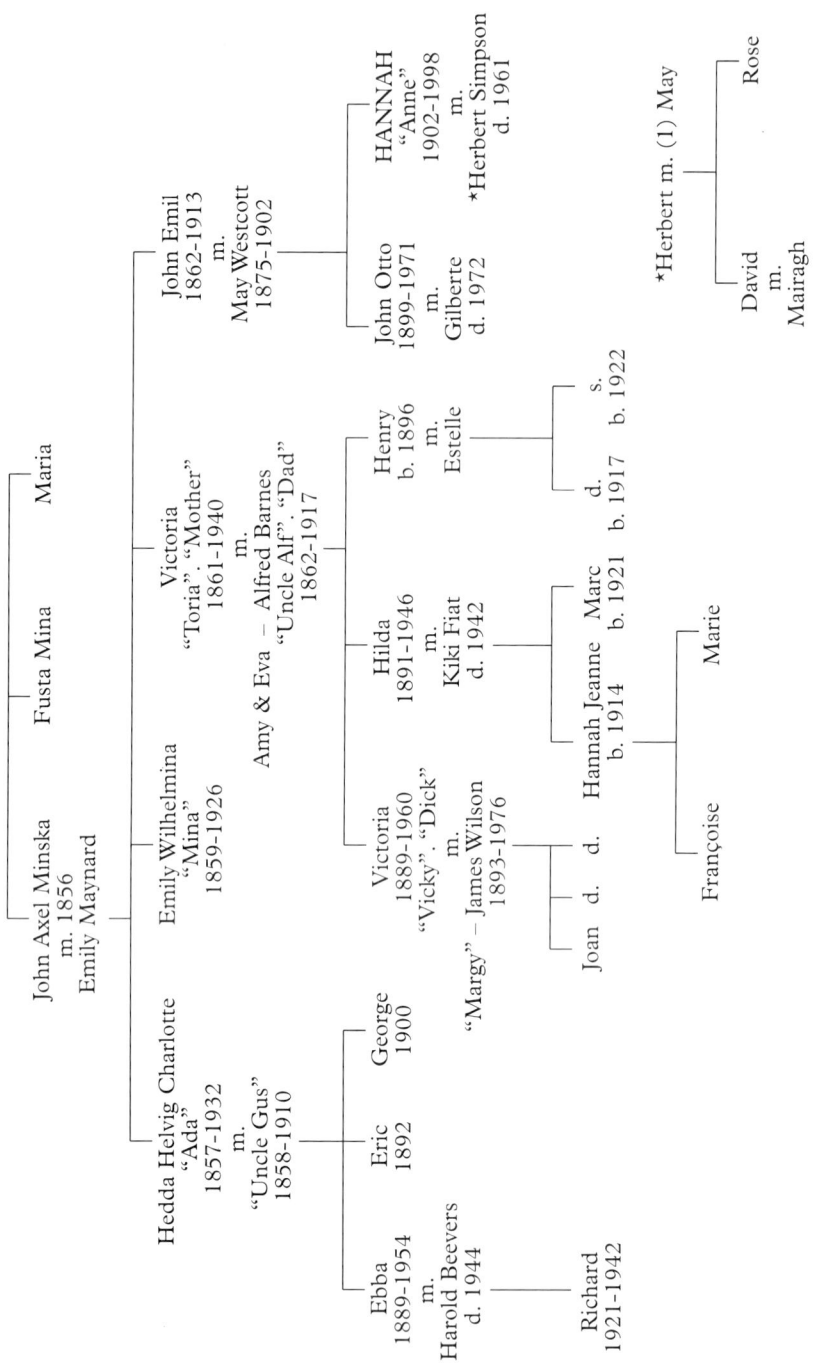

John Axel Minska
m. 1856
Emily Maynard

Hedda Helvig Charlotte
"Ada"
1857-1932
m.
"Uncle Gus"
1858-1910

Fusta Mina

Maria

Emily Wilhelmina
"Mina"
1859-1926

Victoria
"Toria", "Mother"
1861-1940
m.
Alfred Barnes
"Uncle Alf", "Dad"
1862-1917

Amy & Eva

John Emil
1862-1913
m.
May Westcott
1875-1902

HANNAH
"Anne"
1902-1998
m.
*Herbert Simpson
d. 1961

John Otto
1899-1971
m.
Gilberte
d. 1972

Ebba
1889-1954
m.
Harold Beevers
d. 1944

Eric
1892

George
1900

Richard
1921-1942

Victoria
1889-1960
"Vicky", "Dick"
m.
"Margy" – James Wilson
1893-1976

Joan d.   d.

Hilda
1891-1946
m.
Kiki Fiat
d. 1942

Hannah
b. 1914

Jeanne

Françoise

Marie

Marc
b. 1921

Henry
b. 1896
m.
Estelle

d.   b. 1917

s.
b. 1922

*Herbert m. (1) May

David
m.
Mairagh

Rose

HANNAH MINSKA

Adoption, Challenge and Triumph
1902-1998

by

Eleanor Mennim

William Sessions Limited
York, England

ISBN 1 85072 225 0

Printed in 11 on 12 point Plantin Typeface
by Sessions of York
The Ebor Press
York, England

Contents

Preface

THE VICTORIAN FAMILY was normally large. The reasons were many, but not least was a need to assume that some of the babies would die in childhood so the final tally could be expected to be considerably reduced. Some died (with their mother) at birth, some of infection in their first years, others of infectious disease such as scarlet fever or diphtheria before they reached adulthood. In the poorer classes the childhood death rate could reach as much as 50% or more of the babies born, but even in the middle and upper classes where over-crowding and poor general hygiene were not factors, these recurrent tragedies occurred. Child-bearing in a family often went on for twenty years, perhaps from successive wives when the first one succumbed, the elder daughters being brought up to look after their younger brothers and sisters. Later on most of these girls hoped to marry and have children of their own, but any daughter who was less eligible by reason of plain looks, unfortunate features such as a protruding nose or excessive height, was assumed to have her chances of marriage reduced. This daughter was ear-marked from her early teens to be the one who would stay at home as a companion to her mother. Sometimes this occurred naturally in that she received no offers for her hand, but often there was a conscious assumption by her parents that it was her mission in life to look after them in their latter years. There being few careers open to a woman, there was little to entice a girl away from this path, if, as usually was the case, she had no means of her own. She could earn her living at the time-honoured occupations of governess or companion, even nursing, but frequently this was only a way of jumping from the frying pan into the fire, and whilst offering some degree of pecuniary independence, often gave little stability. To live at home permanently not seldom had more attractions, though the common difficulty of parents, particularly of daughters, to realise that their offspring had left childhood behind and was at least able to think for herself, resulted in unmarried girls remaining in perpetual adolescence and indecision, deferring always to Mama or Papa. At length those worthies passed away, leaving their daughter without their support, when she would either blossom into busy adulthood to make up for lost opportunities, being for the first time in control of her own affairs and income, or subside into neurotic and gloomy spinsterhood within an increasingly restricted world.

The onset of the First World War immediately altered this outlook by the sheer necessity for a vast work-force to run not only the normal domestic business world, but to take part in occupations essential to the fighting such as munition production. Girls very soon took the place of men in positions they had virtually never held before, in banks, offices, hospitals, canteens, even railways and buses. Those who did not apply for full-time jobs engaged in voluntary work in one capacity or another. Very few took no part at all in any war-work, paid or otherwise.

Once the war was over, the habit of women going out to work remained to a large extent, particularly with unmarried women, and the idea took root that middle-class girls should have careers. This was the feminine equivalent of 'give a lad a trade', and every wise middle-class father felt that although it might not be necessary financially for a girl to have a training, yet it was an insurance against the day when she might need to be able to earn her living. Out of this grew the idea that 'even a girl' required a career for the pure interest of it and to make use of whatever potential she had been born with, though there were still in the nineteen-thirties people who asked what the point was of her 'passing all those exams' if she was 'only' going to get married.

The Second World War put the final nail in the coffin of objections to women's careers. In this war girls were 'reserved' from joining the forces or industry if they were at a training college or university because it was recognised that they were more useful trained than otherwise. After that they were obliged to enter an appropriate occupation whether in the forces or the civilian sphere. When the war ended it was now normal practice for all girls to have a job, and for the majority of middle-class and a large proportion of 'working class' girls to undergo some sort of training on leaving school. Except in the most lowly families (and even there sometimes) there arose a blur between the different strata of society, and after only two decades, a large number of young women were far better educated than their parents, and had higher expectations financially and career-wise than their mothers and fathers.

This is the tale of one exception to the trend, and how events coloured the outcome for a middle-class woman born when Edward VII was newly on the throne, and only sixteen when the first war ended. With every expectation of a career and marriage, she had to eschew these and to revert to the Victorian view of a daughter's obligations. The metamorphosis of women's suffrage passed her by until the second war broke her bonds.

CHAPTER I

1902

"WHERE'S MY GOO-GOO?" came the warm and familiar voice across the hall, followed immediately by the owner's head round the morning-room door. A young head, with its straight brown hair tied back over the crown and held by a ribbon in the nape of her neck, the side hair hanging loosely almost to her shoulders in the fashion of the time. Her face was open and kind, concerned, and rosy; the brown eyes alert and wide; the mouth turned up at the corners, always ready to break into a laugh; the teeth large and white and slightly protruding. It was a face full of enthusiasm and character; not a lazy or slovenly one. Moreover it belonged to my dearest friend whom I counted as mother, and to whom I went for all my needs, to be washed and clothed and cuddled; to whom I hurried when I fell and hurt my knees – a frequent occurrence – or pinched my fingers in a closing door. It belonged to 'Dick', so named by me and now by the rest of the family, because I did not want to say her full name, Victoria, and could not pronounce her nickname which was Vicky.

"Hallo!" said the face, "Are you coming for walkies now?", and then the rest of Dick appeared round the door, and as she did so, I ran to her, and she spread her arms wide to catch me, and threw me into the air, and then wriggled me round in her hold until I rested with my fat 3-year old legs astride her left hip whilst I clasped her round her neck and bestowed a wet kiss on her cheek.

Dick's was the earliest voice I can remember. There was not a time for me in my babyhood when it was not nearby, except when she was at school. Now at sixteen, and showing the signs of maturity which the eldest in a family so often assumes by reason of its

1

practice, Dick was tall and sturdy, responsible and capable, and only carrying out what nature had obviously and efficiently intended for her, though so prematurely with me – that of inbuilt motherliness. Any baby or toddler found a way straight to her heart; if they were whimpering or crying, all the more so. A motherless waif such as myself could not fail to be loved by her.

I was born in Enfield in February 1902, of an able and rather pompous father, John Emil Minska, and his beautiful young wife, May Evelyn. He was 33 when they married in 1895; she was only 20, and the wedding photographs show a young lady who looks excited and ready to burst into song with joy. She must have been a delight; slim, curly-haired (not entirely under control), enthusiastic, a chatter-box, but so beautiful and so young. She was intelligent, too, and could be serious when the situation demanded. She was deeply in love with John Emil in spite of his bumptiousness, which as yet she hardly perceived, and only respected. The fact that he had a Swedish father, John Axel, who was enormously rotund, so that the family legend related that he had an ellipse cut out of one side of his dining-table to accommodate his tummy at mealtimes, only added to the aura of wonder around his large person. Fair and bewhiskered as all his countrymen, John Axel had come to live in London from his native Stockholm as a young man, and set up as a ship's broker in the docks there, then a busy port. He lived at nearby Haggerston, and there he met his English wife, Emily Maynard, who was born in 1829. They married in 1856, and had four children, of whom my father, John Emil (thus called after both parents), was the youngest. Before him came Ada in 1857, whose full and correct name was Hedda Helvig Charlotta, and who was always beloved of the whole family as a source of unvarying kindness to her dying day in 1932. Then came Emily Wilhelmina in 1859, who was known as Mina, and who had a delightful photograph taken as a chubby little girl standing four-square, with a round, rather bland face, thick legs, and a pretty dress coloured blue by the photographer. Mina was rather a mystery, and I never met her. She worked as a housekeeper for many years, never married, and died in an Eastbourne nursing-home in 1926, when she was 67. The rumour was she was an alcoholic, but I never knew the truth. After her, in 1861, came Victoria Ellen, 'Toria' to everyone, very aristocratic and proud, of whom much more will be said; and lastly my father, John Emil, equally proud but also in his own opinion justifiably so, in 1862.

John Emil was tall, broad-shouldered, but erect and shapely, with the same bland face as Mina when in repose, but different from hers in that it could flare up with fury when he was roused. I cannot sum up his intelligence, but I think that whatever he may have lacked in sheer brain power, he had in unlimited resourcefulness, and what today would be known as 'know-how'. He could talk himself into and out of any situation, but also he was a man of the highest integrity, and in many ways his ever expanding opinion of his own ability was not unjustified. He was extremely capable and reliable, and if he said he would achieve something, he did. All this was born out in his career connected with the Far East, in which he was at first an agent for Guthries, a London exporting firm, and finally their manager. He was known all over Malaya, Singapore and neighbouring ports as a man who kept his word, and the personification of British drive, initiative and honour. His biggest scoop was to arrange the sale of pearls from a London dealer to the King of Siam. All of these negotiations were done by letter, and he never travelled nearer than the Middle East (twice on holiday), or achieved the King's palace. Rather a dandy, with a taste for stylish hats which he wore slightly tilted on one side, and the latest in cravats and waistcoats, the heat and discomfort of the East would hardly have suited him, coming as he did from the Scandinavian and British north.

True to form, John Emil married well. May Westcott, in addition to her youth and many charms, was the granddaughter of a P. & O. captain. Moreover she had a great uncle, George Blagdon Westcott, who was one of Nelson's captains and was killed at the battle of Aboukir Bay. He even achieved a huge statue on an even larger plinth in St. Paul's Cathedral, conveniently in London so that my father could sidle past, nonchalantly swinging his cane, and wondering how he could communicate to other passers-by in the South Nave Aisle, that he was related to, if not actually descended from the good captain. In any case, it was an uplift when necessary to his own self-confidence. My father was not an affectionate person, and my mother must have more than made up for his lack of warmth by her affectionate nature, and with her youth and exuberant joy, and her admiration for her tall and

3

eminent-looking husband, made him feel even more of a personage than did the Captain on his pedestal. Emily Maynard, his mother, had died in 1867 when she was only 38, and John Emil was a little boy of 5. She was buried in Bow Cemetery on October 3rd, from which moment he had been pampered by the rest of the family to make up for his loss, and brought up to feel that he, the only boy with three elder sisters, was of supreme importance. When his firstborn arrived in 1899, and was a boy, he proudly called him John after himself, and Otto for no very obvious reason except that 'John Otto' sounded mysteriously good. That was my big brother, who inherited so nearly his father's attributes and characteristics, but also some of his mother's charm.

Three years later, in February, 1902, I was born, a sickly baby who was not expected to live, after a long, painful labour, quickly followed by my mother's haemorrhage, and death after a few hours.

My father was devastated. Even in those days when maternal deaths were still frequent, he had not reckoned with such an eventuality. It was one aspect of his life which he had not been able to prevent or by-pass. Someone must be at fault for such an appalling consequence, and as the doctor and the midwife were the best in the area, there could only be one person who had caused such a tragedy and loss, and that was the baby herself. He turned away from me from the start, acknowledging only that I existed and that my second name should be inherited from my mother. So I became Hannah Evelyn, unloved and unmothered.

Brother John had been taken to Auntie Ada's house, the Rookery at Belvedere, whilst I was being born, and when my mother died my father refused to look at me and followed John to the Rookery. My mother's sisters, Lily and Annie, were unmarried and did not want me. Toria was thus left holding the baby quite literally, and brought me back to where she was then living at Bowes Park in north London, for what she thought was a temporary sojourn whilst her brother, my father, collected his wits, 'got over' his grief, and made arrangements for John and me to be looked after. John, at three years old, was hardly more than a baby, and soon took to Auntie Ada's kind ways and became part of her happy household, where there were already three other children of her own, and the cousins (Dick and co.) were frequently popping in or coming to stay. Toria was not a motherly person, but she had plenty of

4

common-sense and intelligence, and moreover was fairly well-off both for servants and for household spending money. Uncle Alf, whom she had married in 1887, saw to that. Thus my immediate needs could be met, and she felt almost that I presented a challenge because of my puny size and lack of a mother to nurse me, and so she willingly fell in with the necessary timetable of frequent bottles, changing, washing, and all the other tasks involved in caring for a sickly baby.

Nobody could have been more delighted at my appearance in the Bowes Park house than Dick, who was then 13 and already showed well-developed maternal instincts. She was soon clutching me to her young bosom. and bestowing all the love of which she was capable upon my pasty little face and snub nose, patiently helping me to take my bottles and bring up my wind. She soon showed what a capital little nursemaid she was, and whilst she dandled me or spread her knees to form a lap on which to lie me down to put on my clothes, she was at the same time able to organise the play of her sister Hilda, then 11, and Henry who was 9. More often Henry, who was only mildly interested in me, was out in the garden playing boats, whilst Hilda who thought babies rather "sweet" as long as they did not involve work, was languidly propping up the wardrobe while she watched the nursery procedures.

My father continued to ignore me, and to live with John at Auntie Ada's house. Finally my Aunt Toria tackled him on the subject of my future.

"What are you going to do about Hannah, John, now that the funeral is over?" she enquired. She was a straight-forward lady, and felt she had not so far been appreciated or had thanks due for my care.

My father prevaricated.

"When are you going to find a nursemaid for her, so that you can all three go back to Tremonia?" (our house at Wood Green) she insisted, not noticing that Dick had quietly come through the doorway, and was standing there listening.

"Oh no!" Dick cried, involuntarily putting her hand to her lips. "You mustn't take her away. We all love her here, and I'll look after her, really I will."

"Don't be absurd, Vicky", said Toria, "You're far too young, and anyhow you're at school most of the time."

"But Mother, I do most of the looking-after now and I can feed her before I go to school in the morning, and then when I come home, so you'll only have to feed her the other times in the day. And I'll bathe her just like I do now. Please, please let her stay."

Aunt Toria for once was silent. She could see that very little love and interest was forthcoming from her brother, whilst her own family had already taken me to its heart.

"What do you think, Alf?" she asked her husband, my Uncle Alfred Barnes.

"My dear, if you would like Hannah to stay, of course she shall. She's a dear little soul, and I'm sure we can manage."

"Alright then," said Aunt Toria, "provided that I have complete control of her just as if she was my own." My father thankfully agreed to these less-than-arduous terms, and so it was settled. I became a Barnes in all but name, and sometimes that too. Like my new sisters, Vicky and Hilda, and my new brother Henry, I called Aunt Toria Mother, and Uncle Alf either Dad, or sometimes Uncle Alf, depending on where I was. I called my own father, Father. It was very confusing, but it worked as long as I did not call Uncle Alf Dad in front of my own father. Then the fires of jealousy would show in John Emil's eyes, and I knew I had been foolish, and would bend my head down in shame, my cheeks burning and my eyes pricking with tears. Beyond that, my father took very little interest in me, and of all the photographs I have of my childhood, there are only three taken of me with him. Two are during my first year, and both are posed as if thereby he could retain some hold over me, and the third was on some special day, of the boys in their Eton suits, and me in my sailor suit sitting on his knee when I was about seven. But I was already one of another family, where I felt wanted and secure.

I soon made rapid progress and put on weight, and became increasingly robust, so that by the time I was a year old, my rosy cheeks were bulging round the edge of my bonnet, and my fists and feet were dimpled. In every way I was enjoying being the baby of the family, checked when I was naughty, taunted by my brothers (John, my real brother, when I was taken to see him, and Henry, my new brother almost all the time) and doted on by my two new sisters. Most of all of them, I adored my Dick, and she was the one to whom I ran when life (and the boys) became troublesome.

After Dick, I most loved Dad. Alfred Barnes was the kindest man I have ever known. Not endowed with a high intellect, he made up for it with total concern for others, and was capable of great affection and deep feelings. He had fallen in love with Toria almost at first sight, when they were both at school in Caversham, he at the boys' school, she at the young ladies' establishment known as Hemdean House. Children from both schools attended the same church on Sundays, and Alfred quickly noticed the tall fair girl with the aristocratic nose and upright bearing. Soon he was contriving to meet her in the weektime as well, and I think from the very first he intended to marry her. She was dictatorial and bossy, and Alfred was putty in her hands. He would have done anything for Toria. After leaving school he went into his father's gold-blocking and book-binding business at Hamsel Street in the City of London near St. Paul's. The firm was called 'Glover & Barnes', and in those days old Glover and Mrs. Glover were still alive, and used to take young Alfred on holiday with them to Great Yarmouth. Alfred's paternal grandmother was said to have been a Polish Jewess, and certainly his father inherited the dark looks and Semitic nose of that race, and both Alfred and his sisters, Amy and Eva, betrayed the same characteristics to a lesser degree. Finally the features reappeared in Hilda's face, and when her daughter, Jeanne, married a French Jew in the 1930s, it was difficult to tell whether their children's looks came from their mother's or their father's side.

Whilst Alfred was learning the book-binding business at G & Bs, Toria, radiating her fair graceful appearance, was spending a couple of years in Stockholm with her Swedish relations. Already well-versed in Swedish manners and customs, and having been brought up among Swedish books and furniture (much of the latter carved by 'Fusta', her father's sister, Mina) she was now able to perfect the language. Eventually she returned home, Alfred proposed, and they were married at St. John's Church, Hackney, on the first day of Spring, March 21st, 1888. They then settled down to happy domesticity at 29 Thistlewaite Road, Clapton, and Alf was able to indulge his Toria to his heart's content.

7

Part of this indulgence was to move constantly to better properties as Toria discovered them, and so he soon found himself moving from Thistlewaite Road to nearby Amhurst Road, then to Palmers Green, then Bowes Park, all in North London. At this juncture I joined the family, and it seemed more appropriate to live south of the Thames near to the Rookery, so that I could more easily be taken there to see my father. Thus we came to move to the nicest house I have ever lived in, Chiltern Lodge in Belvedere, a large Victorian residence with a big garden, built on the slopes of the hill which was topped by the Rookery, and overlooking the Thames to the north, only five or six minutes away.

CHAPTER II

1902 continued

THE ROOKERY WAS a really huge house. As I look now at old photos of it, I see that one part of it was a double-fronted regency villa, but onto the back of this had been added a large wing, and subsequently onto that a full-size Victorian house. So it ended up as a vast rambling place, connected by corridors and stairs, and odd steps here and there to make the levels coalesce. Leaning against one windowless wall was a large greenhouse extending up to first floor level, but reduced in height where it came under the tall round-headed staircase window – the one from which it was possible to climb out by hanging onto a convenient drain pipe. The garden was equally huge, with lawns and shrubberies, wild areas and great mature old trees. The whole property was set upon Rookery Hill, with a long, winding drive from the 'front gate' at the top of the hill to the west, which then encircled the house, and continued down to the 'bottom gate' on the east. In between these two gates, there was a third, the 'tradesmen's entrance'. The Rookery was thus an enormous property on very steep slopes, and an absolute haven for children, having unending nooks and crannies and secret corners for hiding, both inside and out.

Here lived my beloved Auntie Ada, who ran the establishment with efficiency, ease, and a great deal of common-sense. Like Mother, of course she was half Swedish, and Uncle Gus, her husband, was wholly Swedish, so that their three children, Ebba, Eric and George, were more Swedish than English in their inheritance, though born and brought up in London. Uncle Gus had come to England as a young man, to work at Vickers' factory at Erith as a draughtsman, and soon met Ada who was part of the neighbouring Swedish community. They were married about the same time as Mother and Uncle Alf, and their first baby, Ebba, was born within a month of Dick's arrival in 1889. Eric appeared in 1892, and then followed a gap until George was born in 1900. Thus my brother John and his cousin George were only a year apart in age, and the two became and remained throughout childhood firm friends, seldom relying on other boys for their games.

Meanwhile Mother and Uncle Alf had been busy producing their own family. After Dick, came Hilda, a dark little girl with big soulful eyes, in 1891, and lastly and proudly a son in 1896. Called John after my father, he was always known as Henry for convenience' sake, and from his birth he was the apple of his mother's eye. All these cousins tended to couple up with the nearest one by age. Dick and Ebba were dumped together in their prams, and played together as small children, but later it was all too obvious who was the leader of the two, and Dick became rather bored with Ebba's lackadaisical ways although she remained fondly protective of her. Similarly Eric and Hilda were at first pushed together, but turned out to have quite dissimilar characters, Eric interested in boyish pursuits, Hilda preferring to tag along behind Dick and Ebba. Henry was the odd man out, but was full of daring enterprises, so that the two younger cousins John and George, admired his lead, and copied his activities until they found how often these led to trouble, and decided to keep themselves to themselves. I, being the youngest of all, typically did not fit into any of these groups, but adoring as I was of my boy cousins, and useful to them as an obedient slave, John and George would sometimes allow me access to their latest project, only rapidly to become irritated with my slowness of wit or action, and to shout at me to go away. This I did with loud cries and copious tears, to be comforted by Auntie Ada or the maids, or of course Dick if she was near. Never did I learn to avoid a recurrence of this situation, and to leave the boys on their own. Instead, so marvellous did I think them that I wheedled myself once more into their games, with the inevitable result.

Thus, when Dick mentioned "walkies" to me, her "Goo-goo", that day at Chiltern Lodge when I was hardly three, I made haste to her to have my outdoor clothes on, knowing that most likely we were going to the Rookery, and I would see John and George. Dick soon had me buttoned into my gaiters and coat, and sat me on her knee while she brushed my long straight hair, and tied on my bonnet. Then into the pushchair she bundled me, and we set off up the hill. Once we had negotiated the wooden gates of the top entrance to the Rookery, Dick took me out of the pushchair, and made me walk the last steep slope up the drive, clutching her hand. On the lawn at the top John and George, dressed in knickerbockers under their pinafores, laced-up boots, and with their caps on the back of their heads, were taking it in turns to pull each other along in a little cart they had been given.

Dick stopped to watch them.

"Give Anne a ride" she directed.

"Oh no, she'll only spoil it" said John, but George, always kindhearted, and anyhow knowing I could be useful to them, said "Let her, John. She'll be alright," and heaved me into the cart, where I sat, plump and triumphant while they pulled me round the house to the top of the slope leading down to the bottom gate. Here they began to lose interest, and too late to realise the cart was gathering speed which they could not control, until down we all went, the cart increasing its momentum and lurching madly from side to side, finally leaving the driveway, and after careering dizzily over the grass verge, ending up under a laurel bush. When I had collected my wits, I could see Dick running down the hill, her hair streaming behind her and concern in her face, and though unhurt I now started yelling in fright. She unravelled us all from the cart and the bush, and began raving at the boys for being so careless with me, whilst cuddling me fiercely to reassure herself that I was alright before taking me back to the house to be washed and restored to rights. The boys followed behind, pulling the cart and muttering against stupid girls in general and me in particular, and disappeared into the shrubbery until the tea gong sounded, by which time all had been forgotten, and jam sandwiches and mugs of milk took up their entire attention.

We often went to tea at the Rookery, not just Dick and me, but also Hilda, usually pulling our little black dog, Rip, along on his lead with one hand, and sucking her fingers with the other. Henry sometimes came too because he liked Auntie's cooking, and also it gave him a chance to show off his tree-climbing skills. On Sundays we sometimes went in after church, which we attended at Belvedere. Uncle Gus was a sidesman and Eric in the choir there, and we knew most of the congregation, anyhow by sight. We became particularly fond, though rather in awe, of the vicar's warden because he always showed us into our pew with a bow, and we preened ourselves on being treated as gentry. His name was James Simms, and later on I came to know his family quite well, particularly his larky son, Arthur. Mother and Auntie sat themselves so as to disperse the more garrulous members of the family, usually Henry and John, and Dick looked after me, and found my place in the prayer book although I could not read, and steadied me as I wobbled standing on my hassock. Uncle Alf and my father seldom came to church with us, preferring to play golf, and this always puzzled me as to why they felt safe from God's wrath for failing to visit His House. I think I assumed that grown-ups were excluded from Hell by other good deeds. Actually it may have been because Uncle Alf had had a Jewish mother that he and Auntie Amy and Eva had never been brought up to go to church. At any rate, he was usually back home sharpening the carving knife by the time we had hurried there, as fast as we could after the service, to be met by the beguiling smell of roast beef, and the cook, red-faced, busy at the kitchen stove. We knew better than to go near her at this critical juncture, and instead tied each other into our pinafores whilst waiting for her to dish up and sound the gong.

Dick was at this time a pupil at the Roan School in Blackheath, then in its old buildings between Greenwich and Woolwich, and she enthusiastically entered into all its activities, particularly hockey. She went off on the top of the omnibus each morning, carrying her satchel and waving goodbye cheerily as she ran down the hill to catch it. I always looked forward to her return at tea-time, when she would rush into the house, fling down her uniform hat and coat, and sweep me up into her arms to give me a great big kiss. When she was 16 in 1905, Mother felt she ought to be 'finished' at a school abroad, and after some enquiries, settled on one in the Harz mountains in northern Germany, at a place called Stolberg. It had been recommended by Anna Adelgren, a friend whom Mother knew through G. & Bs, Anna's father being concerned with supplying the firm with goldleaf for printing. The school was called Rotkappchen-Pensionat, and was run by the formidable but affectionate Fraulein, of whom subsequently Dick punctuated all her conversation – "Fraulein says –", "Fraulein wants –", and so on.

When I realised that my precious Dick was going away, I felt bereft, and Hilda's rather half-hearted efforts to console me had little effect. Even Dad's contribution of a piece of liquorice and a jump on his knee was of only temporary comfort. From this period I went up to the Rookery more or less consistently at weekends, "to play with the boys", which, as I grew bigger and "more sensible", they often permitted. The three of us had marvellous imaginative games, usually outside in the wild part of the garden, often building huts, or playing a form of cops and robbers, where I was most frequently the cop. However I knew it was at my peril that I refused, and rushing on my sturdy legs, I sometimes managed to "tig" them. I became proficient in climbing trees, slithering down drainpipes, crawling through undergrowth, and after one of these glorious days, my father happened to be standing in the side-door as I dragged my well-worn teddy back into the house for tea, my knees scratched and my kilt muddy.

"*Can't* you be a little lady for once, Hannah?" he sighed. But, how could I? The happiest part of my life was spent with the boys, and I liked very much the way they spent their time scrambling about the shrubberies and up the trees.

Sometimes we had big family picnics in the wild parts of the Rookery garden, amongst the lovely old beeches, and then I behaved more circumspectly because there were grown-ups present, but I enjoyed the fun and the jesting that took place in those days when families made their own merriment, before the advent of wireless and television. We had a great deal of home-made pleasure, and Auntie Ada was adept at organising parties. Sometimes these were picnics, but in winter we had sledging parties down Rookery Hill, followed by massive teas in the over-furnished dining-room, with its heavy Swedish furniture, and its drapes along the mantelpiece and round the gas lights. Uncle Gus would seat himself on the revolving stool at the piano, light the candles in their sconces on the front of it, and strum out the latest tunes, 'Lily Marlene' and the rest, whilst we all joined in. Sometimes Auntie Ada would organise a fancy dress party at Christmas to which we all went, and brought our friends, and she would include a number of her Swedish acquaintances who would often be staying at the Rookery for a few weeks. The house was always full and busy, and I loved it for its happy atmosphere. In the summer this jollity spilled over into a boarding house in Margate which we took over, lock, stock and barrel. I don't remember many details except that it had a steep flight of steps up to its front door, sided by low stone 'bannisters' which prevented one falling down into the 'area' at one side, and the other divided our steps from those going up to next door's front entrance. It had, I remember, big bay windows reaching from the basement to the first floor or higher, and we had lovely fish teas there, while our toes were still savouring the grittiness of the sand which had spilled over the tops of our boots.

For several years I thought nothing of my rather ambiguous place in the three families, taking for granted, as children do, that my life was following the same course as everyone else's. Then one day, when I was about seven, I had a rude awakening, and began to think more carefully about it. I was at the Rookery as usual one weekend, playing with the boys, and tea had gone on rather longer than usual. My father was there as he normally was on Saturdays and Sundays, but took not a great deal of notice of me, spending his time mending the greenhouse roof or larking about with his friend Midgely, of whom I was consequently jealous. I kept my thoughts completely occupied with the slide which John and George and I were making on some old planks down one of the steep slopes there. As we were getting up from table to go back to play, my father said "Anne, it's six o'clock. Time you were off."

"Dad said I could have an extra half-hour tonight" I cheerfully replied. I could see the anger rising in my father's face, and realised what I had said. My face went puce, and my forefinger went to my mouth. I was scared. My father was very tall and broad and imperious, and by 1909 or so he was also overweight and developing the Minska tummy. He bent over me and said loudly and firmly "I am your father, Hannah, and don't you forget it." I never did forget this lesson, and so, very early in life learnt the meaning of tact. I never again called Uncle Alf "Dad" in front of my father, but it was difficult to remember when it came so easily to me, and so confusing to imagine the semi-stranger at the Rookery as my father.

I thought about it a great deal for the first time, but I still did not quite understand. I knew my own mother had died when I was born, but she was never ever mentioned either at the Rookery or Chiltern Lodge, and so to me she was entirely mythical, and biology being a closed book to me at that age, I really did not understand my father's contribution to my beginnings, nor entirely my relationship to "Mother" and Uncle Alf. To me they were my parents, and I never had had reason to think about it. Now, however, I began to realise I was different.

Next time I went to play with John and George, I awaited my opportunity, and then I approached John.

"John," I said, "why is it that you only have one father, but I have two?"

"You haven't, silly. You've only got one. Dad is not your real father."

"But then why do I live with him, and not here with you and Father?" I persisted. John looked non-plussed. Truth to tell he had not thought much about it himself, always taking the fact of him and me living in different houses as the normal way of things.

"I think it's so that Aunt Toria can look after you." he said at last.

"But why can't Auntie Ada? I like her much more."

He thought again, wrinkling his forehead with the effort, and then he shook his head, not liking to be defeated.

"I expect it's to make numbers even in the two houses" he ended triumphantly. And there the conversation closed, but I was not placated, and determined to ask Dick when she came home from Germany. Meanwhile I pondered on the strange situation, and compared the loving way Dad behaved with me, with the off-hand manner of my Father, who seemed determined to make me grow up a paragon.

I learnt to hold my tongue when trouble brewed or I did not understand a situation. Always truthful I kept quiet when necessary rather than fib. When arguments arose I often remained silent so that I was not taking sides and afterwards blamed for that. No small girl ever grasped so early, from her own practical experience that silence is often golden. Naturally a chatterbox and excitable like my own mother, I gained so much self-control in this respect that I could melt quietly into the background when occasion demanded, so that adults forgot about me. However, sometimes this did me no good, and my modesty was violated.

One day I was sliding quietly out of the drawing-room at the Rookery, and my father noticed my surreptitious departure.

"Where are you going, Anne?"

Silence.

"Tell me where you are going, Hannah" he repeated more irately. He only used my full name when he was annoyed with me.

Still silence, while I blushed and held my head. I was immediately suspect. Once again he insisted "Tell me at once where you are going?".

"To the lavatory" I mumbled, embarrassed to the core of my being, and rushed off. This was the Edwardian era, and we were all still very modest and polite, and never mentioned such things to gentlemen. However this time it was my father who learned his lesson, and he never again repeated his mistake or disbelieved my word. I think I liked him better for it.

CHAPTER III

1910

AFTER THE BOYS went off to school, I was left very much on my own in the weektime as far as my own age group was concerned, and used to drag my teddy, or sometimes Rip, round the garden for something to do. Having no other children to play with forced me into imaginative games of my own, and Rip was often part of these. He was a nondescript little dog, of dubious parentage, which was perhaps why I had a fellow-feeling for him. But also he was very good-tempered, and did not object to being dressed up in dolly's clothes and being tucked into a pram. I would wheel him up and down the garden path until at last he got sick of it, and, his dress flapping, he jumped out with his bonnet awry, and ran away. Then I had to find some other occupation, and often 'wrote' to Dick in Germany in my scribble writing, and drew a pretty picture for her.

I was rather at a loose end, and eventually Mother decided to find me a governess, as she had little patience herself to give me lessons. One day she took me down to Belvedere Village, and onto a farm behind the church. There we found Mrs. Chapman busily feeding the chickens, and she and Mother started to discuss me, whilst I rambled about the yard, peeping through the half-open gates at the pig-styes. Soon Mrs. Chapman called me across to her, and took me into the dairy for a mug of milk, and then we went into the house to be introduced to her daughter. Before long it was arranged that I should walk over to Erith every day with Miss Chapman, who already gave lessons to the Linscott children there, a boy and a girl just a little older than me, and could include me in her little class. And so it came about.

17

It seemed a long walk to me, but probably was little over a mile, to be repeated on the homeward journey later in the day. However, I was by now very sturdy, and I liked Miss Chapman, although she was strict and we had to work hard at our lessons. She talked to me about all sorts of interesting things on our daily walks to and from Erith, and the time passed quickly.

One day when I arrived home, Mother looked somehow different, and then I noticed she was wearing lovely earrings which sparkled more than any she had ever had before. She always wore her hair in a 'bun', so her fine head was just the setting for pendant earrings, and these glistened with all the colours of the rainbow, as she slowly turned for me to admire them.

"Do you like them?" she asked. "Dad has given them to me for our wedding anniversary", and then I remembered that it was March 21st 1908, and they had been married twenty years. Mother subsequently wore these beautiful earrings every day. Each had two magnificent diamonds set one above the other, and they must have been of the best quality to produce such radiance. I wondered if anyone would ever love me enough to give me such a beautiful present.

Dick came home this year for good, and it was a relief to me to have her common-sense and loving interest at my beck and call once more. When Dad brought her and all her luggage by hansom cab from Victoria Station, I had quite a shock, as I was expecting the same girl who went off to Germany three years ago, but even so, directly she saw me she held out her arms as she always used to and let me run into them for a hug and a kiss. After two happy years in Fraulein's care, she had put up her hair, and gone to work as a 'companion' in Paris. It was the year the Seine flooded badly and all the water had to be boiled, she told me as I shyly watched her unpacking. I couldn't get used to her looking so grown-up, but rather admired it, and as I gradually accustomed myself to the idea, it made me feel safe.

"I didn't like it much there," she said "but I met some nice people called the Fiats and they want Hilda to go as a paying guest. Will you let her go, Mother?"

Mother said she would "think about it", and Hilda, who was listening, said nothing, instead continuing to suck her fingers.

18

The house livened up now Dick was home. Although she was nineteen, she still rushed about in her excited way, and no sooner had she settled in at Chiltern Lodge than she hurried off on her bicycle to see her old Roan friends. She returned later on, resplendent with a badge.

"What's that?" asked Dad.

"I've joined Lily's hockey team" she announced, "I'll have to practice hard to get up to standard again". And she did. Every Saturday whilst I was at the Rookery, Dick went off with her hockey stick, and every Sunday afternoon Lily came to our house to tea. I liked Lily. She was good fun. A real extrovert, she was studying to be a teacher, and was a born organiser. Perhaps that was what Dad disliked about her regular Sunday visits, and I could see disapproval on his kind old face.

Soon, however, he was able to disappear when she came, anyhow for part of the time. He began to have a mysterious expression, and one day Mother looked up from her sewing and said "What's that noise outside?" and hurried to the window.

"Good gracious!" she exclaimed, "It's Dad in a car", and rushed outside closely followed by Rip and me.

There in the drive, perched up above us was Dad in the driving seat of a big open car, its tool box on its running board, and its big brass lamps brightly polished.

"What are you doing in that?" Mother shouted over the noise of the engine.

"I've just bought it" he announced, and helped her in. "It's a Daimler."

"Dam Liar, you mean" called Henry from an upstairs window.

And off they went for a spin, with Rip and me on the leather cushion at the back.

After that we had a great deal of fun in the "Dam Liar". Sometimes she chugged along happily, but other times, going up hills such as to the Rookery, she boiled, and we had to stop while Dad, his hands protected by his new leather driving gloves, unscrewed the cap on the radiator to let out the steam. Cars were becoming popular, and from only seeing one occasionally, we often spotted them driving from Woolwich to Erith, or on their way to the Dover Road and the seaside places on the Medway. James Simms, who had one, even got 'had up' in Purley High Street for exceeding the speed limit of 25 mph. After that we joined the A.A. so that their scouts could warn us, by their salute, of approaching speed traps.

Henry was mad on cars and motorbikes, but he was not yet old enough for a licence. This year, instead, his mind was full of the merchant navy. He was quite a problem, due entirely to Mother's indulgence, and Dad's inability to gainsay her and put his foot down. Mother, faced with this adolescent youth whom she could not control, thought out a splendid compromise. She decided it would be suitably elevated to have a son in the navy, but then on enquiring found it was too late to apply to Osbourne or Dartmouth, and she would have to make do with the merchant navy. Henry agreed, rather fancying the uniform, and so he was packed off to the Conway, the training ship in the Menai Straits near Anglesey. He was there for a couple of years. I never heard about the shock it must have caused him, but the discipline undoubtedly did him good, and his absence from home relieved me of his incessant teasing.

By now I was nearly eight years old, and the puzzle of my double home life continued to nag me. John's answer did not really help, and now Dick was home I felt shy about asking her in case her reply was something I did not like or want to believe. But life already was beginning to toughen me and make me stand on my own feet, and I made up my mind to tackle her. The opportunity came that autumn when I spied her sitting on her own at the bottom of the garden mending stockings. So, calling to Rip who trotted after me, I joined her, sitting on the grass and stroking the dog's ears to give myself confidence. Dick looked very old and wise to me, but just the same understanding person underneath her experience of Germany and Paris.

"I like having you at home", I began.

"I like it too", she said, "but sometimes there isn't really enough to do". She had been home nearly a year, and had spent her time studying languages, of which she now had added Swedish to her German and French.

"Dick," I faltered, "why don't I live with Father and John?" I watched her face change from its accustomed ease to a thoughtful frown.

"Aren't you happy here?" she asked.

"It isn't that, but I don't understand why we don't all live together", I dared not say what was in my mind, which was the fear that my father did not want me.

"You live here because we couldn't bear it if you didn't, and there isn't really room for Uncle Jack and John to be here too", she tried to explain.

"But it still seems queer for us not to be in the same house. Hasn't he got enough money for a house of our own?" I had really thought things out well for a nearly eight-year-old, and came upon this solution as a possibility.

"That's mainly it" said Dick, relieved that I had found this answer myself, but in her simple honesty knowing that it was not the whole story.

"What else then?" I persisted, realising that she had left herself a loophole. It was all rather above my head, and seeing this, she struggled to put it into simple words.

"It was just that he missed your mother so much that he couldn't face a home of his own without her."

So there it was. Dick had managed to express it in words which I could comprehend. I knew about missing people – I had missed Dick herself badly when she went off to school in Germany – and I could see what she meant. It seemed a good enough explanation, and for a few years satisfied me. I was able now to forget the problem and to take life as it came.

It was not long after the excitement of dispatching Henry to the Conway that I was sitting in the kitchen at the Rookery, licking out the mixing bowl as the cook baked the cakes, when the telegraph boy cycled up to the front door. Auntie Ada answered his ring, and I heard a cry, and went into the hall to investigate.

"It's Gus" she said, looking strained and white. The telegram was to say he had collapsed and died of a heart attack whilst busy at his drawing board at Vickers.

21

I was immediately sent to Chiltern Lodge with a note to Mother, and instructed to run all the way. I was scared. This was the second death to affect my life, and I did not know how to approach the people most troubled by it. It was easiest to keep out of their way to save my embarrassment, and so I spent the rest of that day down the garden, and thought about Uncle Gus, and how it would be without him and his jolly smile and his piano playing.

In spite of only being a draughtsman Uncle Gus must have had other income; I never really understood how he and Auntie Ada managed to live so well and in such a huge house, and certainly from now on things were different, and the shoe pinched. Instead of her social life and all the maids to look after the Rookery, Auntie took in Swedish girls as 'PGs', part of the arrangement being that they helped in the house, whilst in exchange she taught them English. They would each come for a year or two, always three or four girls at one time, and were treated as part of the family. They were a nice type of young woman, and joined in all the picnics and parties, now much reduced in lavishment. Meanwhile Auntie Ada metaphorically as well as actually put on her apron (always an embroidered Swedish one), rolled up her sleeves, and worked from morning till night, washing, ironing, cleaning, baking and preparing meals. I never saw anyone work so hard. Before this drudgery started however, my father, seeing how shocked she was, took her off on a cruise to the Mediterranean on a liner called the Vectis. That was the nearest he ever achieved to the Far East, but he enjoyed all the ports of call, not to mention the social life on board, which in those days was very select and mainly reserved for the aristocracy. The following year, as Auntie Ada felt she could not leave the Swedish girls for whom she was responsible, he took Mother instead. Uncle Alf, who was a simpler soul and more parochial, preferred the seaside.

"I'll take Hilda and Hannah to Herne Bay" he announced, unconscious of the alliteration. "They'd like that." We did. The three of us had a lovely time, in spite of the pebbled beach. The Punch and Judy was our favourite treat, and the donkeys next, but just enjoying throwing pebbles into the sea for Rip to run after, and watching the boats with Dad, made it the happiest of holidays. We were not spoilt children, and every day gave us pleasure, with seemingly unending sunshine.

I was beginning to grow out of Miss Chapman, fond as I was of her. She must have been very young, not more than a year or two older than Dick, and although a good teacher for small children, I do not think she had had any training. In any case my education needed to be broadened, and Mother in her wisdom, realised that being a sociable little girl, I would do well to have more girl-friends to wean me from boyish pastimes, and to polish my manners. My father continued to bewail my lack of ladylike pursuits. Mother had big ideas, and with Henry firmly installed on the Conway, she made an appointment to take me to see Miss Roberts, the headmistress of Blackheath High School. So at nine years old, I was duly dressed in my best clothes, with my large Sunday hat on my well-brushed head, and we climbed into the Dam Liar ("Don't mention that name to Miss Roberts, Anne, whatever you do") and were driven by Dad to Weymss Road, just off the Heath, where the School then was. The introduction and talking duly over without me betraying my lack of finesse, I was forthwith enrolled for the Autumn Term, which was still a few months away. This interval was, however, filled by correspondence, enquiries, and visits to estate agents, to acquire a house nearer the school, and quite soon Mother had secured a newly-built one she liked in Liskeard Gardens on the East side of the Heath. It was within easy walking distance of the "High", and backing onto its playing fields, which were between Kidbrooke Grove and St. Germain's Church. Edwardian in style, with bay windows and front porch, the house was detached, and square, with three floors, and with a sizable garden, and was immediately christened "Senrab" by the Barnes family, who liked anagrams.

We were soon installed at Senrab, and I embarked upon my school career with enthusiasm and continuing joy. I loved the High School, and Miss Roberts in due course pronounced that I had had what she termed "a good grounding" with my governess. All my natural extrovert sociability came into action, and my training in tact and self-control helped me to edge my way into all the range of school pursuits, whether or not I shone at them. The girls all came from "good" homes, which included that of the current Astronomer Royal who had five daughters there, and it was a happy, disciplined atmosphere with no distinction into "class", and plenty of competition. If some were "brainy", and some were not, it was recognised that everyone had some asset which was identified and developed by the School, whether it was proficiency on the playing field, musical talent, or ability in domestic science or sewing. As long as one tried hard, no reprimand was forthcoming if the results were less than brilliant. Miss Roberts was a fair-minded woman, and although I was in awe of her, I liked and respected her.

Absorbed as I was in school, I hardly missed Hilda who that summer departed to Paris. Mother had indeed "thought it over", and she and Dick had visited the Fiats at Le Vesinet, liked them, and arranged for Hilda to go to live with them as a 'PG' for a year. It was a matriarchal household like many French families, and Mama Fiat ruled the roost. There were three sons and two daughters, and numerous cousins, aunts and uncles, who were perpetually in and out of the house. Papa Fiat was an old dear, did what Mama Fiat ordained, but disappeared to play pétanque with his friends when he needed some peace. Hilda, who had already spent a year in Stockholm with Mother's Swedish cousin, Maria, was used to being away from home, and enjoyed the Fiat household, which continued in its usual garrulous and argumentative fashion without much regard to her presence. She soon learned to follow their example of shrieking at the other people who were all talking at the same time, gesticulating with both hands in true French manner and making a terrible din. When she came home in 1912 she was much noisier and more assertive than previously.

Thus it was that for a time there was only Dick and me living at Senrab with Mother and Dad, and it was rather pleasant to come home to relative quiet from the bustle of the High. One day Dick was at the school gate to meet me at 4 o'clock. Wound round one hand was the lead of a large black retriever, who though full-grown was obviously still full of puppyish bounce.

"Where did you get him?" I immediately demanded, going down on my haunches to cuddle this most lovable animal. "Isn't he sweet."

"I've just brought him from the kennels on Dulwich Hill. He's called Golly." she said, eyeing me.

"I hope Rip will like him" I queried, controlling Golly's excited movements with difficulty.

"Rip has gone to heaven, Anne. He was so old he needed to be quiet now."

24

Tears welled up in my eyes as I realised what she meant, soon followed by choking sobs. We walked home, Golly alternately tugging at the lead, and dancing in circles with joy, which could not help but be infectious. By next morning I was dry-eyed, though blotchy, and Golly was my especial friend, but never quite erasing the memory of little black Rip, my first dog.

Thus it was that towards the end of 1911, now happily established at the 'High', 9½ years old, and exuding energy and health, my life was as full as could be, and the departure of Mother and Dick for a few weeks to Bremen ("It will do you good, Toria" said Uncle Alf mildly when the idea was broached) came at a time when there was no gap in my timetable when I could mope or feel lonely. Dick's best friend at Rotkaptchen, Luise Dieck, had been married in April 1909, and now was expecting a baby. A year older than herself, 'Lu' and her family had become favourites with Dick, who had stayed with them at Christmas whilst she was a schoolgirl, and from them had come to love the hearty friendship of the ordinary German people, their jovial extroversion, their beer parties and their picnics, their old-fashioned houses with their dark embroidered trappings, their large solid meals, and their warm common-sense. When Lu became engaged to her Fritz Lonsky, Dick was soon drawn into the traditions and preparations typical of a German wedding celebration, not least for the gargantuan feast which followed the church service. Now, eighteen months later, she was anxious to see Lu in her own home, and I soon received a postcard from her. "Dear Goo-goo", it said in her tidy feminine writing, "we are having a lovely time. Yesterday we visited Cologne ---" and on the reverse side of the card was a black-and-white photograph of Mother and Dick in an open omnibus just by the steps of Cologne Cathedral with its multitude of niches and statues, and the ladies in their huge unsuitable hats, their long tight-waisted dresses, and their parasols. How elegant they looked, but, unsophisticated as I was, I could not summon up any envy. All that, I thought, is a far-distant dream unrelated by many worlds from the uncomplicated reality of my life now.

The High and Golly between them kept me busy. When I arrived home at Senrab each teatime with my satchel on my back, my straight hair tangled, my knees grubby and my hands ink-stained, Golly was there to greet me, wildly wagging his long tail and barking directly he heard me open the front gate. I could see his excited face peering over the drawing-room window-sill as he stood on his hind legs, front paws madly paddling up and down the ledge, pink tongue lolling out during the intervals between his barks, and alternately rushing to the door, then back to the window, before finally lunging at me with joy as I came into the house.

"Good grief! Stop your noise." shouted Clarice, the maid, as he welcomed me with licks and nudges and playful bites interspersed with yaps of delight.

"Why don't you take him out for a run to calm him down?" she called. I had discovered that the best way to exercise him was for me to charge along the tracks across the Heath on my bike, with Golly either skeltering after me, or in a flight of exuberance racing across the huge area of grass almost to the walls of Greenwich Park before returning to me breathless and sweating, and with the wind blowing up his long ears and his black shiny fur. Later, as I settled down to my homework at the dining-room table, he would sink down at my feet, circling round and round as if in the grassy Steppes, until, nose on tail, he would curl himself round in a ball, and finally, exhausted, lie out flat on his side with a big sigh, to sleep soundly while I tackled my sums and learned my poetry.

I felt secure and unthreatened by life's problems that December as I concentrated on cutting out a Christmas card for Mother, and carefully crayoned some flowers on the front. Then I sewed a blue ribbon onto the side, a task I enjoyed, before writing my message inside. 'To Mother' it ran 'with love from Anne' – unoriginal but from my heart. My existence just now was predictable and my days filled with pleasant routine, only departing from the ordinary by the usual excitements of childhood festivities. Everything at school was within my grasp although some work was to me more puzzling than the rest. I was only of average intelligence, but I was highly obstinate and determined, and would slave away laboriously at difficult passages of translation or enigmatic problems in arithmetic so that I could retain my place in class. Where I shone was in practical work, especially sewing and dressmaking which I loved, taking my work home to complete in the evenings or weekends. At the other end of the scale was anything musical for which I had little aptitude, though the class singing lessons were fun, and provided an outlet for my noisy exuberance as well as teaching me self-control in the more restrained melodies. Like most Edwardian girls I had piano lessons, for which daily practising was obligatory, and to me distasteful. I usually extricated myself from this chore by 'doing my scales' and my 'pieces' before breakfast so that the rest of the day was free, although at that early hour the house was cold and my fingers soon became stiff on the chilling ivory keys. Mother, as always, was ambitious, and the old upright piano was replaced by a baby grand which added tone to the room if not to my musicality. The Barnes family were mainly unmusical, although Dick enjoyed a rare tinkle on the piano when she had time, and her German background encouraged her to sing her way melodiously and unselfconsciously through all her practical tasks about the house.

I saw less of the boys now that our interests were centred on our respective schools, and our homes much further apart. Auntie Ada still had her family gatherings for birthdays and Christmas, but now had little time herself for her elaborate preparations. Instead she would set the Swedish girls to work on the cookery and sewing, supervising their efforts and providing ideas for them to follow. In place of the time I used to spend with John and George, I was, as Mother had anticipated, developing friendships with girls at school, and giggling away the tea-parties at their houses with all the usual feminine tittle-tattle. My best friend, Edna, often came to Senrab for tea, or I would cycle to her house in Blackheath Village, and we soon would become immersed in some discussion, always accompanied by rollicking laughter as Edna embroidered her anecdote with unlikely detail or I added silly asides to accompany it. We seemed from the first to galvanise each other's idiocy and frivolity with complete harmony and hilarity. Of all my other friends at the High she was the one who most thought and laughed like me, and especially tickled my sense of humour. She could also, however, be serious when conditions demanded, and provide balanced opinion and wise advice. She remained for me a good and dependable ally until her sudden death seventy years later.

1912 provided plenty of change from routine. The first excitement was Mother's and Dad's Silver Wedding celebrations on March 21st. For this event I prepared a special 'card' by embroidering a pattern on canvas in blue and red, and forming their initials in silver tinsel thread with an X to join them. This had to be done secretly in my bedroom, with me indulging in a small

27

number of white lies to put Mother off the scent. Henry, who was developing into a proficient caricature artist, sent them an ink and wash picture on a postcard from the Conway, typically inappropriate and self-centred, of himself in a rugger scrum. Everyone in the family had (and mostly made) his or her own offering, and Dad crowned them by presenting Mother with a sparkling chandelier for the drawing-room, composed of strings of glass nuggets cut to look like diamonds, and indeed emanating colour in the same way. A beautiful thing, it added further elegance to the room and pleased Mother no end, though keeping it clean was a nightmare to come.

Auntie Ada's contribution to the festivities was of course a party at the Rookery to which we were all invited, and which my father enlivened with anecdotes of his clients, and by running the charades after supper with Midgely. He had an amazing knack of inveigling people into carrying out his directions with cheerful obedience, and as always he spent up to the hilt to ensure the event was a success.

Soon after this, letters from Hilda took on a new direction, frequently referring as before to the Fiats, but now especially to Kiki, one of the sons. As she was due to complete her year with them in the summer, Mother thought she would visit the family herself before that, and take me with her "to broaden" me. This suited me very well and I regarded preparations for this, the first of my many subsequent visits to France, with joyful anticipation.

Dad drove us down to Victoria in the Dam Liar, with our portmanteaux strapped on the roof and our best hats firmly on our heads. The boat train was waiting for us, chuffing cheerily as it got up steam, and the whole journey afforded me sheer delight, especially the channel crossing. Paris was another world, with its tooting cars, its crowds of chattering people, and unintelligible street names. We soon arrived at Le Vesinet to be engulfed in the bosom of the Fiat family, and it rapidly became evident that Hilda and Kiki were in love. He was a good-looking young man, very French in his short sturdy build, his self-confidence, and his fair hair and blue eyes. Hilda was quite swept off her feet by his gallantry and polite masterfulness, and gazed adoringly at him with her huge dark eyes. She had yet to learn about his explosive temper. Engagement followed, and the wedding was planned for the next year in England. Mother was in her element at the thought of being the bride's parent, and the three weeks we spent with the Fiats passed happily and quickly, with Mama Fiat and Mother frequently in conclave together over their sewing.

Later on in the year Hilda arrived home to Senrab, almost crossing with Dick who journeyed to Berlin in September to visit Lu and Fritz and to attend the baptism of their baby son, Dietrich, for whom, much to her joy, she stood godparent. The talk at Senrab which had dwelt on babies since his birth, now centred on weddings as Mother guided an excited Hilda through all the plans and preparations which had to be made. At ten years old I was the right age to enjoy a certain amount of this, especially the romantic part, but as it dragged on I found Hilda's continual wide-eyed excitement palled after a few weeks, and I escaped to my own friends. I could not live on a permanent crest of the wave as she was doing.

In the midst of these events, Henry arrived home having completed his two years on the Conway. To me he seemed at first to be very grand in his naval uniform, which he soon nonchalantly cast on one side, but I quickly realised he had changed little when his initial greeting came: "Hallo, Snub Nose," he called, "How's your mongrel?"

I never really understood why he did not go to sea after the Conway, or continue his naval career. Family discussions occurred carefully out of my hearing, and I expect he had found life on board tougher than he had anticipated. Maybe he failed his exams. I never knew. Dad at that period had dubious health and often was under par, at the same time as carrying on the trade at Glover & Barnes. Possibly this influenced the decision to allow Henry to remain at home and go into the business to learn all he could about it so as, in due course, to lighten Dad's burden. Henry himself did not take work of any sort very seriously, though he looked forward to receiving regular wages and thus becoming independent. He had no trouble in visualising himself as the boss when Dad finally retired, and thought the position suited him.

So into the printing works he went, under the manager, Tom Courtney's supervision, and with Minnie, Mother's distant cousin who worked in the counting house, to keep an eye on him. Minnie had gone into the office straight from school on her fourteenth birthday, due to the exigencies of her mother's widowhood, and remained a reliable, hard-working and self-effacing asset there until she finally retired. Now in her mid-thirties, she was ever respectful of the authority of her boss, who was technically Dad, and being a cockney born and bred, with the perkiness and intelligent good-humour of that race, as well as her lack of social standing, exposed herself to resentment and sneers from Henry in spite of his secret respect for her. Her intense loyalty to the firm must often have been severely tried as she found herself torn between Authority and the boss's son, for whom she had a natural soft spot. Henry had great charm and dash when he chose to display it, and soon learned to wheedle favours out of Minnie who would have been his willing slave if she had not been endowed with so much common-sense, not to say integrity.

Henry, who was now sixteen, was old enough to have a driving licence for a motorbike, and hankered after the open road. Dad soon was persuaded to provide him with a machine, and with his usual panache Henry donned gaiters, driving gloves, cap and goggles, and shot off on the bike with gusto and a great deal of noise and revving, to join the Blackheath Motorcycle Club. From now on he spent every free moment with the Club, and his conversation when he was at home seemed to embrace nothing beside the world of engines. With his usual generosity and anxiety to please if it did not upset his own plans, he gladly let me ride pillion one day as it coincided with his desire to show off his wonderful machine. Hanging on grimly to his waist, my lanky hair streaming behind me, and my breath quite taken away, we rode at full pelt round the Heath, before returning to Senrab exhausted. I wondered if Miss Roberts or anybody else from school had seen us careering along, but I heard nothing of it.

Henry, who had a natural sociability, adored the camaraderie of the motorcycle club, and before long was bringing its members home for tea at the weekends. It became a familiar sight to have several of them tinkering away at their bikes in our front drive to the accompaniment of a range of anecdotes and songs, before they roared off on another sortie, or merely to go home for a meal. Senrab entered a new bustling era with the coming and going of all these young people, presided over by Mother, and blandly tolerated by dear kind Dad, who could always tootle off in the Dam Liar for a spin or a round of golf if the chatter became too much for him.

Being only ten, I was of no account with all these young men, but unless they totally ignored my presence, which was mostly the case, they were friendly and kind, and were always ready to adjust my bicycle brakes or mend a puncture for me if I asked them. Mainly though I would sit unnoticed on the back door steps and listen to their conversation, some of it interesting, some such as the mechanics of their machines totally incomprehensible, and when I became bored I went inside and settled down with a book.

Some of the boys were not strangers to me as Henry had been friendly with them in Belvedere. Others such as Arthur Simms, we knew from attending Belvedere Church where his father, James Simms was a warden and had every Sunday ushered us into our pew with a courteous bow. Arthur was a jolly sort of boy, exceedingly kind-hearted, happy-go-lucky and careless, and completely unselfconscious. Occasionally he would bring his younger brother Frank to Senrab, and the two of them would perform remarkable acrobatics on their motorbikes for our benefit. It was only too obvious that Arthur, the eldest of four children, found the sedentary occupation of church-going difficult to cope with, used though he was from early childhood to attending matins. He had all sorts of ploys to combat his insidious boredom there, a favourite one being to tie his handkerchief into the shape of a rabbit and use it as a puppet, even sometimes wildly jumping it into someone else's lap. Once he tied together the pigtails of two girls sitting in front of him until everyone around him was shaking with silent mirth as they anticipated the consequences as they stood up for the next hymn. As expected, the result was well worth the punishment he brought upon himself from his irate father.

Everyone liked Arthur. He was everybody's friend, and his jokes were never unkind or viscous. Now he was twenty-one, I admired his generous easy-going manner which was never too grand to reply to a ten year old. Another boy whom I especially liked because of his quiet pleasant attitude was Arthur's cousin, James. He was notable in that unlike most of the other club members he never showed off or teased either me or the others. It struck me that this was not because he was a cissy, but because in some way which I could not define he was far more adult than the rest, and showed them up for their adolescent self-centred ways. I think that in spite of his maturity he was a shy young man, but when something amused him, his young face screwed up with laughter until the tears ran down his cheeks, and he had to mop his eyes and blow his nose loudly on his dubiously coloured handkerchief.

No one could have been more different from Henry, yet the latter seemed to have an affinity with James who was three years his senior and already at nineteen had been at work for five years. Before long, Henry asked him home for tea, and introduced him to the family as "Arthur's cousin, James Wilson". Mother, who always welcomed our friends warmly, shook his hand and asked him where he lived.

"Charlton" was the reply.

She commented she did not know his parents, and he told her his mother was dead, and he lived with his grandfather Simms. Here immediately was for me a kindred spirit, and I wondered if he could remember his mother, unlike myself. I always burned with curiosity to know what my own mother was like, and supposed he might have the same feeling.

"Is your grandfather the Mr. Simms who owns the factory and the chapel at Woolwich?" Mother enquired. James said yes, it was, and he himself had worked in the factory since he was fourteen, but just recently had completed a year at college learning about optics so that he could understand about the manufacture of the instruments which he helped to produce there. He seemed very knowledgeable, and had a close acquaintanceship with Greenwich Observatory where a number of his firm's products were being used.

James was not very forthcoming about himself after that, but I remembered that one of the senior girls at the High was called Margy Wilson, and it turned out she was his younger sister, and also lived with their grandfather. So from that piece of information I worked out that he must have been at least three when his mother died, and from then on I looked upon him with especial awe and interest. Henry was now established at G&B as general factotum, and in theory at any rate learning the business. His mind wandered constantly from the printing machines to his own beloved motorbike which interested him far more. One day when he was assisting in the gold blocking room with the imprinting of manufacturers' names on the insoles of shoes, he was in one of his daydreams. Having straightened up the run of insoles awaiting stamping, he forgot to remove his hand from the belt before the heavy arm of the printing machine crashed down in its usual way, trapping his hand beneath.

Henry screamed, blood spurted, and the foreman, horrified, had the presence of mind immediately to switch off the power. Henry, by now nearly fainting with pain, held up his hand with the tattered remains of his middle finger. One of the apprentices ran for the First Aid box while the victim sank onto a nearby bench looking a sickly grey. Dad, fortunately, was in the office and soon had him packed into the Dam Liar with his hand wrapped in a towel, and brought him home, leaving a message at the doctor's house on the way, asking him to call as soon as he could.

I think Henry must have been given an injection to ease the pain because by the time I arrived home from school, he was asleep. That evening he was laid on the kitchen table, covered with newly ironed sheets, given ether dropped through a gauze mask, and while he slept the jagged remains of skin and bone were tidied up or removed, and the stump of his finger stitched together. I felt quite sick as I thought of it while I tiptoed round the house getting myself ready for bed.

Already next day Henry was beginning to feel better and enjoy all the fuss as he sat up in bed and lorded it over the family. Factory machinery in those days was largely unguarded, and he had simply not been paying attention. Fortunately the loss of the finger made very little difference to him, and merely served as a good party trick, when he would put on a glove and then, ensuring that everyone's attention was held by his raised hand, nonchalantly press down the third finger of the glove, to his audiences amazement. Gradually the index and fourth fingers grew together and one hardly noticed the gap. After the initial pain I think it was Mother who had suffered most, but from now on she disliked him working other than in the office at G&B as she knew that inattention was to blame for the accident, and she really did not trust him to prevent a repeat performance.

1913 eventually dawned, to Hilda's mounting excitement. This was to be the year of her marriage. The date was set for March 21st, the same as Mother and Dad's wedding day, and Kiki arrived from France a few days beforehand, trim and stylish, surrounded by a tribe of relations who were boarded out at a guest-house or with his eldest sister who was married to an Englishman and lived in Wood Green. The Fiats turned out to be just as noisy when they visited Senrab as they were at Le Vesinet, gesticulating and shrieking "Ooh La La!", or "Mon Dieu" or "Qu'est ce que c'est la". I was amazed at the hubbub and Mother seemed a little overwhelmed as well. Dad silently puffed his pipe and let them get on with it.

Hilda's vortex of excitement was now replaced by dumb nervousness as she suddenly realised that the wedding was next day and she could hardly withdraw at this stage. She was really much nicer in this mood, and it dawned on me that I should miss her when she went off to live in France, a realisation that was tempered by the parallel knowledge that from now on I had a permanent bed to go to whenever I wanted it the other side of the channel. Although not at all sly, I had a pragmatic eye to the future, and was learning to be resourceful.

Not long after Hilda's wedding, when all its excitement had died down and the newly marrieds were settled in their own little house which Papa Fiat had built for them at the bottom of his garden at Le Vesinet, my Father became ill with pneumonia. Then he became exceedingly ill, and I visited him at Auntie Ada's to take him a bunch of flowers from our garden. I felt nervous as I was ushered into his room, but he was blue and breathless and not much interested in my presence. Finally a few days later I was told that he was very seriously ill indeed, and I got panicky. When Mother called me into the drawing-room at Senrab and told me to shut the door, I knew she was going to tell me that he had died, and all the panic disappeared, and I felt quite calm and in control of myself while she was speaking. She was very gentle and understanding, and put it very nicely.

"Of course you will go on living here as one of the family just as you have always done, and Dad will be your father now." she said, so in the end Dad and Mother became my legal guardians, though that was only a formality which cemented what had been true since my birth.

When she finished speaking, Mother kissed me, and silently I wandered down the garden, surveying the cabbages and feeling dazed and unreal. Then the thought struck me that I was now an orphan, and tears began to prick my eyes as I realised how alone I was except for John, and he was around less and less now that school took up his energies.

The house was very quiet that evening, as if everyone was nervous of talking to me. John came round with Auntie Ada, but though he was kind and big brotherly to me and said comfortingly "Don't worry, Snub Nose, I'll look after you", I felt he did not quite understand, he was such an independent person himself. Truth to tell, I knew I should not miss my father very much because my life would go on exactly the same now he was dead as it had done before. One cannot grieve for someone on whom one has had no dependence of any kind. But contrarily, I now recognised how deeply and terribly I wanted my mother whom I had never known; how I ached for her young smile, her girlish liveliness, and even her curls escaping from their hairpins as they did for her wedding photograph. I needed her and yearned to be mothered and cuddled, supported and encouraged by my very own mother who had borne me.

By now I was in bed, the light out, lying with my back to the room, streaming with tears, with great sobs choking me in my desolation of motherlessness. Never had I longed for my young mother so desperately, and she had gone away and left me to face life all on my own. A great sob left my gasping body, and my head throbbed.

The door clicked and a shaft of light flooded through from the landing. I 'froze', hardly daring to breathe. Then I felt Dick's arms round me, pressing my shaking body to her as she petted me and showered quiet sympathy on me. She did not tell me to dry my eyes, or "never mind". She just let me cry until I was exhausted and my sobs hiccuped to a halt, and she went on holding me until I was almost asleep. Then she kissed me, turned my pillow to the cool dry side, cuddled me down, and tiptoed out, her own tears streaming down her face in commiseration.

CHAPTER IV

1914

IT IS ONLY IN retrospect, aware now of the fearful horrors which were then to come, that the words 'nineteen fourteen' immediately cause troubled memories to surface once more. To the general public there was no gathering of war clouds or anticipation of the complete social somersault which so rapidly was set in motion directly war was declared on August 4th, and much more so when the true meaning and portent of hostilities and all their effects became clear during the First Battle of Ypres that October. During the first half of the year, ordinary people continued their normal Edwardian existence oblivious of trouble, and the sun shone. There was more concern over the unrest of labour and the nuisance which the Suffragettes were causing, so that to my twelve years old ears life seemed happily to be swimming along as predicted.

From the previous autumn there had been a continual correspondence between Mother and Hilda, in one direction advice flowing in quantity, in the return mail questions and discussion. Hilda had announced to a hopeful family that she was expecting a baby in April, and a delighted Mother thenceforward threw herself back on her own memories of pregnancy, layettes, maternity wear, and baby equipment generally. Not an enthusiastic seamstress herself, she took up her crocheting hook and determinedly worked little blue jackets and bonnets, a beautiful shawl for the baby and a wrap for Hilda ("for sitting up in bed nursing the baby").

Mama Fiat had obviously taken up her duties of potential paternal grandmother very seriously, and with much exhortation to rest and to "eat for two", volubly produced guidance and information without giving Hilda a chance to disagree. However, it was not in Hilda's nature to argue with her elders, or to exert herself unnecessarily, and she found it much simpler to sit back, receive all the wisdom passively, and follow up the advice. To have to rest every afternoon suited her languid nature only too well, and she enjoyed stitching little garments, and embroidering pillow-slips with tiny blue hearts or the word 'Bébé', whilst Mama Fiat decided what maternity clothes and linen would be needed. Finally, but before Hilda became, as Mama Fiat called it, 'trop enceinte', they had a day at the shops, when they bought a pram, a cot and a baby bath. Kiki seemed to be almost as willing as Hilda to be the inert recipient of these unsolicited goods – it did after all relieve him of the responsibility of making decisions and effort, and more important, the expense – and he confined himself to presenting Hilda with romantic little posies of violets bought from the Paris flower girls on his way home from work. As I thought about them I knew I should adore to be given the flowers, but I felt I should dislike intensely being told by Mama Fiat (or anyone else for that matter) what to do all the time, or having all my baby's needs bought without me having a say. But then, my character was very different from Hilda's, and I wanted to be in control of my life, unlike her. I expect that in the same circumstances I should have been as pig-headed as possible.

In London Mother launched out into a shopping spree at Dickens & Jones and at Gorringes, buying material for dresses and furnishings for Hilda, and sometimes I went with her, which though the actual shopping was boring and I sat on the high-legged Bentwood chairs that drapery stores always provided for their customers in those days, watching the assistant measuring out lengths of cloth by the brass rule which was screwed onto the counter, and vaguely listened to the discussion about the laundering qualities of the different materials, I was thinking more of the café which I knew we should visit subsequently. I wondered whether it would be hot buttered teacakes (which I found hard work as I had to remove all the currants and raisins before I could enjoy the teacake itself) or muffins dripping with butter, which I loved, followed by the decision as to which cake I would like most from the three-tiered stand which the waitress would place on our table – a luscious choice of chocolate and cream confections.

Eventually, a week or two before the baby was due, Mother joined the Golden Arrow at Victoria bound for Paris and Le Vesinet, and for the next month or so enjoyed daily tête-à-têtes with Mama Fiat as they stitched away at baby things, only breaking off when Hilda went into labour, to mop her brow and make encouraging noises. Mother was of course delighted with the baby when she arrived, even though a girl, and thoroughly approved of her name. She quickly despatched a telegram to Dad, "Hannah Jeanne arrived safely this morning. Both well." Dad immediately showed it to me, and watched with his kind smile hovering as it dawned on me that the baby was called after me. I had never in my wildest dreams thought of such a thing, and I was so excited and flattered by this compliment that I felt like crying.

By July the newspapers were sobering, and I noticed that Dad was reading his more diligently. James used to come in more often and the two of them would sit discussing the reports from Austria and Serbia, and shake their heads pensively. James had a habit of half closing his left eye, which he once told me had been 'born blind', and it was this disability which made it quite certain he could never manage to join the army. I remember the excitement when the paper boy brought us an extra edition of the Kentish Independent to announce that war had been declared, and everyone went wild with emotion, and all the boys were looking forward to a scrap with the Germans. James sat very quiet and still, partly, I suspected, because he knew he would have to stay in London, and partly because he was more realistic about war, 21 being old enough to have seen the hospital ships from the South African War landing their battered cargo at Woolwich.

Already Arthur and his cousin William Simms were in army uniform, another Simms cousin was in the navy, and Arthur's youngest brother, Charlie, at Dartmouth. Lots of our other friends appeared at intervals in their newly acquired equipment, showed us how they put on their puttees or their Sam Browne belts, and already had vivid tales to tell of their sergeant majors. The girls turned up in nurse's uniform, or to report they were taking on a man's job to free its previous incumbent for the army. Dick was one of the latter as immediately war was declared, she cycled down to Barclay's Bank in Deptford to apply for work as a clerk, returning later with her eyes shining, to announce that she had to report the following week for training. "They'll pay me eighteen shillings a week once I'm on the counter," she proudly announced. That sounded like treasure trove to me.

Henry, now completely recovered from his accident and full of eager anticipation, but fearing that the 'Show' would be over before he had "had a go at the Huns", rushed off to the army recruiting office. He was immediately taken on as a despatch rider, a position which pleased him mightily as now he could indulge fully his passion for speed on a really powerful motorbike. Even Dad enrolled before long with the civil defence, and appeared at home in army uniform. Only James was left as a civilian. He told me he was afraid people would think he was scared of fighting, and as army service was voluntary at first, although pretty well universal amongst young men, he felt thoroughly out of the swing of things.

"I think I'll go and see what they say at the army depot" he told Dad, and off he went to Woolwich, only to return a couple of hours later shaking his head dolefully.

"No good" he said, and put something into my hand. I looked down to find it was a shilling.

"They even gave me a day's pay," he grinned.

That December James' old grandfather had a severe stroke almost without warning. He was already blind from cataracts, and now was completely helpless. I thought James was going to cry as he told Mother, so affected was he by this tragedy. His grandfather had rescued him and Margy when their mother died and their father was at his wits end to know how to cope with his job as well as look after two small children, and they had lived with their grandfather ever since. He was, as Margy said, "A dear old boy" and they were very fond of him. It was a revelation to me to see a man so obviously upset by sadness, my own male relations being so tough, and I admired James all the more for it.

Everyone's lives seemed to have changed, all, that is, except for mine and those of my friends, which I did not mind about as I was so much enjoying everything we did at the High. Now and then I would notice one of the girls with red eyes and a handkerchief much in evidence, and word would go round that her brother had been killed or wounded. After one of the big battles, huge lists of men would be pinned up outside the town hall, and the number of red-eyed girls would increase. All the grown-ups did 'war work' even if they had no official job, and the ladies would hold afternoon sessions for rolling bandages, knitting comforts for the troops, or inviting wounded tommies from the Herbert Hospital at Woolwich to tea. Auntie Ada, who had had to send all her Swedish girls home at the outbreak of war, now opened her house to Belgian refugees, and enrolled her friends to give voluntary help in running the place. She told Mother she herself intended working several days a week at the local hospital as a V.A.D. (Voluntary Aid Detachment).

"You can't, Ada," remonstrated Mother who hated messy scenes. "You'll wear yourself out." But Auntie, who was a very determined woman, soon started nursing and enjoyed it. Dick, too, started to attend St. John's Ambulance classes in home nursing and first aid, and practiced on the family. Even at school we had first aid classes as well, which was quite fun.

It was as if the whole country was preparing for a huge siege, which in a way it was. But ordinary life had to go on as well, and preparing for Junior Oxford was the aim of everyone at the High.

So we jogged along, my own age group more often than not forgetting about the war until some piece of news startled the grown-ups, and they once more looked grave and worried.

That autumn of 1915 it was my turn to be shaken into the realisation of war. One morning on her way to work Auntie Ada dashed into our house, having propped her bike against the railings. Mother looked up from her desk surprised.

"He's gone, Toria. John's gone to join the army," she shouted, "I knew there was something up, but he never said a word." And she shook a white piece of paper in Mother's face.

"But he's only sixteen," said Mother, taking hold of it to read. It just said in John's adolescent scrawl that he had gone to enlist, and we were not to worry.

"Not to worry!" echoed Auntie Ada. "He must have gone last night instead of going to bed, so goodness knows where he is now."

"They will never recruit him at his age" comforted Mother, "or if they do, they'll only take him on as a cadet or a messenger or something like that. Best to leave him alone and not worry."

So they decided to wait and see, and Dad thought that was best, too. As for me, I thought what a lark it must be for John, and how he would enjoy hoodwinking the authorities about his age.

The next thing was, several weeks later, I received a postcard from France with a black and white picture of a nondescript country scene. The message just read "Everything fine. Don't worry. Hope your mongrel is well. Happy Christmas. Love, John."

Then, of course, we did start to worry. John was tall, well-built and mature. He was very self-confident and could be plausible. Already he had to shave every day, and looked much older than sixteen. What if he told them he's eighteen, I thought. And I could see that Mother had the same idea as she read the card and saw the British Expeditionary Force postmark, but she repeated that he would only be a messenger boy, and went upstairs to put on her hat and coat to visit Auntie Ada, and talk it over with her.

I think we all knew the truth, which was that John had added at least two years to his age, and had been enlisted as an ordinary private. There was little we could do, with the Germans pouring westwards into Belgium and northern France, but hope for the best and trust that new recruits would only be used as back up, and not as front line soldiers. For a few months we relied on that supposition.

I think that had I known on New Year's Day, 1916, in just how many ways the war was going to grasp us in its cruel tentacles that year, I could not have faced it and would, if I had been able to, have run away. There remained the two sides of my life; the calm predictable life of school friends, hockey and music lessons, and the cataclysmic results of war, and for the first time this year I was brought face to face with its horrors. John's birthday coincided with the first day of the year, so we especially thought of him then, though we were still devoid of concrete news but hopeful that someone had spotted his actual age. I ached inside myself as I repeated over and over again like a magic invocation, "Don't let him be killed, don't let him be killed."

Somehow this did not seem adequate, and I felt there must be a more concrete way to help. I thought I would slip round to St. Germain's Church which was just behind our house on the east side of the Heath, and see if I could find the answer there, but I did not quite know how. I felt self-conscious, and hoped no one would see me as I ran into the church. The heavy metal ring handle groaned ominously as I turned it and pushed the door open, and stepped inside. I was very hot and sweaty, and muddled in my mind, and the church was lovely and cool, and quite dark after the sunlight outside. There was nobody in sight, so I sat down in the nearest pew to collect my thoughts and look around. I had been in the church before occasionally with Mother, but always to a service when the pews were full of people, the lights all on, and the organ playing, and I had been so busy watching the congregation and the choir that I had not really considered what we were primarily there for. This time it was all different. I was deeply worried and needed help. The calm atmosphere seemed to invite me into its caring arms, and quite soon I felt less agitated. I just sat still, thinking about nothing much and letting its tranquillity pour over me. Then I got up and wandered round looking at the monuments and coloured windows before returning to the sunshine which at first made me blink. I felt much better and had the feeling that there was indeed Someone who cared about us all and would help us to face all the terrors and anxieties that were drowning us.

After that I often popped into St. Germain's, especially when I felt I needed soothing, and started to go to morning services on Sundays whilst Mother was cooking the lunch. I did not use it like a magic spell, because that would have been wrong, but merely as a rock that was stronger than myself.

The Gallipoli Campaign was meanwhile grinding along at the far end of the Mediterranean, providing a background of horror there. Arthur had been on embarkation leave the previous autumn, coinciding with his grandfather's funeral, and ten days later marrying Peggy, who was a nurse, and whom I liked very much. All the young men in his wedding photographs except James, went straight out to Turkey with the West Kents the following week, and so far Arthur had survived. In Europe there were great rumblings of battle from northern France, and suddenly in early summer we received a telegram from Hilda in Paris which merely said "Arriving Victoria 4.0 pm Tuesday".

The Dam Liar was primed, and Dad and Mother went down to meet her. Several hours later, a boat train packed with refugees puffed into the station and disgorged its hungry masses, and Hilda emerged with a case in one hand and Jeanne in the other, looking worn out, very grubby, and half-starved. Her dark eyes seemed to have sunk into their sockets and her face was lined and anxious. Papa Fiat had packed all his daughters off to England when it seemed likely that Paris would be overrun by Germans. He had been in the earlier siege in 1870, and he was not going to have his children submit to a repetition of the starvation and inhumanity which had occurred then. So Hilda and Jeanne came to live with us at Senrab, and after a good meal and a thorough scrub, the little girl was as right as rain, and Hilda had regained her equilibrium. But it had not been easy for her to leave France, with Kiki away somewhere at the Front, and all their goods and chattels, not to mention Kiki's parents, at the mercy of the Germans. Jeanne was just two years old, and an attractive, bright little girl, who was a joy to have about the house, and a full-time occupation for her mother, who thereby had her mind taken off France's troubles. I was only twelve years older than Jeanne – almost the same amount as Dick was older than me – and I enjoyed looking after her, and we soon became great friends.

Almost exactly at the same time as Hilda arrived in England, Henry was commissioned and came on leave in officer's uniform, to Mother's immense pride, even though it was a well-known fact that statistics showed that 2nd lieutenants comprised the most vulnerable rank in the British Army. Before he had been in the house half an hour he announced that he had obtained a special licence and was going to marry his singer friend, Estelle, that week. Mother and Dad looked nonplussed, and not very happy, but they were so overjoyed to see him and so dreading him going to the Front, that their feelings were all mixed up. If that was what Henry wanted, he should have it.

It was a typical rushed war-time wedding, without any frills except that we had a make shift reception before they went down to an hotel on the coast for their three days' honeymoon. We knew he would almost certainly be going to France now, and in fact he went straight off leave into the trenches that were being dug before the Somme. He managed to survive not only that battle but the rest of the war in the mud of Flanders and France without mishap, or even undue emotional upset. Not so lucky was William Simms, who was slightly older and a captain in the R.A. He arrived on the Somme in July, and was killed within a month. James came to tell us, and although he had not been so intimate with this cousin as with some of his others, it was nevertheless a shock, and he felt sorrow for William's parents. Less affecting, though yet another blow to his family was the news that another Simms' cousin, Alex, had been drowned at sea after his ship was torpedoed. The German submarines were very active now, and this kind of news was common enough, but it frightened me as I wondered about John.

Before long the dreaded news arrived. I saw the telegraph boy dismount from his bike, and push the familiar orange envelope through the letterbox. Mother heard the brass flap clatter down, and came from the drawing-room. Everyone in those years dreaded telegrams, and I had caught the contagion and held my breath as she tore it open. It was an official army notification, to say that Private John Minska had been wounded, and would be returned to England as soon as possible.

It had happened, and so far we had no idea how badly he had been hurt. Mother and Auntie Ada badgered the War Office, and in due course we learnt that he had been hit by a shell in his back and was severely ill in a field hospital, but was due to transfer to a hospital in southern England soon. It took several more weeks before we finally heard he had arrived at Woolwich, and Mother and Auntie Ada went to visit him. They returned looking rather serious, and reported that he was still in pain and was being nursed lying on his front. Bits of shrapnel had penetrated his buttocks, and although some pieces had been removed by the surgeon, others were still working their way out amidst infection and severe pain. Again, as when Henry lost his finger, I felt physically sick as I visualised the wound, but comforted myself by the thought that at least he was not now at the Front.

Either Auntie Ada or Mother went to see John as often as they could, and gradually their reports of him improved as he started to get out of bed and move around. In time he was allowed to dress in the familiar 'hospital blue' uniform and to stroll round the grounds, and then I was permitted to visit him. Even though prepared for it, I was shocked by his appearance. He looked unbelievably old, and very thin and gaunt, but when he saw me approaching and his grin emerged as he greeted me, it was the same John as before beneath the grey face.

"Hallo, Snub Nose," and then "Hi! Not so fast", as I suddenly thrust myself into his arms in tears. But they were tears of relief, and soon turned into a broad smile. I had not realised how pent-up and anxious I had become over the last months, now abruptly to relax into knowing that he was safe. But that was by no means the end of it. When his wound was clean and the bits of metal ceased to emerge from it, John was sent home to recuperate at the Rookery. Auntie was glad to look after him and try to 'feed him up', and I cycled over to see him as often as homework permitted. We played draughts and chess and card games, but he soon became tired and irritable, and then I knew it was time for me to make some excuse to leave. He complained very little but I knew he still had a good deal of pain and was not sleeping well. It was like having a constant severe series of carbuncles, and the effect on his general health was similar. Every few months over the next years the pain became unbearable as yet another piece of the shell found its way to the surface. Sometimes the doctor lanced the infection to hurry things along. I once was at the Rookery when that happened, and never shall I forget the scream of torment followed by groans and finally tears as that poor boy submitted to this torture. I simply could not bear to hear it, and rushed into the garden with tears streaming down my own face. War is terrible.

At Senrab we also had a patient. Dad was very unwell that year, and was in bed for several weeks, with the doctor coming to see him frequently. I was told it was something called 'Bright's disease', which meant nothing to me, but Edna said knowingly "Kidneys, you know", and I could see Mother was worried. After a while he started to get up for a short time each day, then gradually more and more, but he never seemed to be really well again. James used to come and see him often, but then James was often in our house anyhow, and becoming increasingly one of the family. With Henry in France and Dad unable to do much about the house, he was very useful mending fuses and things like that. He and Dick got on very well together, and the two of them would go out on long walks, or sometimes they went 'up West' to a show or for a meal. On Sundays they went to the Congregational church at Blackheath together. One evening in the summer James and Dad were closeted for ages in the drawing-room in earnest discussion, and I found Dick wandering round the garden with an odd look on her face and nervously picking flowers in an absent minded sort of way. After a while James came to the back door and waved to her, and she rushed anxiously up to him, and to my astonishment he nodded and then kissed her full on the mouth. Then of course I realised that they were engaged to be married, and Dad brought out the glasses and we all, even me, had a little sherry to drink their healths. I felt so happy and pleased for them both as they were my big supports in life.

"We shall be married as soon as the war is over," Dick said, and then they went off across the Heath, him with his arm round her waist, and she all smiles and excitement. So, in a romantic haze, I took myself off to bed.

Not long after that, Dick announced that her friend Lily Pennell, who was now Lily Cook, was expecting a baby early the following year. Lily's husband was in France, so Dick went over to Greenwich where Lily had a little house, as often as she could, and sometimes Lily came to us for a meal at the weekends. But as time went on this was not very satisfactory for her, and in the end Dick told Mother and Dad that she was going to stay with Lily until after the baby was born so that she was not on her own. I could see irritation rising in Mother's eyes, and Dad looked uncomfortable as he said "Don't you think you ought to stay here with us, dear." And Mother, much more forthright, exclaimed "Of course she ought." Hilda got up and went upstairs with Jeanne. She hated trouble. I felt the same and went out into the garden. What actually happened I don't know exactly, but I think there was a big argument, and in the end Dick lost her temper and said she was going to pack, which she did.

I missed her at home very much. I would cycle over to visit her at Lily's place, or at other times she would visit Senrab to see the family and collect some of her belongings. It seemed reasonable to me for her to go and live with Lily, especially as the German zeppelins were liable to come over London to drop their bombs. I should think Lily's husband was very glad when he heard in his trench that she was not alone. I really did not understand why Mother had made such a fuss, except that Dad was not very well. I noticed however that though Lily's baby arrived safely in January 1917, Dick stayed on with her until the summer, going to the bank each day, but helping to look after the baby, which she loved doing, at other times. I would sometimes find the two of them, Lily and

Dick, sitting like a couple of old dears, each with her sewing, discussing all sorts of interesting things like weddings and marriages and babies, and back again to weddings, and very happy they were in their ménage.

I think it must have been the continual fighting in the first half of 1917 that forced Dick and James into a decision about their marriage. The war seemed to be going on and on without any hint of an end to it. Now the Americans were entering the fray, and the slaughter continued, particularly at sea. James had been seconded to the India Office in Whitehall, where his knowledge of optical instruments was being put to good use in sorting out the scientific side of weaponry for their forces. His income was secure and he had also been left some money by his grandfather. In the mid-summer Dick and James made their minds up to go ahead with the wedding, and started house-hunting.

"We'd like you to be a bridesmaid, Anne, if you will," Dick said, to my complete surprise and delight. A bridesmaid! How marvellous! I had never thought of such a thing.

"What shall I wear?" I immediately asked, with true feminine instinct. Dick had worked it out, and had all the answers.

"You'll have a goldy-brown dress like this," she said, producing a pattern, "a straw hat, and brown shoes and stockings, and a little autumn posy. We can't have a white wedding with the war as it is, so I thought you'd both better have things that you can wear afterwards."

"Both?" I queried.

"Yes, Margy is going to be the other bridesmaid."

"Oh." I tried not to sound crestfallen. Margy was six years older than me but miles apart in every possible way. She seemed to have everything that I had not; money, good looks, nice clothes, confidence, intelligence, and she was very gifted musically. She could sing and play the piano well, and also paint and draw, all the things I much envied and was hopeless at. But on top of all this she was very lofty in her attitude to life, and could be very scathing. I remember once overhearing her say to a friend "Poor Mrs. Barnes doesn't have a cook. How does she manage?" I felt she looked down on everything to do with my life and family, and I could never reach her standards however hard I tried. I could not imagine how it was she was James' sister, he was so easy to get on with – just the opposite.

I knew Margy would look just beautiful in her bridesmaid attire, and show me up for my gaucherie and lack of poise, but equally I wanted nothing to spoil Dick's joy, and so I hid my disappointment, and tried to concentrate on my new dress.

The wedding was set for October 6th at Blackheath Congregational Church, with a small family reception afterwards at Senrab. Anything more pretentious would have been inappropriate just now when there was so much heartache in the world. However, as plans blossomed, and wedding presents (some of which I eyed with awe) started to arrive, there was the usual hustle and bustle and excitement as I helped Dick to make her new little home in Bromley ready for occupation. Dad too, although not really well, enjoyed giving a hand where he could. However, it was his swan-song. The very day before the wedding, he suddenly complained that he felt "funny", and the next moment had collapsed. He had suffered a massive stroke, and the doctor said he was almost completely paralysed and speechless. It had all been too much for him.

Once more the garden offered refuge from a crisis, and as I wandered aimlessly round it, imagining my dear old Dad lying helplessly in bed, I just could not believe he would not the next moment appear at the bedroom window to wave, or ever again offer his kind words of encouragement, or greet me when I arrived home from school. Dad, my Dad, was leaving me. Like my own parents had done; like John had almost done; like lots of friends had done in battle. It could not be true, and somebody would soon say "Hannah, wake up."

Instead, the word went round that a nurse was coming to look after Dad next day, and the wedding would go ahead, though there would be no proper reception, just wedding cake and a toast to the bride and bridegroom. Suddenly the sun which had been shining so brightly in my life, had been veiled in cloud and mist and shadow. All the dreariness which other people complained of, but which for me had been camouflaged in the bright colours of adolescence so that I had hardly noticed it, became grey and gaunt and predominant. The security and fun of my life became obscured by care and worry. The first chapter of my life, happy in the midst of my adoptive family, was over.

CHAPTER V

1917

DAD MANAGED TO live a few more days, but Dick and James had to be telegraphed whilst still on their honeymoon to return home as he deteriorated. After the funeral I went back to school oblivious of the fact that it was to be the last term I should do so.

A quietness had descended on Senrab, only broken by Jeanne's baby chatter, and the visits of Mother's friends wearing black armbands, and numerous tradesmen calling with commiserations and their bills. The solicitor came for several long sessions, when he and Mother shut themselves in the dining-room, and I could hear the low hum of their voices which, even though I could not make out the words, were so obviously sober, concerned and intense. Mr. Courtney arrived from G&B with a bag full of account books, and I had my tea in the kitchen that day. Mother was white and strained and preoccupied. With her fair Swedish appearance and her upright carriage she looked so aristocratic in black that I wondered she had not worn it before. She hardly seemed to notice Hilda or me, and even Dick who understood accounts and money matters was brought into the discussions only after some time, and emerged looking even more worried than before. Then James arrived on his motorbike one evening, and went with Mother into the dining-room, where the table was permanently covered in papers and ledgers.

Finally all the visitors left, and Mother, dry-eyed but taut, called me in.

"Hannah," she began. "We have been going over Dad's affairs, including G&B, and it is clear that we are going to have to economise." I looked her squarely in the eye, in as understanding a manner as I could, and said nothing.

"I'm afraid we shall have very little money now," she continued,"and we must sell Senrab, and go to live somewhere cheaper."

"That's alright, Mother," I agreed in my ignorance, "We'll manage." She inclined her head in acknowledgment.

"It will have to be somewhere very small. I don't know where."

"As long as I can cycle to school, it doesn't really matter," I said helpfully. She looked at me without expression.

"You will have to leave school at the end of this term,Hannah. We can't afford it any more." I could not believe my ears.

"Leave school?" I echoed. "You can't mean leave the High."

"Yes, I do," she repeated.

I was completely speechless. Then as the words sank in, I wanted to scream, to stamp and rage, like Jeanne in a temper, but Mother looked so sad and vulnerable, and almost frail in a way, I knew I must not hurt her further.

"Oh Mother," I cried, and put my arms round her as we clung together.

And so that was how my career at the High School ended, how the domestic science course I had just joyfully started had to finish, and how Edna and my other friends all went back to school after Christmas without me. Now I had to earn my living, and so on January 1st, 1918, I caught the train to Cannon Street in the City and walked to G&B in Hamsel Street, just off Aldersgate near St. Paul's, where I started my sojourn in the office. This was the only way I could think of to make money.

G&B occupied a whole house in this busy commercial street, and typical of City buildings, was Victorian, self-important and cumbersome, and faced with huge blocks of stone which were blackened with London grime. It had an imposing front door, but after that any pretence of grandeur or charm ended in the bleak hall and stairway, the dark lincrusta dado and brown paint. There was a cellar used for storage of paper, as also was the ground floor which was too dark, in spite of its large windows, in which to work without artificial light owing to the tall buildings opposite shading it from the murky smoke-laden daylight. The first floor contained the office where Mr. Courtney had his desk and many of the files were kept, and next door at the back of the house was the counting house where Minnie spent her days. The next floor up housed the gold-blocking equipment, and piles of materials waiting to be stamped with their manufacturers' names, very largely the insoles of shoes made in Northampton and Norwich, and also the hard covers of books to be bound, though this side of the business lapsed during the war. Upstairs again was the book-binding department where women as well as men laboured away with a mixture of machine and hand sewing, and the top floor contained more storerooms.

About thirty-five people were employed in this building, for which there was one w.c. squashed into a tiny room in a corner of the staircase between the first and second floors. This poky hole also boasted a minute triangular wash-basin with one cold tap, a small mirror, towel of dubious colour dutifully changed by Minnie on Mondays, a forty watt light without a shade, and a small sash window kept permanently open. There were gas fires in the work rooms, controlled carefully by Courtney, and pegs on the walls at strategic places to accommodate coats and hats. The whole thing was incredibly Dickensian, and the discipline firm, but amazingly, all seemed cheerfully absorbed in their tasks, and the general atmosphere was undoubtedly content.

Minnie greeted me cheerily.

"Come along, ducks," she said, "You can work at this desk," and she showed me where to go, and started to explain the office routine by spreading a huge account book before me.

Minnie was a round little person with smooth rosy cheeks like newly-baked bread buns. Her gold-rimmed spectacles, which obscured her cheerful eyes, had forged a deep crease across her nose. Her hair was cut short, and pin-curled at ear-lobe level, carefully parted on one side and kept in place by an 'invisible' hairnet. Her floral-patterned dresses reached to her calves, and in summer had elbow-length sleeves. In winter she wore a capacious woolly cardigan well pulled down over what she called her 'embonpon', and her shoes and thick stockings were brown and serviceable. She had artificial dentures which showed a lot when she talked, and caused her to excuse herself from the room after lunch, especially if she had partaken of anything pippy. She had beautifully ironed white handkerchieves with her initial on, which she shoved up a sleeve or down the front of her dress, and then had to go fishing for them when they were needed. Her handbag was large, capacious and mysterious. Amongst other useful items, such as extra handkerchieves, safety pins, kirby grips, a comb, a bag of acid drops, and a notebook and pencil, it held a bottle of lavender water which was one of her few self-indulgences. She was a busy little individual, exuding common-sense and kindliness, and was one of the most unselfish people I have ever known.

From the moment I entered that counting house, homesick for the High, lonely without my friends, yearning for all the activities I enjoyed, I hated the place. One half of me said Mother had rescued me when I was a new baby and nobody wanted me; now in her agony I must do all I could to help her in return. The other half of me, the selfish, adolescent, joie-de-vivre half, felt squashed and repressed and rebellious. I loathed it all; the dreary rooms, the curtainless windows, the bare floorboards, the black ledgers and pens, even poor Minnie's kind Cockneyisms trying to break through my moroseness. I suppose she thought I was mourning Dad, and did her best to help me. I was indeed mourning Dad, but I was mourning my past life even more. I knew I was meant for a physically active existence, and here I was sitting on a horrid stool all day, kicking its legs with my own, and chewing the end of my pen with self-pity.

Somehow I stuck to the work – I had to, there was no alternative and my sixteenth birthday in February passed miserably. Minnie was strict but fair, and did her best to relieve me of the boredom of deskwork by sending me on all the errands that occurred. I made the office tea, took the cash to the bank, visited the post office with the mail, and bought the stamps. Sometimes I acted as delivery boy with parcels of printed matter for offices about the City, and as long as I was reasonably careful not to overstep the time, she did not reprove me for being slow. I enjoyed these outings along the bustling streets, and was able to look at the shops as I passed, or stare at the crowds.

At one o'clock each day we put down our pens and got out our packets of sandwiches. If it was fine I took mine out to St. Paul's churchyard, and ate my lunch sitting on a wall with the other office workers from neighbouring buildings. I became quite friendly with some of them, although they were mostly older than me. Sometimes I would wander into Smithfield Market to watch the meat vendors washing down their stalls after the morning sales, or past Bart's Hospital to see the nurses scurrying along. Other days I walked round the Guildhall or past Bow Church and its 'big bell', and wondered what they were doing in my form at school and how different life was here in the City. If my spirits were particularly low, I went into St. Paul's to look at George Blagdon Westcott's vast statue. "Nobody I know has an ancestor like that," I cheered myself.

On Fridays Minnie and I made up the wages. She stressed to me that this was highly confidential work, and I noticed that she did the office staff packets herself, and left me to count out the factory men's money. Then I had to stick up the envelopes and name them, while she checked the ledger. Finally she placed my own envelope on my desk with a nod.

"There you are, ducks. Nicey picey! Don't spend it all at once."

Nicey picey indeed! I would certainly not be spending it. It all went to Mother for essentials. Every Friday it was the same, until that remark too started to rile me, and in spite of myself I waited each week with irritable glee for her to say it. I knew I was only hurting myself by such silliness, but it was all part of my sneering hatred of that beastly office.

Meanwhile much of our furniture at Senrab had been sold, and so had the house. One of James' relations suggested the basement of their house at Shooter's Hill as a temporary retreat for us, and that was where Mother, Hilda, Jeanne and I moved.

My feelings about that flat were similar to my attitude to the office. Without reservation I loathed it. It was dark and damp and crowded, and there was no garden for us. I slept in a sort of boxroom: it was either that or sharing with Mother, and I couldn't bear the thought of that. I needed to be able to cry at night without anyone hearing me. I expect Mother felt the same, though she was so weary by bedtime that she said she went straight to sleep. To do her justice, no sooner had she arranged the move than she started work at the Foreign Office translating Swedish. She was no more used to office work than I was, and the constriction must have been just as daunting for her. From her relatively leisurely life she now had become an ordinary office worker.

I think I missed the fresh air and exercise I was used to as much as anything, and the strain of a full day's concentration at a desk for five-and-a-half days a week was probably responsible for the perpetual colds that I developed. The tension of detestable office routine possibly caused my wheeziness which began this winter for the first time. In spite of cycling and walking all I could at the weekends, often to Edna's house, or Dick's, or to see John, or indeed anywhere to get away from the flat, I did not get rid of it for any length of time, and when I was tired or worried it was always worst.

The best news in 1918 was twofold. In October Dick and James produced their first baby. I thought she was lovely, and although I liked to think I was invulnerable and self-contained, I could not prevent the motherly feelings which assailed me when Dick put her into my arms. Marriage and babies appeared to be a natural progression of events to me, although I did sometimes wonder, when the casualty lists were especially gross, whether there would ever be any eligible men left of my age group to marry. However, shortly after the baby's arrival, came the overwhelming joy and excitement of the Armistice, and for a day or two life seemed worth living again. John was improving, and it appeared as if at least one side of our existence was going to become normal.

Gradually people we knew in the forces returned home and became civilians once more, and Hilda was talking about going back to France with Jeanne, where Kiki had come unscathed through four years in the front line. Mother found that there was less and less translating required in her section of the Foreign Office, and decided she would be better occupied in learning the business at G&B. Stevens, the manager, offered her £2 a week "to come and help", but she said no thanks, she was going to come and run the place, which completely took the wind out of his sails. So now, just coming up to sixty years of age, she commenced her daily train journeys to Cannon Street, and settled down in the premises at Hamsel Street to take over responsibility for the firm. Old Courtney was only too glad to have some of the burden taken from his long-suffering shoulders, as he was getting on in years himself, and he preferred that Mother, even though a woman and inexperienced in business methods, should grasp the helm and be firmly in control before Henry reappeared from the army to claim that position.

Mother was intelligent, forceful and persevering, not to say obstinate. She must have been all those things to have coped at her age with this entirely new world. Minnie remained in the counting house, and Mother knew she could rely on everything running smoothly there. The accountant, Fitzhugh, had final say on the books, and Courtney ran the factory and the commercial side. Gradually Mother found her way into all aspects of the business, and quite firmly and unmistakably was the boss. It says much for her strength of character that she made a great success of it, and very soon had turned the debit which Dad had left into a remarkable profit.

Meanwhile John was improving so much that he was becoming bored at the Rookery, and was thinking about his future. He wrote to Father's firm, Guthries, and must have used all his guile and charm to persuade them that he was exactly what they needed, as they offered him a job straight away in Singapore to do with tea planting. How John bamboozled them into assuming that his health was up to Far Eastern hazards I do not know, but as I mentioned before, he could be very plausible, and he was also determined and had more than his share of Minska obstinacy. It was a characteristic that had been highly useful to all of us.

So, some time in the Summer of 1919, with the last pockets of fighting now at an end and the Peace Conference convening at Versailles, John set sail in a merchant boat from the Port of London. I felt utterly wretched and wobbly-kneed as I waved him off, trying hard to keep back my tears. But I knew he had to go, if only to prove to himself that he could do the work. I dared not wonder when I should ever see him again. However, somewhere in the Middle East, perhaps at Suez or Port Said, he picked up a tummy germ, and began to be alarmingly ill. This new infection started up his war wound again, and he was so bad that he was landed at Colombo, more dead than alive, and the ship went on without him. After weeks in hospital there, Guthries arranged for his return to England, where I felt as if it was a re-run of 1916, only this time he was an absolute skeleton and you could more or less see the light through his hands.

Auntie had his bed brought downstairs at the Rookery, and the drawing-room was turned into a special retreat for him. He even spent his 21st birthday, on New Year's Day 1920, in bed, and celebrations were somewhat circumscribed in consequence. Once

55

more, with careful nursing by Auntie Ada, and as much nourishing food as he could take, he gradually improved and put on weight, but it was obvious that his future could not be other than in Europe, and he needed plenty of fresh air and proper care. In the end it was arranged that he should go to live with Kiki and Hilda in France, where they had a pig farm at a little place called Goursat near Condé-Busac, and help as much as he could on the land. I felt much happier about this than having him at the other end of the world where I should probably never have been able to visit him. France was easy to get to, and as soon as I could save enough I would go. I retrieved my school books from the bottom of my wardrobe, and set to work to rub up my French vocabulary in the evenings – anything to take my mind off my present life which was so hateful, and give me something to look forward to. I used to read a great deal at that period, especially in the winter, and would always be happy to curl up with a thriller and an apple to while away the time, but this new interest was a pleasant alternative, anticipating as it did future bouts of French sunshine.

By 1921 Mother evidently could see the light at the end of the tunnel, and determined that she and I must have better living quarters. I do not know how she worked out the finances, but at any rate she started house hunting, and in spite of the shortages of accommodation after the war, managed to find a small semi-detached house not far from where Dick lived. To help pay for it she suggested that Henry and Estelle, who had had their first baby in-1917 and were now expecting a second, should live on the first floor. I did not relish being in the same house as them as they were so noisy and overpowering, and Estelle was given to singing loudly in her resonant contralto, but it must be better than continuing in that damp flat which not only affected my spirits, but Mother thought my health also.

It was an unutterable relief to me to move, and at Avondale Road we now had a small garden which I began to look after at the weekends. The other major advantage of having Henry and Estelle upstairs was that now I felt Mother could be left on her own at night, as they were within call, and when Dick asked me to go on the Broads with James and her that year, my joy knew no bounds. They left their two little girls with Lily, who turned not a hair at the extra work, and the three of us set off in an Austin Seven borrowed from Bill Strong, a friend of James. Clad in long army-style leather coats, felt trilbies, and strong leather brogues, we arrived in Norfolk cold but with an unwonted sense of freedom. The Cygnet was a small single-cabin yacht with a minute galley in the forepeak. To me, fresh from the jaws of the office, this was more than nicey-picey. It was idyllic. We sailed and walked and ate and read. We shopped at the little Broadlands stores for our milk and bread, and bought an array of tinned food from Roys of Wroxham to heat up on our primus stove. It was a complete change and a thrill, and I returned to Mother with a smile on my face and my wheeze disappeared, to find that although she had missed me, she was quite cheerful in spite of a row with Henry over something or other at the office.

The fact was that Mother simply did not trust Henry not to make a mess of the orders or to squander the profits. She did not even value his opinion to any extent, preferring her own. It reminded me of the relationship between Queen Victoria and the Prince of Wales, except that Henry had few alternative modes of employment. But I knew what she meant although I was sorry for him, and thought she ought to give him a chance to prove himself, instead of which she made all the decisions herself. Much as I hated the office myself, I knew he hated it more, and in a way it was worse for him as although neither of us could see an alternative because of the mounting unemployment problem in the country, he now had a wife and baby, and could not risk his income by leaving. Besides, it was degrading for him to be passed over like a child by his mother when there were decisions to be made, especially when she did it covertly in front of other employees. Even old Courtney would sometimes try to guide a discussion in Henry's direction in his deferential and kindly manner.

"Do you think, Mrs. Barnes," he would venture, "that Mr. Henry would prefer such-and-such?" knowing full well that Mr. Henry didn't care two pins either way as long as his cheque came in each month.

"No, Mr. Courtney," she would answer, interpreting Henry's supposed opinion to fit in with her own, "Mr. Henry would definitely not prefer that."

"I just wondered" Courtney would try again "whether we should ask him so that he feels more a party to the policy."

"I'm sure Mr. Henry will feel that anyway, Mr. Courtney," she would firmly reply. "I will speak to him about it on the way home." Which really meant that she would tell him when whatever it was had become a fait accompli.

I liked old Courtney more and more as he bowed gently and withdrew respectfully both from the subject and from the room. His first loyalty was to Mother because she owned the business, and his second was to G&B for which he had worked all his life. After that came his due to Henry who was the boss's son, and here he was placed in an awkward position where he could rarely balance the different forces acting on his better judgement.

So Henry was never really encouraged to participate in management or become more than superficially involved in the firm, and accordingly any spark of interest or enthusiasm he may have had was snuffed and all but extinguished.

For me it was different. Mine was a long hard daily slog at work which I found distasteful and very boring. I could see no end to it, and yet in the far distance I knew there was a bright light because assuredly there was more to life than sitting at a high desk adding up figures which never gave the same answer twice running. By the time a column had been totted up three times and still produced a deviant result, Minnie would notice my sighs and failure to progress to the next page of the ledger, and, looking over my shoulder, would remove her pencil from its perch over her right ear, and soon produce the correct total that had evaded me.

"Come on, ducks," she would exclaim, "see if you can't do better." Or she would try her best to find another job to divert me, with her kindly perception that my sixteen years were being sorely tried to their utmost.

"It will soon be time for lunch. Nicey-picey!" she would conclude, replacing the pencil to its previous resting place on her ear. Poor patient Minnie, who was herself resigned to the complete predictability of her grey and changeless future, and humbly grateful for the chinks of light which so rarely broke through her London fog.

"That's a nasty cough you've got, ducks," she said one day after I'd been hacking my way through several weeks. "Got another cold, have you? Better ask Mother to rub your chest tonight."

And Mother did, with great vigour, back and front, and with large quantities of camphorated oil or Bengues balsam. It was lovely and warming, and the smell and the friction made me sleepy, but did nothing for my cough, which had a rather satisfying barking quality to it. When the bark gave way to a loose fruity choke, and I was obviously losing weight, Mother took me to see Dr. Pitts Payne, who looked at my chest, listened to it, tapped it all over, and made me cough again and again, before repeating the whole performance. Then he sat down at his desk with his stethoscope dangling from his neck, changed his glasses, and wrote out a prescription.

"Hannah has got a great deal of fluid on her chest, Mrs. Barnes," he announced, "and in view of her father's illness, it would be quite wrong for her to remain working in an enclosed atmosphere. She must have as much fresh air as possible. Switzerland perhaps?" he hedged.

Switzerland! But how?

"What about the office?" queried Mother.

"Quite unsuitable. She must on no account continue there," he replied firmly in a tone that brooked no nonsense.

Once more in my short life I could hardly believe my ears.

"Leave the office?" I broke in, amazed and incredulous, whilst Mother looked more and more worried.

"Do you mean she has T.B?" she asked in an accusing voice.

"She may well have. We will take some sputum for testing," was his reply.

Hurray for T.B., I thought recklessly. What matters T.B. if it gets me out of that hateful office, and I coughed all the more in my excitement, until I wheezed to a standstill.

So that was the end of my daily grind at the office, and rejoicing, though trying to appear as ill as I was supposed to be, and accepting Minnie's concerned commiserations with grace, I almost danced out into the sunlight of Aldersgate, with a lighter heart than I had had for three years.

CHAPTER VI

1922

"LUCKY THING," SAID Henry enviously when he heard the news. "Just like a girl to get out of it." But then he remembered the seriousness of the diagnosis and said no more.

Switzerland was, of course, quite out of the question in our financial state, but Mother wrote to her Auntie Maria in Sweden, and after some exchanges of correspondence it was arranged that I should go to friends of hers in Norway for a few months. So in January 1921 I set off from Harwich with all my winter clothes packed into one big valise, including a good supply of woolly vests from Mother, knitted scarves and gloves from Dick, and several detective novels from Henry to while away the time on board.

To my joy I discovered that the friends, who were called Mr. & Mrs. Amundsen, lived in the mountains above Christiansund, and were keen skiers. Their daughter, Helven, was about my age, and the whole family spoke good English which rather discouraged me from trying to learn Norwegian. To tell the truth, I felt weary after my years at the office, tired of trying to understand things I found difficult, and exhausted too in a physical sense. At first I was treated as an invalid, and had a very lazy time, but gradually as I perked up I went with Helven to the ski slopes, and while she performed with great gusto, I soon acquired the knack of remaining upright and controlling my obstreperous feet with their long appendages. I was a natural athlete, but I was out of practice and my muscles were sloppy and weak from lack of use. Increasingly they regained their lost tone, and very soon I was off the nursery slopes attempting more ambitious runs. The Norwegian air was crisp and clear, the sun shone around noon most days that year, but so dry were the mountains that the bitter cold did not deter us from skiing all the daylight hours, which at that latitude were few. However, the Amundsens were very sociable, and there were skiing parties in moonlight, or skating parties by floodlight, and not only was my physical health restored after a couple of months in these beautiful surroundings, but they gave me back my enthusiasm for life, and I found myself chattering away with all their friends as if I had known them always. My 20th birthday coincided with this visit, and was spent in the mountains amongst the snow-laden trees, with a huge bonfire and an alfresco meal to finish the day.

My faith in human beings completely restored, I began to think about my future. I dreaded Mother insisting that I return to the office, but my instinct told me that Dr. Pitts Payne would not allow this, so I felt fairly safe. But I was unable to solve the problem of how I could possibly earn my living other than in an office, as I had no other training. My own love was cookery, but as I had left school so precipitously, I had only achieved one term of the special course they ran for that at the High, and consequently my knowledge in that direction was embryonic. I adored needlework and embroidery, but my efforts were anything but professional, and certainly no-one would pay me for them. So I scratched my head and tried to solve the problem, but with little success beyond the most vague ideas.

After about three months in Norway, I felt really well, and had regained my appetite and was putting back on the weight I had lost. I began to realise that I was perhaps imposing on the Amundsens' kindness, although they never indicated any wish for me to leave, so I wrote to Mother and arranged to come home.

The sea journey was to me a joy, as always, whether rough or smooth. This time it was quite smooth.

"Goodness, Hannah! You do look fit," said Dick when she met me at Liverpool Street. "A bit different from the scraggy creature we sent away. I think we'd all better go to Norway," she laughed, her own weight having only too obviously increased since her two babies had arrived.

"Do you think Mother will want me to go back to the office, Dick?" I hardly dared ask her.

"Oh no. Absolutely no chance of that, she reassured me. "I think actually she has got a good idea about your future, but you'd better wait and let her tell you herself."

Mother's 'idea' soon became clear, and I rather liked it. Now that we lived in the house at Avondale Road, and she herself continued to spend all her time at G&B, she really needed a housekeeper, and I was to be that person. In other words, as long as I looked after the house, including preparing the meals and doing the shopping, the rest of my time was my own. Mother would pay me pocket money for my own personal expenditure, clothes and so on, as well as housekeeping money for running the home, and we had a maid for the cleaning.

This is going to be lovely, I thought. And so it was. I had a great deal to learn, which was good because I needed something to get my teeth into, and being on my own in the kitchen without anyone looking over my shoulder, I could try out new recipes and quite complicated items with only myself to blame if they went wrong. I saw quite a bit of Estelle at this time, as she and Henry and their two babies (the younger had been born whilst I was in Norway) still lived on the upper floor, but I carefully kept my own counsel and my own timetable, so that I maintained my independence. Estelle was a great chatterer, and I knew that if I became too involved with her, my life would not be my own and she would continually be coming downstairs for a gossip or a cup of coffee, and the children would be in and out, too. So I put down my foot mentally, and in this regard remained polite but formal, and she soon got the message and only occasionally imposed on me.

"You're so obstinate, Hannah," she would say for the thousandth time. "Why won't you come up for a chat?"

However, in a way it was reassuring to have someone else in the house as long as she learnt to respect my privacy. There was some social gain for me, too, as we all went to the same tennis club in the summer, and although Estelle was not very good at tennis, and anyhow had to keep an eye on the children, I got to know her friends as well as making more of my own – a very easy process for me as forging acquaintances was never a thing which caused me a problem. I supposed I was a natural extrovert, and easily became involved in conversation. Quite a number of my Blackheath friends, including Edna, were still in the vicinity too, and I could visit them during the daytime as long as I was back home by about 5 o'clock to receive Mother back from the office with a welcoming cup of tea, and later a meal.

Henry now had a car (bought, I suspect, on borrowed money), and always ferried Mother to the City in the mornings, but it was becoming more of a chore for him to bring her back in the evenings, as he often wanted to go to his Club, the Seven Seas, to meet his naval cronies before returning home. In the end he and I came to an arrangement that he would teach me to drive in return for me fetching Mother from the office when need be. This seemed a good 'quid pro quo' as it also would give me greater freedom to have a car to go to my friends or the tennis club. It only remained to persuade Mother to buy a car for herself and me, and as business was rapidly looking up under her guidance, this was not difficult. Not only was a car a useful tool, but it was already in 1922 a status symbol, which she rather fancied.

Henry was not in fact a very patient teacher any more than he was a tolerant driver. He still liked speed, and he considered most other drivers were fools. If annoyed, he would quickly wind down his offside window when in a traffic jam such as frequently occurred in the City, and shout abuse at a rival for the road ahead. At other times he would without warning bellow across the street whenever he saw a chimney-sweep with his brushes on his back.

"Morning sweep!" he'd yell.

"Morning guv!" the man would shout back above the traffic noise, aware as all Cockneys are of the luck it gave his interlocutor to greet him thus.

More peaceful was it for me to be given driving lessons by James, who now had an Austin 7 of his own, and would quietly sit and puff at his pipe in the passenger seat, giving the minimum of instructions and the maximum of confidence whilst I drove him round and round the neighbourhood. Soon launched into the traffic of the City, I quickly learnt to negotiate the Old Kent Road, arriving at Aldersgate unflurried and calm, and was waiting for Mother when she emerged from Hamsel Street, which was always packed with waiting cars. The London bobbies were my greatest aids, with their big burly 6ft 2in height and their hearts as large as their size, as with Cockney humour they controlled the City firmly and efficiently. On the way home we were travelling with the flow of taxis and buses and carts, and if profits were good, Mother would direct me to stop at the Evelina Hospital for Children so that she could put a few pound notes into their collecting box. She could be very generous when she chose, though she did not always show her feelings.

One day in January 1923, as we were driving home, she said without warning, "Anne, you're coughing again."

"Yes Mother. I think it's the fog that catches my chest." She was silent for a mile or two, and then she said, "Perhaps you ought to take a trip down to see Hilda and Kiki for a few weeks until the spring arrives here."

Hilda and Kiki now lived in Merignac near Bordeaux; indeed their erstwhile small-holding at Beaudesert has now been absorbed into the outskirts of the town and is known as Bordeaux au Port. John had been staying with them until recently, but found that he became bored with pig-farming, and now that his health was good, yearned for a more sociable and forceful life of a city. After several attempts, he found himself a job with an English insurance firm in Paris where his perfect grasp of both languages and his persuasive plausibility enabled him particularly to deal with British expatriates there.

"How was it that at last John's war wound healed up?" I asked Hilda one day soon after I arrived at Beaudesert.

"Oh, mon dieu!" she exclaimed in her French English. "It was terrible. The docteur come and say to John, 'You will never recover like this; we must do something radical.' John was so fed up of the pain and not feeling well, he said 'alright'. So the docteur he put a small towel between John's teeth and told him to bite on it. And he tied another towel to the bed head and told John to pull on it when he said so. Then he cried 'Maintenant!", and John bit and he pulled, and at the same time the docteur he stick a red hot needle into the flesh. Oh, Hannah, it was je ne sais quoi! The smell! Oh, la-la!" and she blanched at the memory. "John screamed. I never heard such a scream, and his language ----! I felt so sick, and Kiki felt faint." She paused, lost in the memory. "After a few minutes John shouted 'If that docteur ever comes near me again, I will kill him.' And he meant it."

"But the needle did the trick?" I ventured.

"Yes, it did. There was no more trouble and no discharge or pain. So after all those years he was cured. But, oh Chérie, I never want to hear such a scream again. The war, it was terrible what it did to people," she finished, her grammar becoming more and more confused as she echoed what I had so often thought lately as I still saw the limbless and destitute, the blind and shell-shocked, about the London streets.

Here at Beaudesert war was far away, though Hilda and Kiki were only just making ends meet. It was still very rural in Merignac, and life was simple. They were largely self-supporting, with their pigs and a couple of cows and their chickens and vegetable patch. I helped on the farm with all the lesser jobs, where methods had not changed for generations, and milk was still brought home in buckets strung from yokes carried across the shoulders. The air in Merignac was clean and dry, and my cough subsided, and soon I lost my wheeze and felt well.

For the second year running I spent my birthday abroad. This time it was my 21st, and for a treat at Mother's expense, Hilda and Kiki and I went to see 'Carmen' at the Opera House in Bordeaux. This was my introduction to opera, and I loved it. I remember how in the little bone-shaker of a car that Kiki owned, he and I sang the Toreador song at the top of our voices all the way back to Beaudesert, and only on tea and coffee at that!

Once the English Spring had arrived, Mother's letters urged me to come home. Henry and Estelle were moving to a house of their own in Bromley, and so she would be by herself at Avondale Road. I don't really know why, but it was assumed by us all that Mother could not be left on her own for the night, and she never had been since Dad died, and never was for the rest of her life. She assumed it herself, and arrangements were always made so that either I or Dick was in the house. It seems ridiculous at this distance that a healthy 60 year old needed 'company', but this was a piece of Victorianism that had become ingrained.

In any case, I wanted to get home now the tennis season had begun,and also to tend the garden which I knew Mother would never touch, but which was one of my loves. In addition my conscience dictated that it was not fair to leave her on her own any more, or to impose on Henry and Estelle any longer for her evening meals. Besides, I was longing for a gossip with my own friends. So back to England I travelled, crossing the Channel in a little boat which bounced about like a toy duck in a bath.

Mother was pleased to see me back. Almost her first remark, after she had kissed me and commented on how well I looked, was "Dick and James are going to live in Yorkshire."

"Yorkshire?" I repeated in my dotty fashion.

"Yes. He's being sent up by his firm. They're going in June."

"Do you mean for good?" I asked.

"Yes. The whole firm is moving, so they've got to go too."

"Oh dear! How awful!" I had the usual Londoner's view of Yorkshire as being a far distant land filled with uncouth individuals who worked in mills and lived on Brontëesque moors.

"How really awful," I said again, and as soon as possible walked round to Dick's house for confirmation of this horrific piece of news. It was quite true, said Dick. As soon as they could find a house they would be going.

"But how on earth shall we get up to see you?" I exclaimed.

"There's a good train;" she said, "only four hours from King's Cross."

"But I can't take Mother on a long journey like that."

"Why ever not?" she said in her practical way. "She goes far longer journeys in France." Which was true, but seemed different somehow. Anyway, it was a real blow to me. Dick had always been my big standby in times of trouble and I could not visualise life without her nearby to discuss problems, or merely for a nice cosy gossip.

"How absolutely awful," I sighed once again.

"Not really," she said. "But the most difficult thing is that it does rather land you with looking after Mother, although I'll come down to stay with her now and then, so that you can go off on your own. We're going to get a mother's help, so I shall be able to do that all right."

And that was really that, and I had to learn to accept it, but I didn't like the idea of only seeing my Dick very occasionally. Mother must have realised how I felt, and indeed she probably dreaded them going as much as I did, for before the end of the year she announced that she and I were going to Sweden for a month in the spring to see all the relations there. She adored travelling, and in fact after that we went to France every year, and in addition we always went somewhere else as well, and Sweden was the first of many trips abroad. Profits at G&B must have increased dramatically, and quite against the general trend of commerce which was recovering only slowly from the post-war slump. Even in the early thirties when unemployment was in the three million range, and the figures did not even include the many women who would settle for lowly cleaning and office jobs if they could find them, we still could afford to go off each year for several weeks.

I was now 22, which was just the right age to enjoy travelling, particularly as I did not have to worry about the money side of things. I had a busy week or two sorting out our clothes and making Mother's mind up for her as to which items should be included, and persuading her that more than three hats was excessive. In those days all our headgear went into a hatbox, which was a standard piece of luggage, but one hatbox would barely take the four or five hats she wanted, and I also had skates and tennis racquet and other essentials to take.

There were always porters to help with their barrows and so as long as everything went onto one of those, it would be simple.

Mother was a good sailor, so we enjoyed the voyage to Stockholm, and Auntie Maria met us in when we landed. The weeks in Sweden passed quickly and pleasantly, with all the sociability I so much liked. There seemed to be an unending list of relatives to meet and visit, and as Mother was greeted warmly by them all, and old times were recalled of her previous visits, I was introduced to all the cousins and soon embraced into their friendly community. Mother even forgot her Victorian background of chaperonage, and said nothing to my going to evening parties on my own.

Once more English was spoken universally and I never felt the need or inclination to learn Swedish, so the time was spent in pure enjoyment and self-indulgence on my part, only broken by lady's maiding for Mother. This I did not dislike, because I felt some responsibility for seeing that all was made easy for her to enjoy her holiday. Some of my duties I positively took pleasure in, such as brushing her still beautiful waist-length fair hair, before pinning it up into its habitual bun.

After three weeks of this luxurious life, Mother suggested rather illogically that as we were 'abroad', we might as well take the opportunity to travel down to Paris to see the relations there. She telegraphed Hilda of her intentions, and indicated like a queen that Hilda's and Kiki's presence would be welcomed. I think she had not quite reckoned with the distance, but having crossed to Germany and arrived in Hamburg late at night, we were unable to obtain 'sleepers' and had to put up with an ordinary compartment for the rest of the way. In those days I wore my hair in 'ear phones', which, although they had been à la mode since the war, were now becoming superseded by bobs and shingles. All night as I sat in that train, my head wobbling from side to side with its motion and I slept fitfully, my hairpins stuck into me mercilessly. I wonder now why I didn't just remove them, but the answer must be that it simply wasn't done to let one's hair down even at night, in public. Mother seemed quite unmoved by the discomforts of night travel, and we obtained coffee and rolls from one of the stations at which we stopped. Next morning, arriving (irritably on my part) at the Gare du Nord in Paris, we were met by Hilda and Kiki, obediently as directed, and I flounced out of the station announcing that I could not stand my hair another minute, and before doing anything else I was going to the coiffeuse, which I did, watched by all three. As the first of my ear phones were snipped through and fell to the floor, Mother protested it was too sad, but now like a hound to the hunt, I turned my lop-sided head to her and remarked caustically that I could hardly go about like that. She saw it was no use objecting further and the second side also was shingled, and I emerged a new, up-to-date young miss, self-conscious but feeling most avant guarde and Parisian.

The week we spent in Paris was fun. We stayed at Le Vesinet, but the four of us, Hilda, Kiki, Mother and I went out each day on an expedition. The children were looked after by the Fiats, and Mother 'treated' the rest of us, so that Hilda and Kiki were able to have a real holiday. Notwithstanding this, Kiki, who still was the dapper little Frenchman he had always been in spite of his years on the pig farm, majestically 'allowed' us each to spend so much every day on our lunches. It preserved his self-respect to do so even though Mother actually paid. Hilda liked to be bossed about by him, and still gazed up at him admiringly with her dark eyes as though they were just engaged. I rather envied her this feeling, though I thought it somewhat soft for a woman of thirty-three.

Back in London, Henry appeared on our doorstep quite cheerfully the first morning to drive Mother to the office. It seemed that all had run smoothly there whilst we were away, and I guess Mother ensconced herself with Mr. Courtney most of that day listening to his account of events. At any rate she came home tired but unruffled in the evening, so I concluded that he had kept his hands firmly on the reins all the time, and although allowing Henry the misapprehension that 'Mr. Henry' was boss, actually had managed the business in his own way. From my point of view this was all to the good as there would not be any deterrent to Mother and me repeating our lengthy absence another year.

Now the business was progressing smoothly and profitably, and I was running our home, Mother began to be rather bored in the evenings, especially at the weekends. She had some friends who were near-neighbours called Mr. & Mrs. Scott, and they were keen bridge players. With total lack of forethought as far as I myself was concerned, I suggested that they be invited in one Saturday evening to teach her to play. She had a good brain, still very active, and I anticipated she would enjoy the challenge of the mental exertion. All was arranged, though as Mr. Scott said "We need a fourth; Hannah had better learn, too." Nothing loathe, and always ready for new experiences, I light-heartedly agreed, and as the Saturdays went by, it became a habit for the Scotts to come round at 6 o'clock for bridge, which was only broken off at 8 pm for coffee and sandwiches, continuing otherwise relentlessly until 11 or 12 o'clock at night. At first I rather enjoyed the concentration and achievement of remembering the suits and hands, but as we become proficient, Mr. Scott did not relax correspondingly his vigil on our progress, but persisted in tutoring our efforts. To me then it ceased to be a game and became hard work which progressed to a drudgery. Mother still seemed to be enjoying it, but I began to feel I should scream if anyone else said "Two no trumps", or worse still egged me on to hurry.

"Come on Hannah, we've not got all night."

"Oh no?" I thought bitterly. "It seems like it."

So the next Saturday I made up my mind. I simply would not play on any account.

"I shan't be home until late tonight," I said to Mother.

"Oh, Anne, you must be here when the Scotts arrive. We can't play with three," she replied, apparently oblivious that I might want to do anything else.

"I promised Edna I would go to supper," I parried.

"Well, you must just tell her you can't. What would the Scotts think?"

I weakened.

"She'll be so disappointed," I said lamely, knowing I was on a losing wicket.

"What about the Scotts?" was her reply. "How do you think they'll feel if you're not there. You really must not be so selfish."

"Selfish!" I muttered under my breath. "Crumbs!" But my wretched conscience came trotting out, and I knew I must be home by six or Mother would be upset, and that wasn't fair.

After that I really had no leg to stand on, and Saturday after Saturday I was home from whatever I was doing, by six, no matter how much I longed to join a party or go to the theatre. All my friends were aware I was unavailable on Saturday evenings – "Anne's bridge night" they called it – "How exciting!", they teased, their eyes twinkling, while mine scowled blue murder.

I had my own back on them all though, with the freedom I had most of my other days, and this they envied. Moreover, Mother was very up-to-date with London life, and we often stayed in Town for a meal and then went to a show. I adored this, and became familiar with all the current playwrights' work; Ben Travers, Noel Coward and the rest. Musicals with a really good score such as 'The Desert Song', or Ivor Novello's 'Crest of the Wave', or Gilbert and Sullivan, filled my head with lovely tunes and romantic situations. Owen Nares in straight plays was my idol. Mother enjoyed all these productions, though I expect she never realised how much they affected my emotions and left me limp with envy of the heroine for her loved one.

It was quite apparent now that there was a shortage of men due to the carnage of war, but I was still very young and it never entered my head that there might not be one for me. I assumed there would be, in time. I would certainly never consider marrying an 'old' man such as Margy did that summer. Mother and I were invited to this very grand affair in Blackheath in June. As always for Margy, I thought jealously, everything was perfect; a fairy-tale white wedding, a marquee in the garden, six bridesmaids, everyone in lovely clothes, quite stunning wedding presents such as I had never seen before, and as if that was not enough the sun shone brilliantly. Margy looked more elegant and aristocratic than ever in her beautiful dress and her mother's Brussels lace veil, but when I saw her husband-to-be, even his kind smile could not prevent all this splendour paling into insignificance for me as my envy turned to scoffing. Fancy, I thought, getting landed with someone of forty-odd. Not for me, I decided. Even being an old maid is better than that. I was twenty-two at the time, and life was before me still.

Meanwhile, not only were my friends envious of my frequent visits to the theatre, but they were quite bowled over with admiration for my frequent trips abroad. This more than made up for their twitting me for my 'bridge nights'. Every year now I went to France, sometimes on my own now that John was installed in Paris, when Dick, bless her, would come down from Yorkshire for a week to stay with Mother. On other visits, such as to Hilda in Merignac, Mother accompanied me, and though we would stop off on the way for a night or two in Paris, we would stay on the farm for a fortnight or more. Perigore and the Dordogne were lovely areas, and if Kiki was busy, I would borrow his car and take Mother and Hilda and the children to see the country or on a shopping spree to Bordeaux. Mother, who now apparently had spare cash burning her pocket, had grown attached to the coloured glass which was a local product, and would return home with sets of wine and liqueur glasses which sparkled with cut designs in brilliant greens, deep blues and blood reds for all the family's next Christmas presents. She was never mean when something beautiful caught her eye, and she had good taste. I think Dad had seen to that with his generosity. She was much more light-hearted these days, and although domineering to the point of selfishness, it was all with such charm and poise that one automatically fell in with her wishes, usually without question. It was nearly ten years now since Dad's sudden death, which with its complete unexpectedness, had knocked her off her feet. She had been through a deep trough of unhappiness and insecurity since then, in which I had accompanied her with similar misery and disease. She, however, had her share of Minska obstinacy and tenacity, enough to make her toss her beautiful head at the Fates, and rise above each hurdle by sheer determination and calculated drive. I admired her beyond words, irritating though I often found her, and doubted whether I myself would have had the guts to achieve what she had. Her aristocratic manner had paid off, and she had managed to build up a financially and socially sound life for herself without, on the whole, damaging anyone else on the way.

Or, at least, that was what I liked to think. Perhaps I myself had been used as a tool, though I do not believe she would have seen it like that. She had after all provided me continuously with a home and a job, and both she and I assumed it as my duty to look after her, so blind were we to the changing mores of the time. Never completely from my mind was the picture of her bringing me home as a new baby when my mother died and my father could not bare to look at me because he thought I was the perpetrator of my mother's death. I almost had come to think so myself, although my common-sense resolutely forced me to reason that a helpless infant could hardly have willed such a thing.

Thus I gradually came to accept that my life's work was to pay back this inestimable debt which I owed to Mother, and bit my tongue rather than speak out when riled. Likewise I accepted gratefully the credit side of the coin without demur, such as her sudden decisions about travel which surfaced without warning or reference to me.

"I think we'll go and see Anna Edelgruhn while we're down here," she announced one morning at Beaudesert. Anna now lived at Lugano in southern Switzerland. Mother had become acquainted with her years ago in connection with G&B to whom her family supplied material for the gold-blocking process. It was she who had arranged for Dick to go to school at Stolberg, a very successful venture.

As usual, Mother had not looked at the map or considered the mileage across France, or indeed the complications of the French rail network. We were 'abroad' and 'in the south', so it must be possible to flit from one place to the other. After various telegraphing and studying of timetables, we eventually stayed a night in Lyons, where I had never been before, so that was a bonus, and an enjoyable one. The old city was fascinating and the Rhone Valley, too, delighted me, as did our journey next day through the mountains to Geneva, and then on in a circuitous route to the huge and most lovely lake of Lugano. After the filth and litter of France with its grimy streets and smelly piscines, Switzerland was a joy of clinical cleanliness, and its gateaux out of this world.

By now my French, though of dubious grammar, was full of idioms and expressions, and in Lugano, although Mother and Anna conversed in German, I could mainly understand them, and added my part in French. It is a lovely language, expressive and lilting, and I enjoyed its cadences and characteristics. "Alors" I would start every sentence to make it sound genuine, "Alors, je vais là." John had taught me a large repertoire of French swear-words, but I kept them in reserve, and used them when I got back to England where no-one understood them.

Lugano was a memorable visit. I had never stayed near a mountainous lake before, and the reflections of the peaks and the rising sun over the water were scintillating. The guttural German spoken in the launches by the overfed Teutons pleased me less, but I thought of the millions of Germans who were next door to starvation, and was glad that at any rate some were free of that horror. But the realisation that I was becoming critical made me homesick for ordinary English people who did ordinary predictable English things, and moreover spoke a language in which I could easily converse without effort. I needed to be back home in my own little niche with its familiar routine and its discipline, and I was relieved to find that Mother also had had enough of the vagaries of travel for the time being. Within two days we were on the train to Basle and home.

The next Christmas Mother and I went up to Yorkshire on the train. I was a bit frightened she would get one of the bad colds to which she had recently become prone, and I took a hot thermos of coffee to have on the way in case she felt chilly, and a big thick rug which I wrapped tightly round her. She started to giggle as I pulled it up under her arms and folded it across her back.

"Don't be absurd, Mother," I said severely. "We don't want you catching cold, do we?" And I heaved it up higher round her chest and tucked it round her legs until she looked like a mummy.

Dick and James had got three little daughters by now – 'The Girlies' Mother called them. She adored them and took the greatest care over her choice of Christmas presents for them. On the other hand, she appeared very severe with them, and this became more evident as they got older. Her logic was that all her other four grandchildren had less advantages and stability in their home lives and thus she must even things up so that these three Yorkshire children had less indulgence from her. She was very fair in her dealings, and I don't think they ever knew of this difference, accepting her devotedly as she was when with them. They were not 'spoilt' by their parents, and the result of this attitude of hers towards them was that they appreciated quite astonishingly the presents she gave them, always I must say, most generous and appropriate.

Mother had missed James' advice and wise guidance since he had left Bromley, which she had previously extracted with gratitude, from the date of Dad's death. He was experienced in the world of industry and commerce, and he never proffered advice unless he had a copper-bottomed answer, with which in the event she always agreed. Whilst the mothers' help was putting the children to bed on our first evening in Yorkshire, and the cook-general was busy with our dinner, Mother and James retired to one room for a 'committee meeting', leaving Dick and me pleasantly free in another to catch up with each other's gossip. Later, as we dined, conversation turned to holidays, and so it was that we four sailed off on a cruise ship from Tilbury the next summer to Madeira and the Canaries; a wonderful trip, much envied by the High School faction. Not realising it then, I now can see in perspective the way Dick's and James' thoughts had developed. Assuredly they would have preferred to holiday on their own, but they were aware of Mother's increasing hold on me, and that if they joined their holiday to ours, I should at least have that much respite to join in all the social activities and dancing on board the cruise, to my heart's delight. They themselves were only mildly interested in that side of shipboard life, James not at all, much preferring to observe all the navigational conundrums en route, and to read. They were quite content to keep Mother company whilst I cavorted round playing deck tennis, 'horse racing', and quoits. I did bless them for their thoughtfulness.

But there was another kind of stability that they provided for me. Ever since my first visit to St. Germain's Church during the war when I was so confused and frightened, I had continued to attend services there until I became Mother's housekeeper.

74

After that, Sunday mornings were busy ones when I prepared the traditional Sunday dinner which Mother had always previously done. But I missed the tranquility and the mysticism of the Anglican matins, and instead I used to pop into one of the churches nearby on my own during the week. This gave me a quiet time for reflection, but I still missed the corporate worship with its indefinable reassurance. Although not particularly musical, I regretted not having the opportunity to join in the canticles and hymns of set services, and to enjoy the organ voluntaries. It was all part of a pattern I needed and had proved to myself. When we were with Dick and James, attendance at Sunday morning worship was a quietly organised routine, whether at their home church or away on holiday, whether on board ship or at an English church abroad. Going to the services with people I loved and respected gave me a firm basis on which to tackle the week ahead, and I felt that now I was more proficient in the kitchen, I could arrange to go to matins at Bromley and still manage to get the roast on the table by 1.30. I told Mother that this was what I wanted to do in future, and to my surprise and pleasure she gladly fell in with the idea, and nearly always accompanied me. I still found the occasional quiet visits to a church during the week was calming and helpful, even uplifting, and I continued to do this quite secretly when I felt the need.

CHAPTER VII

1926

I FOUND MYSELF DOING a good deal of chauffeuring for Mother during these years. I loved driving, so it was usually no penance for me. I was a 'natural' when it came to managing a car, and negotiating traffic or finding my way through an unfamiliar district presented a challenge, which I invariably won. The car and I functioned happily as a unit. There was none of the screeching of gears or wobbly steering which accompanied Dick's erratic performance in the driver's seat and which had made her children dread hills when she was driving. In those days of relatively low power in domestic vehicles, the steepest slope did not make me fearful; I had even on occasions in the Lakes been known to go up backwards, the reverse having so much more power than the other three or four gears. Resorting to this ploy, however, was a rarity, and more usually I had to contend with traffic which in London was already formidable, partly because it combined the internal combustion engine with horse-drawn carts and bicycles. Other visits would entail map-reading over a distance, but this too caused no difficulty to me, as long as Mother did not chatter whilst I was negotiating a complicated route.

In the twenties and thirties we went to visit Dad's elder sisters now and then. They were what was known then as 'maiden ladies', born in the early 1850s, and as different from each other as it was possible to be, except that in their individual ways they both appeared unequivocally Jewish. They were Londoners born and bred, but their mother was whispered to be a Polish Jewess (as if there was something disgraceful in such an admission), and no doubt had fled to England in one of the early nineteenth century pogroms. She married Alfred Barnes, who with his dark colouring and prominent nose, must have belonged to the same race. History related that he became friendly with old Glover, and together, from nothing, they started the printing firm in Hamsel Street which turned out in a few years to be a wild success.

The Aunties, as they were collectively and distinctively known, had never married, always lived together, and had not changed their routine or their opinions since their parents had died in the mid-1870s. They were christened (I should say 'named') Amy and Eva, and invariably used the prefix 'Auntie' when talking to or about each other – "Auntie Eva does so-and-so". "Auntie Amy said something." Auntie Amy was short, dumpy and bossy, with straight hair pinned in a bun. Auntie Eva was tall, thin and amenable, with wavy hair cut short. They both were dark complexioned, and dressed in black, with strings of beads of varying lengths dangling down their bosoms, and they lived lives of the most excruciating dullness which they seemed to take for granted. They were narrow, prim and self-sufficient, but in their own ways they were kindly, though the world never demanded that they put themselves out for anyone else. They did not even attend church pursuits because of their origins.

When I knew the Aunties best, in the 1920s, they lived in Southgate, North London, with their two maids (also spinster sisters), their two dogs, and their blind niece, Madeleine. It was the most Victorian ménage I had ever experienced. The house was very dark, as in spite of large casement windows reaching from the ceiling almost to the floor of the lofty reception rooms, the glass was swathed in patterned lace curtains from top to bottom, and lined with heavy tasselled velvet curtains in dark red, with deep pelmets of the same material. True to form, the square mahogany table was protected by a huge covering of the dark velvet reaching almost to the ground, and providing a private hidy-hole for the two objectionable and snappy Pekineses they always kept. There was a big upright piano, with a carved fretted front and attached brass candle-holders, which blind Madeleine used to play, sitting on the red plush covered stool, and removing her rings before commencing. Piano, table and various whatnots and tallboys were all covered in china nick-nacks and photographs in silver rococo frames, and there was a big brass fender surrounding the fireplace, and a vast aspidistra in an ugly jardinière in a corner.

The room where the Aunties received visitors was always stuffy and very warm. Auntie Amy, the rotund one, usually remained seated to greet one. Auntie Eva, who was more active, rose to do so. I think they were genuinely pleased when we visited, although they could not have contended with the upset too frequently or for too long. The front door was answered by a maid in a 'stringed' cap and a white frilly apron, who formally knocked on the parlour door before showing us into the room. "Mrs. Barnes and Miss Hannah" she would announce as if we were at the Lord Mayor's Banquet. Later, Auntie Amy would bid me ring the long tasselled bell, and the maid would reappear with the silver tea tray on which would be laid a teaset of beautiful porcelain, apostle teaspoons, and silver teapot on a spirit-flame silver stand. Upon the table she would unfold a pristine white lace cloth, and place on it sundry dishes with currant bread and cucumber sandwiches, surrounding the pièce de résistance which was a large fruit cake, not yet cut, on a china stand. Tiny starched linen napkins and bone-handled tea knives completed the arrangements, and we were then invited to 'sit up'.

Tea at the Aunties was actually a frugal affair and all show, as everything was cut so daintily that one had to eat very slowly to avoid continually having an empty plate. However, it was anything if not elegant and the one thing to refrain from doing was to ask for a piece of the central cake. Mother and I often laughed about this as we were never positively invited to have a slice, nor had we ever seen it cut. One day, when Auntie Amy in her usual flowery way said "Now Hannah, what may I offer you to follow?" I looked at her, then at Mother who imperceptibly shook her head as if to say "No, don't you dare", and then at Auntie Eva who always followed Auntie Amy's lead, and I boldly replied "May I have a piece of the central cake please, Auntie?"

Silence. I could feel the atmosphere pulsating around me.

"Oh no, Hannah," Mother said. "It's a shame to spoil it," while Auntie Eva fussed over to the sideboard for a special silver knife, and Auntie Amy popped another sandwich into her mouth in desperation, and Madeleine – sweet Madeleine – said "Good for you, Hannah. It's just wanting to be eaten. Cookie will be pleased."

The Pekineses got up and stretched, and wandered over to catch the crumbs before settling down to sleep again. The cake proved to be full of cinnamon and fruit which I loathed, but I could not very well leave it now. I was not offered a second portion.

After tea the Aunties and Mother started to discuss all the family. "Have you seen Mina lately?" said Auntie Eva in an unguarded moment, then stopped abruptly and looked guiltily at me. After a pause, Auntie Amy suggested I might like to go and look at the garden, and as it was very hot in the drawing-room, and although I knew it was a ploy to get rid of me, I said I would, and Madeleine took my arm and said she would come, too.

Mina was Mother's eldest sister, and was something of a mystery. Another old maid, I knew virtually nothing about her, and had never seen her. In recent years I had been asked now and again to drive Mother down to Folkestone so that she could visit Mina at her nursing home, but I was always left outside in the car though Mother never gave me the reason. Born in 1856, Mina had been a housekeeper for many years in a private house. Now aged around seventy, this alone did not answer the question of why I was not allowed to see her. I often wondered if she was an alcoholic or an epileptic, or some other then unmentionable category, and even when I took Mother to Mina's funeral in 1926, Mother never divulged anything about her, although Mother's very silence struck me as significant.

"Why did the Aunties never marry?" I asked Mother one day, not daring to include Mina in the question. Mother thought for a moment as if she had never considered this before. Then she said she supposed they had not met anyone they liked enough to do so. From this unhelpfully obvious answer I concluded that Auntie Amy was too bossy, and Auntie Eva too submissive, and together they happily were complementary. But it made me think about myself and hope that, although they were no blood relations of mine, being Dad's sisters, I should not inherit the same boring fate. Mina was a different kettle of fish, as she was an actual aunt to me, as my true father's sister, as well as Mother's. I wondered if that was why I always loathed alcohol, however faint a trace. But then, I reflected, I was fussy about all sorts of foods – oranges, tomatoes, cheese, and so on – perhaps a by-product of my insecure origins, or was it because I had been pampered as a small child owing to my frail start and my motherlessness?

By 1928 Mother was becoming restive. I often noticed her pause during her evening game of patience while she apparently was considering some project. If the cards did not work out and she had to start again, she would flip through them with dexterity as she shuffled them, and with decisive movements re-deal. I knew then by her manner that she had come to a conclusion and that sooner or later she would announce her decision. Then one evening as she rose from the card table and took up her crochet, she said "I think this house is too poky. We'll try to find somewhere better, nearer to Henry."

By the autumn all was arranged, and we moved out of Avondale Road which had been our refuge for seven years, and found ourselves owners of a large semi in Park Avenue; a very much more spacious house, with a larger garden, a downstairs cloakroom, and four bedrooms. The dimensions were all a little greater, and the ceilings higher than at Avondale Road, so that our grand piano and the glass chandelier, both of which we had retained through all our vicissitudes, came into their own again, and Mother's heavy Victorian furniture could more happily be accommodated.

Leaving Henry with the key and instructions about the water, the cleaning, and the transference and arrangement of the furniture, we then departed from the gathering winter and the chaos of our belongings, on the Balmoral Castle bound for South Africa. Mother felt she needed sun and warmth to recover from her exertions with estate agents, and as usual delegated efficiently and successfully for her new house to be ready for her return in January, thus avoiding further agitation or fatigue herself. I admired enormously this ability of hers to organise others to carry out her ideas. She was a born aristocrat, who could loftily acquire and expect others to execute her instructions, which they invariably carried out obediently and efficiently down to the minutest detail.

Meanwhile, as these henchmen were sweating over our house, we complacently travelled the hundreds of miles of our tour in luxury and elegance and what I call a civilised manner; dressing for dinner, attending evening dances, morning deck games, and with stewards and handsome young officers to bend continually to our will. Moreover, we visited lovely places on our route, starting with Santa Cruz in the Canaries, still in its winter balminess, and where the very evident poverty did not strike a chord because it

80

was so similar to what one saw in Europe, only here the weather was warmer, and the sun masked the dirt.

When we arrived in South Africa, Cape Town was in mid-summer, and we spent an exciting Christmas in brilliant sunshine under a cloudless sky and the eye of Table Mountain. Later we sailed up the east coast and called at Port Elizabeth, East London and Durban. Here we left the Balmoral Castle, sadly for my part – the parties on board had been any young woman's dream, as had the young officers in their romantic white tropical uniforms, and all so friendly too. From Durban we caught the train to Ladysmith where we stayed two nights, Mother's one aim being to visit the battlefield. The heat at Ladysmith was shocking, and as we bounced along in our hired car over the bumps and ruts of the rough terrain, I thought how much the poor souls had suffered during the siege, under conditions which must have been appalling. After a tedious ride through almost featureless wastes, our driver jolted to a standstill and announced that we had arrived. There was no other indication to confirm the site of the battle, but Mother climbed out of the ramshackle vehicle, looked about her at the bare plain surrounding us, and evidently was satisfied. I made no comment, and soon we were trundling back to our hotel to relieve our parched mouths.

"Really Anne, you might have shown a little enthusiasm," she complained.

"But Mother, I couldn't made out what we were supposed to be looking at."

She sniffed and shrugged her shoulders and said nothing more, but when we got home she thoroughly enjoyed giving a lurid and somewhat romanticised description of the place.

Next day we caught the train over the Drakensberg mountains to Johannesburg where we saw the gold mines. Then on to Pretoria where I sat in Kruger's chair in the parliament building, and visited his home, a long white one-storied house, roofed, to my surprise, with sheets of corrugated iron, and where all the contents remained as they had been left thirty years before when he returned to Germany in 1904. These memories impressed me most, but the deep colours of the myriads of flowers also left their effect on me, and increased my penchant for travel.

As we returned to wintry Britain on board the Armadale Castle, wrapped in our cloak of warmth and plenty, I felt quite guilty as I saw others scurrying about the docks at Southampton earning their daily bread. Later that year the Wall Street crash resounded through the world, but affected me personally not at all. I did, however, become very aware now of the ragged men lounging at street corners with nothing to do, and bare-footed children in the gutters where their legless or war-blinded fathers were inducing tunes from a cornet or a fiddle for a bob or two. I realised that I had complacently assumed that poverty in hot countries such as we had visited, was bearable, but was quite definitely not so in cold, foggy, damp Britain. I began to contrast my own unutterably fortunate existence with what I saw, and I did not grumble when Mother ordered me to slow down as we drove through London on our many journeys from Hamsel Street, so that she could throw a coin in a proffered cap on the pavement. Even the Aunties' existence was sheer luxury in comparison.

CHAPTER VIII

1932

NINETEEN THIRTY-TWO was a watershed for me as I look back at it now, though at the time it was yet another period of what I had grown used to expect out of life. Every day was busy. If I had no particular tasks in the house or appointment to meet a friend, I filled the time with all sorts of activities which I so much enjoyed, dressmaking, embroidery, knitting, or cookery. How dull this sounds, but I suppose I was a born home-maker, and loved all the practical crafts to which I could turn my hand. When the weather was good, I spent every minute I could in the garden, coaxing flowers into bloom, trimming hedges and bushes, and labouring to produce a range of vegetables in a plot at the far end, coming in at tea-time with shoes heavy with mud, filthy hands, and frequently a dirty face, too.

At that time I had a companion in my dog, who watched my every movement with interest, now and then yawning with an ascending note as if to indicate it was time for a walk, and then off we would go, round the houses, to the shops, or across Sundridge Park, anywhere to give him a run, to his great satisfaction. Almost all my life, except in the second war, I had a dog, and this one, Peter, was one of the best. He replaced Golly, the black mongrel, who died at a great age when we were in one of the horrid rented flats we had after Dad died. I was so upset at that period that despite our poverty, Mother thought it would help me to cheer up if I had another dog. Peter was bought as a tiny puppy feeling as forlorn as I was, and was brought up mainly on scraps so that he cost very little. Part collie and part terrier, his 57 varieties seemed to ensure his health, and he was the most intelligent and pleasant animal I ever had. Easy to train and essentially faithful, he was a reliable house dog, and a gentle nursemaid to the children when they visited. I adored him, though I now wonder why, as I was just as much at his beck and call as I was at Mother's. Perhaps it was his ingenuous way of sitting himself beside me when I was sewing or reading, and placing his muzzle on my knee where it remained without moving until later, often much later, I rose to do something else. Peter died at a ripe old age in the mid-1930s and was succeeded by a small black mongrel as like a terrier-cum-scottie as anything, who I called Flash owing to his propensity to rush about. Unhappily this characteristic foreshadowed the fact that he was mad, and try as I would I could not tame him. When war was imminent in 1938, as we thought, I felt I could cope with him no longer, and took him to the vet for speedy and painless despatch to a doggy hereafter. I did not have another dog until the bombing had finished and we settled to a peaceable existence.

Back in 1932, Peter provided me with companionship and, when necessary, consolation. I was not quite sure whether the latter was required or not when in February I reached the grand old age of thirty. My fourth decade! Good gracious! How ancient I was. But the day passed as usual with a party for all my friends, and the week previously was spent preparing the supper and those intelligent paper and pencil guessing games we all played before television induced us into a trance.

Any introspection or depression that might have been caused by the event was eclipsed unexpectedly by Auntie Ada. She was now over seventy, and had given up the Rookery after the war. Without Uncle Gus to sustain her or John Emil to organise, or even Midgeley to do odd jobs for her now he had married, she felt she could not continue into peacetime with her Swedish girls as before the war. After several attempts at returning to her old routine, the place really got on top of her, and she gave up and went to live with Ebba at her little house, typically called 'The Moorings', at Erith. Ebba had been inveigled into marrying Harold Beevers, who had previously been an underling of her father's in the drawing office at Vickers before the war. More accurately she had somehow just slipped into marrying him, almost as if by accident, I really do not know why. Harold was tall, dapper and persuasive. I disliked him intensely because I thought he treated Ebba abominably, even when they were engaged. He would order her about, break appointments, be late for special meals she had prepared, and spoke unkindly to her. I could not understand why she allowed him near her, or why Auntie Ada had not perceived what he was really like. They must all have been blinded by the fact that his mother was a most capable and conscientious person who was a baby nanny with a string of positions in the most aristocratic families, and who later was to be present in that capacity at the birth of Princess Elizabeth in 1926, and later her sister Princess Margaret Rose. There must have been something about Harold, a glory reflected from his mother's dabbling in the homes of the nobility perhaps which bamboozled both Ebba and her family. At any rate she and Harold were married in 1920. Next year a son, Richard, was born, the only happy occasion in a miserable union, for he was a gifted artist, intelligent enough to gain a scholarship to Colfe's grammar school, an all-rounder in every activity, and with an attractive personality into the bargain. Almost from the start of their marriage and with little respite, Harold was on the dole, and Ebba who like her mother was a proficient linguist, went 'out to business', working in a commercial office in the City. Now in the early nineteen-thirties, Auntie Ada had been a member of this unhappy household for several years.

One day she appeared at our house when Mother was out. After sitting her down and bringing in the tea-tray, she indicated she had something personal to ask me – she did not know who else to go to and I was "always so sensible about such things". She looked embarrassed and then she said, "I've got a lump in my breast, Hannah. Do you think it matters?" She undid her dress and put my hand on the place, which I could feel very easily. My head spun, because even with my lack of experience I knew what was the probable cause.

"I think you must go to your doctor right away, and ask him to look at it," I said, very calmly. "It will set your mind at rest," knowing very well that it would do the opposite. Auntie quietly finished her tea, and then she got up.

"Thank you, Hannah. I knew you would give me good advice. You have so much common-sense. Anyone else would have tried to bluff me."

She went into Erith Hospital a week later for an operation, and once she had recovered from that, seemed well again. Mother, as usual in a crisis, was controlled and practical, and gave Ebba sensible advice on how to cope with the situation, without giving her too gloomy a view, and Ebba really rose to the occasion and was a great strength to her mother over the next worrisome period of time. She was not as weak as she often led one to believe, and within her lackadaisical exterior she fostered enormous resources of courage, with not a little of the Minska obstinacy thrown in.

It was while I was pondering over all this selflessness and concern that we had a visit from Margy, who was visiting friends in Blackheath following her father's recent death. I could not help comparing attitudes although I knew I should not do so. She had written a few days previously to say that she would be in the area, and Mother had replied to invite her for a meal. True to form she appeared on the doorstep exactly at the appointed time, and Mother welcomed her in as I emerged from the kitchen where I was busy with the dinner. She was affable enough with Mother and soon engaged in conversation with her. I could not believe my ears when, looking up and noticing my presence, she dismissed me.

"Please don't feel you have to stay in here; I know your place is in the kitchen," she remarked peremptorily.

I am not often speechless or dumb-founded or at a loss. This time I was, if possible, all three. I had never heard anyone speak unkindly on purpose, apart from family teasing, and I did not believe people in Britain behaved like that. Flushing furiously, without a word I went back to the kitchen where I belonged, and pressed a towel dampened under the cold tap to my forehead. I could not understand, believe, take in, that anyone, much less a sister of James' who I so much loved, could treat me so. Perhaps she had not meant it, it was a clumsy way of saying I was not to be bothered with greeting her when I was busy. But no, I knew it was not that, but merely Margy putting me in my place.

I said very little at all that evening, addressing my remarks, such as they were, to Mother, trying to forget that all my hard work in producing that meal was going toward someone who cared not a jot for me, and only wished to degrade me. What mattered it if my silence marked me out as uncouth. As if sensing my fury, Peter laid his head on my lap under the table, and I stroked his silky ears to comfort myself.

This episode resurrected once again all my previous feelings of rejection and complete worthlessness. Stupid, I knew, and yet with a glint of truth. The world could have done very well without me, and only Margy was truthful enough to say so to my face. I did not think of probing the reasons in her own background why she should be prompted to such unkindness, and it was not until many years later that I realised the insecurity of her childhood.

This humiliating sense of being the Cinderella, the poor relation, thus overwhelmed me once more, and my self-respect and reassurance fell in a heap at my unworthy feet. Margy and Mother chatted happily, but then, Mother was an aristocrat in all but fact. She spoke and appeared and behaved like the Lady of the Manor, of which Margy would approve. With my flat nose, my wholesome rosy cheeks, my habit of dashing about with wisps of hair blowing across my face, and my impetuosity, no-one could be illuded into supposing I was one, and Margy openly sneered at any pretensions that I might have.

It was in this frame of mind that I packed our bags for our next sortie. Mother had a wish to explore the West Indies, and at this moment I felt I would do anything to leave my mundane, submissive, useless existence in London. Shipboard life at least would give me the illusion of quality for a while, and when we returned I would, I speculated, have forgotten the cruelty and possible truth behind Margy's remark, or at least it would be blurred into insignificance.

Leaving the Evans to find other bridge partners, we departed for Southampton with lightening hearts, and once on board I found myself immersed immediately in the now familiar social routine based on 'let's pretend'. I was determined to enjoy our trip to the full, and fingered through the timetable of events planned for the cruise with enthusiasm. However, even these surroundings could not divorce Mother from her Bromley routine, and every evening after dinner I tried, unsuccessfully as it turned out, to find some excuse to avoid playing bridge, which was even here rearing its ugly head. Mother seemed to attract the bridge-playing fraternity like a magnet, and I could visualise all my evenings being swallowed up at the card table, whilst from the saloon the dance music was drifting enticingly over the ship, and my feet were itching to join in. It was most peculiar the bland way Mother did not sense my restlessness. It was not exactly selfishness that caused her to ignore my hints – "Doesn't the music sound lovely, don't you think, Mother?" – so much as lack of imagination; indeed memory of what it was like to be young herself. She did not intend to be unkind. Fortunately, on the third evening of this unacceptable restraint, fate in the shape of Herbert and May Simpson came to my aid. They were introduced to us and immediately took a friendly interest in our game, and after the first rubber settled themselves down at our table in place of our previous partners. They were kindly, unassuming people, easy to get on with, and sympathetic in their attitude. I liked them very much and they already had lightened my burden of boredom by their happy approach to life, and particularly to cards, when at about ten o'clock that evening, Herbert began to collect up the pack at the end of the rubber, and pushed back his chair.

"Would you like a dance, Hannah?" he said.

"Would I just," I thought, and before Mother could interfere, thanked him and stood up in one movement. As we walked off, May nodded encouragingly.

"We'll be alright here," she said. "Mrs. Barnes and I will have a nice chat while you're gone."

"It's a bit boring playing cards every evening, isn't it?" said Herbert, as we slid at a smart pace into a foxtrot.

"Awful!" I replied with fervour. "But Mother loves it, so I don't like to disappoint her."

After that it became the rule that we played cards with Herbert and May after dinner each evening, but about ten o'clock every night Herbert would get up and take me off dancing for an hour or two while May entertained Mother. Often there was an excuse-me dance, when he stepped aside as I was whirled away by someone else, or we would be strung out in a veleta, or dashing along with the 'Gay Gordons'. Herbert was a good deal older than me, nearly twenty years as I later discovered, and although he certainly did not fail to enjoy the dancing, I know he did it out of the kindness of his heart, seeing my despair at my evenings being whittled away in the tedium of cards. May was just as aware of my disappointment, and willingly took on Mother so that I could escape for a while. Not only in the evenings, but on some of the day trips we joined, particularly in Nassau, they were attentive to Mother so that I could really enjoy myself with people of my own age. It was an act of sheer kindness and understanding, for which I was ever grateful, and made the greatest possible use of, and from that time I started to call Herbert 'Uncle', and so did Mother. It just seemed to suit him. May demurred from being called 'Auntie' however, so we called her 'Sister', which pleased her, and 'Uncle' and 'Sister' they remained. Moreover, their thoughtfulness had completely restored my faith in human nature. Life seems to be all ups and downs, I decided, and here was an 'up' just when I needed it. I returned home feeling quite a different person from the misery in which I had left it, and with all my old optimism revived I felt strong again.

Soon after we arrived back, Auntie Ada came to tea. I had a shock when I saw her, as she was unmistakably and frighteningly jaundiced. I had never seen anyone so yellow before, and the whites of her eyes especially were the most surprising colour. She looked thin and haggard too, and I could see that Mother was shaken by the change in her.

After this, it was a gradual unremitting downhill path, until in October she died. Poor simple Ebba was shattered, but bravely saw to all the arrangements at home, whilst Harold organised the funeral. Ebba found great comfort in Richard, who was now about eleven, and already developing into a considerable personage in his quiet sensitive way.

But she had lost the prop of her capable warm-hearted mother, who had always been a foil to Harold's obtuseness, and much as I admired the way she had spared Richard any feeling of friction between his parents by always submitting to Harold's whims or quietly ignoring his unkindness, I felt deeply sorry for her now in her loneliness. With her long hours at work, in a way Harold's unemployed status was at least helpful in that he was always around when Richard came home from school, and needless to say the boy was the apple of his eye, though to do him justice he did not indulge him. He was enormously proud of his son, and fortunately Richard's nature was able to take on board his successes in every aspect of school life without becoming spoilt.

"How do they do it?" I said to myself when I found myself tussling with one of Dick's children who came to live with us while she attended college in Kensington. It looks so easy to bring up children when other people do it, but full of pitfalls when one is involved oneself. Joan was their eldest, and at that stage of life very argumentative. Moreover she dawdled around, vaguely gathering herself and her possessions together, as she prepared to make off for the train each morning, and the daily fracas to achieve this started every day off on the wrong foot for me. She seemed to have every reason for not putting her things ready the night before, so each succeeding morning we had a fuss.

"Where's my bag?" she cried accusingly. "Who's taken my gloves? What's happened to my manuscript book? Oh dear! Where on earth is my bag? I know I shall miss my train." And so it went on. Moreover, when I finally found myself alone and able to have a quiet cup of coffee and a cigarette at last in order to calm down, I knew without doubt the trail of mess and disorder I would find upstairs. I was right. Bathroom, bedroom, and even landing were a muddle of her belongings; stockings and grubby undies thrown on the floor, stacks of skirts and blouses she had considered for that day and discarded, flung on the bed, or even on the side of the bath; lipstick and powder on the basin; books and papers scattered regardless. Such a confusion I could not live with, and in the evening the problem re-erected its head as she no doubt dawdled around at college and missed her train back to Sundridge Park, whilst her meal hardened in the oven. I felt that this sort of selfish behaviour had certainly not been tolerated at home, and did not see why I should put up with it now she was with us.

In the end, and after much previous endeavour, I decided it must stop as it was ruining our peace – mainly mine, as Mother had her breakfast in bed and probably did not realise the disruption, only enjoying having her granddaughter with us so that she could boast about her to her cronies. So, one Saturday I launched in, prepared to do battle if necessary, feeling a worm, and wishing I had had more experience of how to deal with fractious adolescents. After a furious argument – "You don't understand, Auntie," – stamping of feet, and finally exit slamming the door, there was quiet while both Joan and I calmed down and regained our respective equilibrium. To my great surprise, the result was almost perfect, peace and order reigned,and the house was more or less returned to normal.

This was the only time I ever had a problem of discipline with any of my nieces and nephews, and in after years they said, shivering at the very thought of it, "Oh no, you never disobeyed Aunt Hannah. I would never have dared." In fact I never had to raise my voice to any of them again, so it evidently taught me how to deal with young people and served me well in the future.

CHAPTER IX

1938

IT WAS NOW THE mid-thirties, and I had become used to being
past the first flush of youth. Some of my nieces and nephews
were already grown-up and yet treated me deferentially as one of
the older generation. I was a sort of mezzanine floor between Dick's
generation above, and Joan's below – neither one nor the other. I
was beginning to be taken for granted by them all, in the nicest
possible way, I suppose, as the steady, reliable member of the family.
I did not feel too flattered by this assessment, which in any case
was in some ways so untrue. They thought I was predictable, and
would give unbiased viewpoints of every circumstance, and they
all, young and old, had begun to rely on me for common-sense
opinions, even advice. I found myself often in the position of
listening to their worries, and if possible helping them through the
problem. They all knew also, whatever their age, that their secrets
were safe with me, and I became a repository for all the family
skeletons. Conversely, they sensed that it was no good them trying
to worm gossip about each other out of me. I had learnt very early
in life when I lived between two households always anxious to know
each other's affairs, the value of saying "don't know" to leading
questions.

But for myself I felt envious of the young ones with their
ability to be flighty and adventurous even if they sometimes came
a cropper; starting new careers, now ever more the norm for
women, and having a stream of boy-friends. On the other hand I
envied Dick, even Estelle for their settled way of life, with husbands
to depend on, and their own homes. In many ways I had a better
life than either group, as except for my commitment to Mother, I
was splendidly independent – too much so, I often felt. Within a

limited budget, I could spend my days as I liked, although this very freedom itself was the master of my existence, and I knew I had to compose my disciplines for myself rather than the far easier rôle of having them imposed from above. The predictability of my life irked me, and yet I could not see it altering. It was as if I had no ultimate goal to achieve, but merely had to keep going on the flat course ahead. I could admit to myself all the advantages I had over the rest of the family, in my freedom, my visits to the theatre, trips abroad, tennis parties, time to read, and so on; but it was aimless and endless.

The one thing I found so easy, that of making friends, saved me from becoming down-hearted. It was natural for me to chat to people, to make acquaintances, and to forge long-term friendships. But I still needed a basic routine and a purpose to work for. In order to provide the latter during these years, I set myself to become a good skater, a peculiar ambition in a way, but being athletic and enjoying ice-skating both as a sport and an art, I wanted to achieve extreme proficiency in this beautifully sensitive dance form. I was already going to the ice-rink at Streatham two or three afternoons a week, from whence I could drive straight into London on the A23 to fetch Mother from the office. I thought I would save up to have some skating lessons, because I so much admired the exotic prowess of some of the professionals there. Cecilia College was the star at that time, and did most of her practising at Streatham. Although the general public was allowed onto the rink much of the day, at about hourly intervals a bell would be rung to clear the ice, and only those who could waltz or tango or even dance the paso doble were allowed to participate for the next quarter of an hour. Everyone else had to stagger off onto the sidelines still on their skates, to collapse onto the cinema-like seats where they had to remain until the bell rang again indicating free use of the rink once more. No one minded this enforced interval as they were thus able to watch exhibition dancing of the highest calibre, interspersed of course with the not-so-goods like myself.

My tutor's name was Robert. Straight away when I first met him, I sensed this was going to be a pleasant and easy association. Just because I was a woman, he did not talk down to me, and he quickly assessed my ability and expected neither more nor less than I could achieve. And yet he immediately gave me confidence so that even by the end of the first lesson I was far and away better and lighter and more flexible than before. This ability of his to bring the very best out of his pupils was quite extra-ordinary, and the wonderful sense of truly dancing was intoxicating. The half hour passed all too fast, and with a flushed face I booked my next session. After that I did without visits to the cinema, new silk stockings, shoe-mending, make-up – anything I could think of to save money for further lessons. Ice-dancing became my number one priority. Here at last was a way of feeling on top of life, poised, confident, supreme, even attractive, with my short skating skirt swishing round as I twisted and turned, and my hair blowing up in the gusts of air, my hands and feet in unison this way and that, and my knees bent to control my balance. Leaps, arabesques, rotations and reverses, all with confidence and evenness; Robert holding me lightly by hand and waist, gently guiding with but the softest pressure one way or the other; him leading, me following; only to change into my turn to lead, him to follow.

It was like a drug. A smoothly beautiful concoction which turned my head, controlled my body; where speech was superfluous, eyes were essential, so that we were dancing as one.

Robert was a splendid teacher. Not only did he bring the best out of me, but he completely sublimated his own feelings and personality, concentrating totally on his pupil. After I had been dancing with him for months without any conversation other than my asking questions about technique and his answering these and introducing me to further patterns of movement, it occurred to me that I knew not one single thing about him personally. Then one day I received a postcard signed by him to say he had to cancel my next lesson as his wife was ill, and would I keep in touch with the rink to find out when he would be back. I attended there on my usual days, and practised my steps, and after a week or two called in at the office to enquire about him.

"Oh, Robert," said the girl absent-mindedly. "His wife has been ill for years, you know. He does everything for her. Wheel-chair and all that."

I felt slightly stunned that I could have spent so many hours with a person and not fathomed the anxiety under which he lived, not to mention the hard work and devotion entailed in caring for his wife. I wondered whether there was something wrong with my sense of perception that I had missed this; but then I comforted myself that Robert's and my relationship was entirely a professional one of teacher to pupil, and there was no reason why I should have detected his own troubles in his manner to me. He was just a good tutor whom I paid for his services. All the same, my conscience did not like to be stilled, and he now appeared in quite a different light from before, so that instead of aiming at proficiency for its own sake, I found I wanted to do well at my dancing to please him, with the muddled idea of easing his pain at her illness.

"This is ridiculous," I at last announced to myself. "It's becoming too personal. Why on earth should the fact of his having private concerns alter one iota our businesslike attitude to each other."

So, with this firm avowal of the position, the matter was closed.

When I arrived at Hamsel Street, Mother was waiting for me in the doorway of G&B's.

"I thought you'd forgotten to fetch me," she grumbled.

"Mother! When did I ever forget to come?" I expostulated.

"There's always a first time," she answered as she sat herself down in the car, edging in backwards and letting me swivel her legs round, and then tuck her skirt in under her behind before slamming the door firmly.

"Have you had a good day?" we both said simultaneously, and then laughed.

Next day there was a letter for Mother from May Simpson – 'Sister' to say she and 'Uncle' would be in our area to look at some damaged cars, and could they call on us. He was an insurance assessor, and his work took him all over the country to calculate claims, most frequently in the various docks where goods may have arrived after a stormy journey or been damaged on unloading. This time Uncle was going down to the Surrey Docks on the Thames, and they would be at our place for tea. I was glad to hear this. They had kept in touch with us ever since our West Indies' trip, and I enjoyed the quiet consideration they always showed us. Their thoughtful attitude had a calming effect on me, and I liked them also for themselves. They were very alike, except that Sister was rather plump and bosomy in a motherly way, whilst he was exceedingly thin, but as they were both tall they seemed to fill our house to capacity with their goodwill once they were within the front door. Both with quiet voices and slow speech with a mildly London accent, I immediately felt at ease with them even if we had not met for some months.

"Well, Hannah," Uncle said when they were settled in their chairs, "where are you planning to visit next? Not the West Indies again?"

"No, but we're going through the Panama Canal once more, and then down to Valparaiso and Concepción. It should be lovely."

"Lucky girl," he said approvingly. "Whose idea was that?"

"Oh, Mother's as usual. You know what she is." His eyes twinkled.

It so happened that 1938 started off for me as one of the most travelled years I had experienced, as if the Fates knew that soon we should be confined to our own shores. I had already promised to go skiing at Innsbruck with Edna early that year, and in the event had to rush home after a fortnight in order to get myself and my clothes ready for the different climate of South America. In Austria we were fairly isolated with the skiing fraternity, but there was a mixture of European nationalities – though not of race – on the slopes. The talk was of Hitler Youth, and how smart they looked in their uniforms, and of the huge gatherings in the major German cities to hear the Fuhrer speak. In England we had heard some of these rallies on the wireless and were aware of the hypnotising effect of the excitement they engendered as the tumult simultaneously all shouted "Heil, Heil, Zeig Heil" in unison. There were stories coming out of Germany of Jew-bating, oppression, even persecution. Jewish families were arriving in England seeking refuge, with frightening tales to tell. Edna and I listened intently to conversations we could overhear in the 'après ski' bars, but in the main did not join in. We thought that safer, even though we were British citizens. Amongst most of these holiday-makers trying to enjoy themselves in a light-hearted manner and forget the threat hanging over them, there was an unmistakable feeling of gathering darkness, as if a storm cloud was gradually enshrouding all Europe. Only the British on their island were free to say what they thought of it all.

I felt almost besmirched by all this underlying gloom and the cruel stories we heard, not to mention the inability of the Germans to believe what was happening under their noses. They seemed drunk with the charisma of Hitler and his new Reich. The photographs which came through to this country of the Jews sweeping the streets, and being chased and rounded up by the S.S. made me want to vomit. It affected Dick even worse as she thought of all her German friends and knew that they would never behave like that on their own initiative. Had they all gone mad, we wondered.

I was glad to feel cleansed by the Atlantic winds blowing on my face, to counteract the grime of Europe as Mother and I crossed to Panama and then down the west coast of South America, though it was rather like clutching at last straws before we drowned. Chile, outwardly at any rate, was light-hearted, bright-coloured, careless and sunny, and did me good. Song seemed to permeate the streets, and the donkeys with their huge loads cut us down to size. The old men and women lounging at corners smoking their pipes as if they were timeless, put German aggression into perspective. Above all, the warmth and the attitude of 'manãna' despatched the clouds I had been under at home.

We arrived back to a beautiful English Spring. There was a letter from Hilda on the mat when we opened the front door.

"Do come to Paris for Easter," it said. "We shall all be there, and it may not be easy to meet again for a while."

So, aware of the urgency of her tone, Mother and I did another quick turn-round, packed up again, and bought our tickets for the Golden Arrow. Hilda's language was veiled, but we knew what she meant.

When we arrived in Paris, John whisked me off to stay in his pretty villa in St. Cloud, whilst Mother was met by Hilda and Kiki who drove her off to stay with Jeanne and Jacques in the house at Le Vesinet where they now lived, the same house that Papa Fiat had built for Kiki before the First War. The weather was lovely, and Paris looked its best in the sun and was full of flowers. The Seine was calm, and its banks decked with multi-coloured awnings over the stalls of second-hand ware, books, pictures and all sorts of bric-a-brac. The piano accordion and the fiddle could be heard all over the City, as if it was gasping its last breath of gaiety. But there was no denying the ominous presence of sandbags being piled up in the streets; shelters were being dug, men in uniform were much more in evidence than usual, and in the cafes the talk was of war, although the colours of the blossom on the trees in the Champs Elysée and the clothes in the Rue de Rivoli were as bright and fresh as ever.

"We will come to England as soon as we're certain Jerry means business," John said. "We'll get a bit of warning."

"What! And leave all your things here?"

Gilberte, his young wife of two or three years, said nothing. As always she left it all to John.

"We can fight them better from England," he replied. "I'm too old for the army, but I'll go into the Civil Defence. I can't have Gilberte in Paris if they come."

"You seem very certain France is going to be overrun. What about the Maginot Line?" I queried, but he shook his hand.

"We'll see, but if necessary we'll get out."

Mother and I left Paris with heavy hearts, wondering where and if we should ever meet any of our relations there again, and what was in store for us all. Paris had been bombarded in two wars within the last sixty years. The authorities evidently expected it again. As I waved from the carriage window while our train drew out of the Gare du Nord, I caught the last glimpse I ever had of Kiki, and was not to see Hilda and Jeanne again until after the war. It was with a sense of shock that I sat back in the compartment to digest the sombre prospect in front of us.

Henry met us at Victoria, and it was obvious as he drove us back home across London that preparations for war were going on there, too, though not with the same urgency as in Paris. Sandbags were making an appearance, and some windows in large stores and office blocks were boarded up. As we rode up Whitehall I suddenly realised the policemen had 'tin hats' on instead of their usual helmets, and large hessian bags slung across their shoulders.

"Gas masks," said Henry briefly.

Next day we were fitted with ours, small civilian ones in flimsy cardboard boxes, which made us look unearthly when we wore them. The Air Raid Warden who checked them sent us into a van filled with tear gas to make sure they were not leaking, which was an eerie experience, but they completely protected us.

"You should carry them everywhere with you now," he said as he ticked us off his list. "Best to make strong canvas bags to put each one in. Don't forget to take a leaflet about blackout. I'll be round to your house to check it as soon as I can," he said.

So that afternoon I bought a roll of thick black cotton material, and got out my sewing machine, wondering as I did so how all the Austrians we had met only three months ago were weathering their own storm of invasion by the Germans. It was hardly credible that the streets of Innsbruck were now overrun by Hitler's storm troopers, and the mountain roads we had so recently travelled on to the ski slopes were patrolled by German soldiers. Even while I was making those curtains, the sound of Hitler's ranting came over the wireless with his demands for the return of the Sudeten Germans from Czechoslovakia.

"You'd better get some stocks of tinned food in, Anne," said Mother as she listened.

All this war fever was wearing, and that afternoon I rang up the ice rink to find out if Robert was back. I felt I needed to reassure myself that life was going on just as usual, and everyone had not deserted their senses. The girl in the office said yes, he was back, and fixed an appointment for my lesson.

"Do you know if his wife is better?" I hedged, not wishing to appear too interested.

"No, ducks. She died about a fortnight ago" she said unemotionally.

There were noticeably fewer people at the rink now as everyone took up their wartime roles, and gradually more uniforms appeared on the ice. Robert was swerving around with another pupil when I arrived, and did not see me at first, and then he turned and smiled faintly.

My lesson passed well, and I fixed several more dates with him. Still he did not mention his wife, and I hardly liked to do so until one day, when my half hour had finished, he said suddenly "Let's go and have some coffee," and followed me up to the cafe.

"I'm sorry about your news," I said, hoping that he could follow this up or not as he wished.

"That's alright," he said. "Her life wasn't worth living anyway."

"You must be lonely without her." He nodded.

"Wish now we'd had some children, but she couldn't," he said. I had the impression of his unutterable loneliness like a big black void as he spoke, but did not want to break up his train of thought.

"Will you have a meal with me one evening?" he broke in suddenly. "Then we can talk."

"Oh dear, I can't possibly. I have to look after Mother."

"Every night?" he said with disbelief.

"Well, really, yes. She works so hard all day," and I started to explain. He listened without interrupting, shaking his head slightly with comprehension as I ran over my life so far.

"You must have an evening off now and then, surely?" he argued.

"It's very difficult," I parried. "What about lunch."

"Alright" he said at last. "On my day off. We'll go to the Kiosk in Purley. It's quiet there."

So that is what we did, and gradually he told me all about his marriage, and how lovely his young wife was at first, but how soon the truth about her illness had become plain, and although with remissions now and then, there had been a general downhill course over the last ten years. He spoke quietly and factually, but I could tell how hurt he had been by this cold touch of Fate, and now he was glad to be able to speak to someone outside his family of his sadnesses at watching her deteriorate.

"It seems that we have both had problems, you and I," he said "though you've managed to cope with yours. I am still learning to accept mine."

After that we often had coffee together after my lesson if his next pupil had not arrived, and sometimes we went out for lunch. They were quiet peaceful times, often without much conversation at all, but with almost palpable companionship. He asked me over and over again to meet him in the evenings, but I never felt I could. Partly it was because to do so would have meant telling Mother about him, and I wanted to keep this friendship private. I did not want other people to intrude into our mutual warmth and understanding.

All summer we met, but by late August the news from Europe was so threatening, and Hitler's strident voice on the wireless was becoming so enveloping that I thought I'd better take Mother up to Yorkshire, away from London's vulnerability. There was not much work for her at the office, and likely to be less. I was trying to make up my mind as to whether it was too drastic a step to take, when the phone rang.

"It's Dick," said the voice. "You'd better bring Mother up here for the duration. We've plenty of room."

"Talk of the devil!" I said, but that decided me. If a sensible person like Dick thought it necessary, it must be.

So I packed up our belongings, all the tinned food I had stocked up, and a few precious bits and pieces such as Mother's jewellery, gave the key of the front door to the Evans next door, voiced thanks to heaven that I had not replaced Peter by another dog, and with the car crammed to the roof, and just room for Mother, a picnic basket and myself, set off up the tortuous route of the A1.

Only a month later Neville Chamberlain was at Berchtesgaden, and the Munich crisis gave us 'Peace in our time'. It was only a breathing space, and we knew it. Meanwhile I could not just sit twiddling my thumbs at Dick's house with nothing definite to do, but having no training whatsoever I had a problem. What could a raw thirty-six year old do for a living temporarily whilst Hitler made up his mind about our future? I made some enquiries and looked at advertisements in the papers, but none of them seemed suitable. It appeared I was of no use for anything. Finally, in bored desperation, and only too aware of my lack of substantial income, I decided to see what I could make of a 'companion' job which had materialised through friends of Dick's in Barnsley. The duties were not onerous, and my employers were an elegant old couple whose family were now spread around the world, so that their large stone Victorian house was dark and lonely and quiet. There were several maids and a cook, and my job was to supervise them, and generally to run the house. In fact the house more or less ran itself, and my duties were totally undemanding. As I dressed for dinner on my first evening, in my velvet 'après ski' frock made more prim by the addition of a lace collar, I wondered what on earth I was doing here. The old couple were delightfully unworldly and courtly, and treated me more as a guest than an employee. They were grateful to have someone relatively young in the house, and told me proudly about their own children, especially 'Freddie' who was an Air Vice-Marshal. I could sense what a disciplined and united family it was, and the big house and extensive garden reminded me of the Rookery. Perhaps it does not matter growing old when you have had such a complete life, and successfully reared your children so that you can bask in self-respect reflected from their achievements. I found myself wondering what Robert was doing, and whether he ever thought of me or missed me. Probably I had played my cards completely mistakenly, and should have managed to meet him one evening as he asked. I had thrown away that precious friendship without more than a thought from my stupid conscience, and now I was lonely and aimless again. He was probably in the forces anyhow now, whilst I was fancying myself as a working girl.

Despite all these high-flown ideas which returned to me many times in the future, I could not but be bored. The house was built on a steep hillside well outside Barnsley, in good solid limestone grit. The countryside was rich and grand. But beauty on its own, unaccompanied by purpose is not enough to thrive on, and I still needed something more definite to get my teeth into, and feel I was achieving worthwhile goals. As soon as the A.R.P. was well-organised in Yorkshire I asked to go back to Dick, much to the old people's concern. "Have you not been happy with us, Hannah?" they asked sadly. My conscience hurt me once again as I left them, but the Country needed me now, and I needed it, and their family must look after them. The months with them had not been wasted. They had been happy, and I had had time to think, away from the family or my old associations. Now I had to go back.

York was the nearest large town to Dick, and it was there that I applied to join the Civil Defence as a driver. The A.R.P. was still fumbling, with little experience to go on. It had a certain number of full-time employees, both in the office and in practical jobs, and other permanent but part-time placements which could be combined with civilian jobs. As well as these there was the whole army of voluntary staff covering every nook of the City, but who had to be trained, organised, and kept up-to-date. Everyone was very keen, and raring to go.

I was full-time, but on shift work, and although it included long hours when maintenance and training were done, yet we still had to be available immediately for emergencies, day or night. Our headquarters, where we could sleep or relax, was a tumbledown sort of terrace of old houses in a less salubrious part of the City by the river, and here all the ambulances and fire-tenders and vans were parked so that they could be sent out at a moment's notice. We all learnt a little about every job so that we could carry on each other's work if necessary. Officially there to drive a van converted into an ambulance, I learnt first aid, field cookery, fire fighting theory and the use of hoses and stirrup pumps, not to mention the servicing of all kinds of A.R.P. vehicles. Working in shifts, where absenteeism was practically unknown, we came to know other members of the team well. The fire-fighters, who were all men, inhabited the far end of the terrace, but came along to our end for meals. These were efficiently cooked and prepared by 'Violet', a factory hand with a choice vocabulary. In fact my grasp of language broadened quite considerably whilst I was with the York A.R.P., but also I learnt a good deal about camaraderie and other people's personal lives. We were all middle-aged or nearly so, and had already seen something of life, though our experiences ranged over a wide spectrum. Mainly not a cultivated group, we did include a retired botanist and a professional singer. Mostly, however, we comprised housewives whose families had grown old enough to leave home on their own, or unmarried women like Violet and me, and people (both men and women) who had never thought it necessary for whatever reason to have a permanent job before, plus well-preserved retired men. It was a remarkable mix, and as we tucked ourselves into our camp-beds at night, or drank our evening mugs of cocoa, I heard about sides of life and modes of existence, family squabbles, and matrimonial intricacies, I never knew existed. They were a warm-hearted group once one dug beneath the often coarse exterior.

CHAPTER X

1939

THE DAY WAR finally broke out was a Sunday, and I was home with Dick. As I walked back through country lanes from church where the failure of Chamberlain's ultimatum had been announced from the pulpit, I felt extreme anger more than any other emotion. It was only twenty years since we had ceased the idiocy of the last war, and evidence of its effect on people was still with us in the maimed bodies one saw in the streets, and the gassed lungs and damaged minds of people one met in their own homes. How could man be so foolish as to throw away the bounty of peace for goodness knows what risky future? The sun was bright that September morning, the cornfields covered in brown stubble, ploughing just starting, the hedgerows full of movement and life, a few trees beginning to show their autumn colours. What stupidity could encourage anyone to throw this away wilfully? Then I thought of the unarmed Polish peasants tackling oncoming German tanks; I thought of the Jews in Europe; and I heard in my memory the 'Zeig Heils' we had witnessed on the wireless. Then I knew we had to fight the evil of Naziism.

"Hullo luv!" said Violet when I reappeared at the A.R.P. next day wearing dungarees and my 'tin hat'. "Well, Jerry's done it now, b----r him. We'll show 'em." And she produced more expletives to show her opinion of Hitler, as she poured the Camp coffee into our mugs of hot water. "Fire drill today," she announced. "Better check your pumps before You-know-who comes round," and returned to the latest copy of Reynolds News which she had brought with her that morning to enliven odd moments.

I stayed with the York A.R.P. for two years. It was a time for me for consolidating all that had gone before in my life, and was a bonus that Hitler brought to some of us whose lives had previously had no aim. Now we were all completely under the control of the war, and our one united endeavour was to win it. This was a great opportunity, unasked for by most people, to learn what it meant to be in a team, even if only a small part in it. All now had their value and their worth and were needed to achieve our aim. Personal pettiness was buried beneath the common objective. As at no time in peace, we were all lumped together in a great big melting-pot, subduing our personalities to some extent so as to be part of the group, but never losing them to the polyglot atmosphere of our struggle. It changed us all to some extent, mostly for the better, and made us much broader minded in our handling of our fellow humans, sharing their joys and troubles with more understanding than previously.

During 1940 Mother had died, very peacefully, at Dick's house. She was eighty, and London had already had a preview of the destruction and horror to come. I was glad she was not to see G&B razed to the ground in future blitzes, and her beloved 'City' devastated, as seemed so likely by then. Business at G&B was just managing to tick over, and kept itself alive by printing government forms in a small way and doing some book binding. Minnie and old Courtney and a couple of elderly operatives remained to keep an eye on it. Henry, who adored uniform, the more glamorous the better, but was too fat to squeeze into Civil Defence gear, achieved the much more eye-catching apparel of an R.A.F. squadron leader by dint of joining the Balloon Barrage Service.

"Rather a cheat, don't you think?" said Dick, who was none the less proud of her 'little' brother as she studied a photograph which showed him on an airfield straining on a rope attached to a balloon flying above, as if his weight alone kept it in check. "Typical!" she said.

Summer 1940 produced beautiful hot weather over the whole of Europe, so much so that the cornfields of France were firm enough to take the rumbling weight of the German tanks as they bypassed the Maginot Line and made for the Atlantic coast. The skies were full of aircraft engaged in dog-fights as news came over the wireless that Paris was about to fall, and later that it had fallen. We held our breath as the epic of Dunkirk came to fruition with the heroism of the little boatmen of southern England. No word arrived from John, and I worked hard at my maintenance jobs to keep my mind occupied and prevent my imagination frightening me. Were he and Gilberte in one of those civilian convoys being machine-gunned as they escaped through the French countryside westwards? Were Hilda and Kiki safely on their farm in Merignac, and what about Jeanne and her obviously Jewish husband? We had the wireless on all the time listening to B.B.C. bulletins. The battlefields were changing so rapidly it was impossible to keep abreast of the news, and when the last British journalists escaped with the remnants of the British Expeditionary Force from France, a thick impenetrable blanket came down between us and Europe, and the only bulletins were the official ones, the significance of which we then had to unravel from between their lines.

My heart sank. There was no word from any of my French relatives. Not for the first time in my life I wondered if John was dead.

Then suddenly a telegram arrived out of the blue. "Arrived Southampton" it said. "Going to Bromley. John Gilberte."

I couldn't believe it. I told my supervisor the news, was given five days' leave, rang the Evans to tell them to look out for John's arrival next door, and rushed home to change and pack a few things. As I walked up the road at Bromley, my heart thumping, I knew at once they had got there before me.

They were both alright, just very tired from loss of sleep and continual fear for the last fortnight. They had managed after several days' wait in crowds of other refugees, to get on the last boat out of La Rochelle before the Germans walked into the town an hour later. The place was packed with anxious terrified people, and so were all the roads leading to the coast. There had been strafing from the air, and continual sound of gunfire in the east. The boat was crammed full, but they had managed to find a space to sit down in a corner of the deck, protected by a lifeboat from German gunfire. It had been very scary – "And oh, les toilettes!" cried Gilberte, as if that was the greatest insult "Oh la-la! C'est terrible." They were exhausted, hungry and worried about their families, but otherwise unscathed, and John was already raring to join the London Fire-fighting Service, and "pay back Jerry". He was thinner than before his recent privations but his hair was neatly brilliantined back as usual, and his face had its old determined look of self-confidence and cockyness, the gold tooth showing as he grinned, and his Gallic habit of hand-display active as it illustrated the bombing he'd experienced by the German planes. More sanguine and less excitable than the French, he combined his English phlegmatism and his Swedish obstinacy with their conversational characteristics, accompanied, like all his Paris acquaintances, by a cigarette balanced on one end of his lower lip.

"We'll show 'em," he said, echoing Violet's Yorkshire pronouncement.

Those few days we talked and talked as only the French can, and it seemed to be therapeutic for John and Gilberte, and to lift the load from their shoulders as they quickly recovered and settled down in their new circumstances. Leaving almost all their possession behind in Paris had been hard, and although Gilberte's sister would try to look after their affairs as well as she could, it was inevitable that their empty house would be taken for refugees' or army use. It did not bear thinking of, and in any case as the Battle of Britain continued in the air over southern England, they had plenty to occupy their minds.

Before I left to return to my job in York, I was able to broach the subject of my own future with John. I did not mind doing a lowly job such as I had undertaken in the A.R.P. as my contribution to the war effort for a circumscribed period of time, but I was again in the position of not being stretched mentally. The only air raid alerts in our part of the Country had so far been due to enemy aircraft passing over to drop their bombs elsewhere, and up to now there had been none dropped on York, though in the future there might well be as it was an important railway centre. It was, however, of only minor importance industrially, and we did not then visualise the crass objective of the Baedecker raids. Surely I could be of more use to the Country in the long run if I was in a position other than the one which I now held. Everywhere I had turned to find a solution to this question led me to the same reply. I must have a training. John agreed, the more so, he reiterated, because after the war I would still need a satisfying occupation and there was no likelihood of achieving that without a qualification, and a certificate to prove it. Something in what in those days was called 'domestic science' seemed the right thing.

"But would any course take me on at nearly forty?" I queried. "And if it did, would my brain be so out of practice that I should simply not be able to keep up with it or (awful thought) pass the terminal examination."

John, always so practical, pointed out that as the war progressed, men and women would be discharged from the forces for one reason or another, and having enlisted straight from school, would need the tools to develop civilian careers. The whole attitude to students would have to change, and rather than only eighteen year olds, older groups would have to be catered for. He had not quite coined the phrase 'mature student', but that was what he meant.

"And you're not such a fool that your old brain won't tick over adequately, he cheerfully encouraged me with typical brotherly frankness.

I left them after four days happily digging in, quite literally,as their Anderson shelter had arrived, and I returned to the North. I chewed over what John had said about my need for a career after the war, and knew he was right. I just had not faced it before. Now there was no Mother to look after, I could not simply fritter away the rest of my life, and anyhow the little money I had must be augmented. Marriage had passed me by, and with it the chance of a sure income. I had to come to terms with that fact whether I liked it or not. It was the hard truth.

Like John, Dick and James were equally matter-of-fact when I approached them about this, though Dick was immediately worried about the obvious practical difficulties, not least the financial ones – there were no student grants in those days.

"I shall blue the money Mother left me," I said, somewhat to her consternation. Dick always liked to save for a rainy day. "This is my rainy day," I forestalled her before she could say her piece.

James, the businessman, said he thought that it was a good way to invest it, and it would bring 'lifelong dividends'. He was more interested in the type of course I envisaged.

"Well, cookery is really the thing I enjoy most," I began selfconsciously.

"There's no call for high-class private cooks just now, and goodness knows about the future," he said. "What about institutional cooking?" I did not like the thought of that, as it brought to my mind uncarpeted Dickensian establishments with long bare tables and wooden forms, and nothing but bowls of porridge to eat.

"I don't know," I hedged vaguely.

"Boarding schools, factories, hospitals?" he encouraged. "Think it over," and he produced from his daughter's file in his desk an old prospectus for the 'Pud School' in Leeds. "This will give you an idea," he said. The 'Pud School' was a much respected training college in all types of domestic science where that daughter had filled in a year before starting to nurse. She had enjoyed it and had a high opinion of the place. I took the brochure up to my room and did 'think about it' and tried to visualise myself as a student there.

After much writing, interviewing, and considering ways and means, I finally left the A.R.P. in 1941 and entered my new Alma Mater next month. My set of students turned out to be a mixed age-group of girls, half of them straight from school, another quarter following on from other courses, and a very few old 'aunties' like myself. I was scared!

"Are you Aunt Anne?" said a cheery voice my first day as I was settling my file for the initial lecture, sitting as obscurely as I could, as I thought away from the tutor's eye, in the back row. The owner of the voice plumped down gracelessly beside me. She had a pink round face, a mop of curly hair, and an obvious problem with her weight. Immediately I felt better. "I'm Anne, too," she announced. "I was at school with one of your nieces."

I liked this Anne. She was easy-going, and kind, and being a very perceptive person, realised how I would feel on my first day, with so many younger students. She turned out to be my saviour on that course, and besides helping me with my notes, we giggled silently together on the back row throughout the year, and life became fun once more. Fresh from school, she was enjoying the freedom of student life, but had the maturity to understand how restricting it was for me, and did her best to help me through. The practical work was no worry for me, though as I had anticipated, it was hard to make one's intellect react sharply. However, the course was sensible and interested me, and I worked very hard to keep up with the theory, whilst turning out to be a star pupil at the practical work. Meanwhile I lived free of charge with Dick and

James, who could not have been more understanding, and all in all it was a happy year, though with little time or inclination for social contacts.

Next summer, equipped with a certificate and a glowing reference from my tutor, I started to apply for jobs, with my eye firmly on the south London area, hoping that I could return to my roots, and if possible Bromley. My age must have helped, perhaps also my unglamorous no-nonsense attitude to work during the interviews, and almost at once I obtained a post of supervising cook for a Vickers' armament factory on the Slades Green marshes, near Dartford, and this in every way suited me perfectly. The firm was working a twenty-four hour day during the war, in three shifts, and I was responsible for all the food for the employees, including when I was not actually present myself. Then my assistant, who turned out to be another Violet, took over control under my instructions, and if she was not there, a real Cockney called Lila supervised. Violet and Lila had hearts of gold and infinite loyalty, and under them was a team, mainly women, of varying ranks in the kitchen hierarchy, who did the preparation work and the cleaning. Here at last was something for me to get my teeth into; to organise a motley collection of Londoners into a credible unit, instruct and train them, and to carry out our brief to feed the factory workers satisfactorily whilst maintaining co-operative contentment in the kitchen. Moreover I was welcomed by John and Gilberte to live with them, which made that side of life easy, and gave her some company when he was away for long hours with the A.R.P.

I jumped in with both feet, feeling that all my previous experience was going to be put to good use now, right down to dealing with giggly adolescent girls. I aimed to be open and fair and straight with my staff, and they soon learned that if they behaved that way with me, we got along fine. I found I had a penchant for effortless discipline, both with the factory workers and with my own staff in the kitchen. It never caused me trouble, partly because they could see that I was working quite as hard as they themselves, and was not prepared simply to organise and give orders. On the other hand we shared the same sort of London sense of humour, which helped us through some of the terrifying episodes of the bombing. We were a prime target for the German attack on the capital, being easily located by our position beside the Thames,

109

and certainly required all the humour we could assemble to cope with the fearful circumstances that sometimes faced us.

The air raid sirens were still busy in 1942, but there was no return of the ferocity of the earlier blitz. However, the warning went off if enemy aircraft approached the south-east coast, and they only needed a few minutes to fly up the Thames to reach us, so that now and again we found ourselves scooting for the shelters at top speed, or if we left it too late, under the kitchen table. We often heard the guns on the coast, and if the sound gradually came nearer as the ack-ack fire followed a plane on its course to London, we knew we were in for it. Sometimes there were huge explosions as it jettisoned its bombs or even was shot down. Thud, thud, they went ominously, followed by a shower of gunfire as if the latter was applauding. I never could forget that there were actually real live men – young ones – up there in those planes, even though I knew they were hoping to kill me.

It was not until 1944 that the un-manned 'doodlebugs' began to fly over us. They were, frankly, terrifying. Whereas we had previously heard the sound of aircraft approaching before the screaming of the bombs warned us of danger, the flying bomb was psychologically traumatic. Its engine had a recognisable sound like a rather tinny motor, to hear which was unrelated to an explosion. It was when it cut out, and suddenly one realised one could no longer hear the engine that one's wits abruptly gathered to indicate that the thing was falling, perhaps aimed at you. No whining like a conventional bomb. Just an unearthly silence, and perhaps time to dash for the kitchen table if one was lucky. We heard many of the flying bombs making their way up the river past our factory, and wondered which poor devil was going to catch it as we ourselves kept covered for fear of flak from the guns. Sometimes an R.A.F. plane came racing after it at a tangent to try to head it off, and sometimes they managed to shoot one down before it reached us. Mostly, by the time it got to us, it was destined to produce devastation somewhere in central London, and sometimes we heard the cut-out after it had passed us, and saw the explosion somewhere 'up West'.

On these occasions, I thought of John with the Fire Service and wondered if he was in the thick of it, and whether he had been able to help alleviate the suffering caused. I knew he would not spare himself, and I could only hope his luck would hold, as it did

110

eventually, throughout the blitz. Throwing himself into danger to help others was his answer to what he knew the Germans were doing to his French friends and relations. After a bad incident we would not see him back home at Bromley for a day or two, and Gilberte and I would try to carry on as usual, and make as light of it as we could. At last he would stagger in, having been dropped off by an A.R.P. van, dead tired, filthy, and very hungry, but from under his care-worn expression his grin usually surfaced as he managed to find some happening amongst all the horror which struck him as funny. Once he had had a wash and a shave, a meal and a sleep, he was ready to go back on duty, but both for him and for me it was not unusual to find buses were erratic and diverted from their usual routes, so one or other of us sometimes slept at our work places. Gilberte was used to this. "You're becoming a real Londoner," I would say as a form of congratulations to encourage her, and although she looked pleased, she obviously had reservations about that particular compliment.

I never failed to be amazed at how philosophical the ordinary Londoner was about the bombing. Not once did I have to face panic, either from my 'girls' or from the men and women working at the munitions. "Worse things happen at sea" they would say cheerfully as they swept up glass and debris after a near miss. They were always entirely phlegmatic, matter-of-fact, and sensible, even if in extremis. For myself I had no time for personal fear because I was kept occupied with my responsibilities for the others, which automatically subdued my own feelings at the time, although after a bad episode I often wondered why I had not been frightened out of my wits. As a protection against fear we all built into our systems a characteristic fatalism – if your number was on a bomb, there was no possibility of avoiding it; if it was not on, you would be alright regardless of what happened. It was a cheering view because it meant there was no point in worrying one way or the other, and certainly, like all inevitable traumas, it made the possible disaster easier to bear just because one did not dwell on it. It was a question of destiny, although it did not stop people taking cover when necessary. On the other hand they were nearly all superstitious. They avoided ladders like the plague, rejoiced in black cats, crossed their fingers hard, and would recite all sorts of magic mumbo-jumbo in times of stress. Most wore charms or mascots, either for themselves or for their menfolk in places of danger, searched for four-leafed clovers amongst the weeds surrounding the factory, and were a little dubious about ghosts. Mostly they sneered at each other's foibles in these matters, but continued with their own. It was a natural way to ward off rational fears, and it worked well in that respect as I realised one night when Violet and I found ourselves squashed together in the cupboard under the stairs whilst the whole kitchen shook with an explosion. She let out her breath in a sigh of relief, and brought out a wishbone from her overall pocket, which she held towards me. "Hang on," she said, "silly really, ain't it, but you never know."

No, you never did know, so together we hung on to the wishbone until it was safe to leave our cupboard.

Meanwhile I struggled with menus in an attempt to avoid monotony in the meals. But I was sorely tried. How do you inject interest into your catering when nearly every category of food is rationed, and some are totally unobtainable. Being a munitions factory we received a fair ration of what was available for each worker, and certainly cooking in bulk made the meagre amounts appear to go further. Almost everything was in short supply, but particularly meat and eggs, cheese and other fats, and of course sugar and syrup. We had to vary the vegetables, and disguise the same dishes judiciously with colouring or herbs and spices to make them look different. I would never have believed how much I missed the humble banana for instance, and even the sponge puddings were made with powdered egg from Canada, and the meat was said to be whale from the Argentine. It had a horrid fishy odour. We renamed it and produced it as steak and vegetable stew, added potatoes in their jackets, with which indeed we filled up the men every day as potatoes were grown locally on waste ground, and were just about the only bulky food not on ration.

Every Monday morning I worked out my menus for the next seven days, which was the most brain-wrenching job of the week, but I could at least console myself that had the workers gone home for dinner they would have fared much worse. The Government preferred everyone who had access to a canteen to use it, as communal cookery used less fuel than each individual preparing his own little meal, and, illogically, seemed to use less food for the same number of portions. We were at the height of the submarine warfare, when every item coming into Britain from abroad was liable to be sunk in one of the little merchant ships crossing the

Atlantic. Because we all knew the danger these seamen were exposed to in order that we should be fed, no-one grumbled at the poverty of the food and the boring diet of 'Woolton' pies which consisted of vegetables mixed with other vegetables and covered with potatoes.

As I carried out my weekly stock-taking on Monday mornings, I sometimes felt panic-stricken wondering if I should ever make the ingredients go round. There would be no more coming in until the next ration-load, and I just had to make do. All the 'girls' knew well enough not to interrupt me these mornings. "Don't go near Miss Minska. She's in 'er cupboard," they would whisper, and tiptoe past, hoping to hear what my favourite swear-word was today. Usually 'damn and blast' sufficed, but with it I produced a good deal of sweat and near-tears as I faced the bleak prospects in my stores. There was no doubt that this fear of failure to provide for 'my' workers adequately wore me down more than all the bombs and doodlebugs, because it was so difficult to equate with what was expected of me. We somehow came through with sufficient meals each day of those years, but nobody other than myself and Violet ever knew what a near thing it sometimes was, and I shuddered to think what I should have done if I had simply run out of an essential item such as flour. Each day began by my weighing out the total ingredients for the next twenty-four hours. I noted every item down in my notebook most meticulously so that I knew exactly where everything had gone, and I kept the keys of the store cupboards on my belt, and only handed them over to Violet or Lila, whom I could trust, when I went off duty. I could not afford to have anything stolen, because there would have been no replacement, and the workers would simply have had to go without. This atmosphere of policing was very wearing, and not a bit the way I liked to work, but it was the only method I could use. Every now and then some remark in the canteen would make me feel it was all worthwhile. "Blimey! Miss, you don' half make a good pud" spoke volumes. "Bet ol' Hitler wish he ate here." There was a good deal of banter too – "Not veg rissoles again – cor – we'll turn into blooming carrots, we will." None of it was vicious though; they appreciated my difficulties which they experienced even more at home where they had to juggle with their own rations.

All had their 'war-work' in those days, whatever their age, and the young only remained civilians if they were in reserved occupations. Even then they did their bit in civil defence, fire-watching, and a range of social work. I had one niece who was nursing in London, and another in the F.A.N.Y. – the army nursing service. Of my three nephews, two were in the Forces, and one (Hilda's son) was 'somewhere in France', as the B.B.C. would put it. We had no idea where this last one was, and could only hope and pray for him. He might even have been taken to Germany as forced labour. Another, Henry's son, was in a bomber squadron, nightly flying over Europe's towns, and the third had gone with the R.A.F. to Canada on a training course. Not quite twenty-one, he had recently become a pilot officer. He was Ebba's only child, one of those boys who was good at everything he tried, including being a fair artist. Ebba and Harold, in their otherwise cheerless marriage, together took great pride in this young man, Richard, and breathed a sigh of relief when he was sent away from the theatre of war to what they saw as the safety of Canada for a few months.

It therefore came as all the more of a shock for them when they received a buff-coloured envelope from the Air Ministry to announce in officialese that Richard had been in an accident whilst flying. A visit from his previous Squadron Leader rapidly followed to break to them the news that he had been killed outright, and that his body would be flown home.

I received a phone call at the factory from Harold. "Please come over at once. Richard's been killed" his altered voice told me flatly. I could not believe it. Of all the youngsters one could think of, he was the most promising and most needed. How could fate be so hurtful and cruel? Then came the anger against Hitler, swept immediately away by agony over what Richard's parents must be feeling. Leaving my keys and a mass of instructions with the kitchen staff, I caught the bus to Lee Green where Ebba and Harold lived in a little semi, feeling light-headed and unreal as I hurried up their road. Harold, expressionless and yet with excruciating pain evident on his haggard face, was sitting motionless in the front room. Ebba, with anguish in every part of her thin body, flung her arms round me, and together we cried as we tried to grasp the truth, writhing in torment and unreality until she was exhausted.

The funeral took place the following week. Ebba did not want to see Richard's body, and Harold was not allowed to. The R.A.F. Officer from the Ministry told me on the side that it was 'only bits and pieces', and perhaps Harold realised this as he did not insist.

114

Never had I experienced such heart-break as that day, and so much harrowing pity to the very depths of my soul as I watched Richard's parents follow his coffin to its grave. This was war at its most bitter and most tragic. They were in a daze, as if hypnotised; still in a state of shock; dry-eyed, white faced, unable to speak, to comfort each other, even to hold each other's hand to share their sorrow. I was devastated for them, and all my petty concerns evaporated rapidly into pointless obscurity.

Harold and Ebba never recovered from this blow. She managed to smile again after a few months, bravely went back to her office work, and tried to live a normal life. Rather than consolidate their marriage, it separated them completely. Harold was a broken man. It was as though the only thing he had lived for had been wrenched from him, and he had no wish but to sink into the grave himself. There was no consolation for him after such a tragedy.

There was little I could do to help, but I kept in much closer touch with Ebba than I had done previously. Her colleagues at work were gentle and understanding, and helped her back into the office routine without pressure. Harold took himself off from home a good deal, as if he could not bear to look at the walls hung with Richard's paintings, and the memories in every room and each piece of furniture. I began to wonder if I was not blessed in my failure to marry and have children if this is what one risked. At least my sights were not lifted by expectations that might come crashing down, smashing my whole being in the process.

Almost the same time that Richard was killed, I received a letter from Herbert to say that May had died after several months of illness. I realised then that I had not heard from them for a considerable time, but so much had happened to me and to the country in general that I had not thought anything of it. Herbert and May were a good deal older then me, and now that Mother was not around, it seemed natural that we should have ceased to correspond. He sounded more sad than devastated by May's death, as it occurred more in the normal course of events when compared with all the younger people being tragically killed in the war. He had a son and a daughter, both married and living fairly near him, but even so he sounded lonely, so I replied, asking him to come over to Bromley for lunch with Gilberte and me one weekend. After several years' absence, it was pleasant to meet him again, and the old feelings of tranquillity he had always instilled in me in the past by his quiet presence and slow measured speech with its London accent, immediately returned. He was still working on much the same lines as before except that now he was employed by the War Office to assess damage to their civilian cars and trucks in England, some of this due to war, and some due to the ordinary hazards of life.

Herbert had a very calming effect on me; the sort of man who never got excited or flamboyant over problems. So different from myself who had to use extreme self-control to suppress my fury at even petty irritations. When a few weeks later he wrote to suggest we might meet for a meal at Lyons' Corner House in Coventry Street, I felt his soothing influence was just what I needed to counteract the effect of my running battle with menus and rations, and wrote back to accept. He was waiting at the door of the restaurant when I came puffing along, late as usual and in a rush. He quietly guided me into the brasserie where he had booked a table, and after taking my coat to hang it up, ordered a glass of lemonade each to drink whilst I collected my wits and cooled down to consider what I would like to eat.

This was a pleasant interlude, and after much chatter and laughter, I returned home feeling much more composed and tolerant. His own imperturbability and common-sense was catching, if only for a short duration and I found him easy to talk to without effort. He lived in Ealing, which is a long way from Bromley and involved a double journey, so we continued to meet halfway in central London, which broke the journey and gave us both an outing. We had a meal together about once a month or six weeks, and I found myself looking forward to these meetings because I felt so much more serene afterwards, as if he cast a spell on me. He seemed to see everything with cool common-sense tinged with optimism, but also appeared pleased to tell me about his own life. I rediscovered his deep kindliness which was the first characteristic which had so impressed me about him on board ship, and I was astonished now to find that it dipped into every aspect of his activities however formal. It was a basic tenet with him, and although he would have denied it, he was deeply religious in a most veiled manner, and had firm and unshakable standards of behaviour for which he would have died if need be, so important did he consider them. Of these consideration for his fellow creatures was foremost.

CHAPTER XI

1944

I HAD BEEN AT MY factory job for three years, and in truth it had been one hard slog in spite of the pleasant camaraderie and the sense of success and achievement I derived from my busy kitchen and the healthy faces of the workers. But I was unutterably weary. I had been working very long hours, at least ten each day in the building, and often getting out my account books and records at home to balance them up and write notes at night. Apart from my occasional meetings with Herbert, and infrequent trips to the theatre or a meal up West with John and Gilberte or Edna, or seeing old friends on leave, I had had very little social life. Mine however was probably no more curtailed than other people's in those war years, and five years of restrictions were beginning to tell on us all.

The V1s (alias the Doodlebugs) in 1944 had been almost the last straw because they were so demoralising by virtue (if that is the correct word) of their engine cut out and the nail-biting silence until their explosion. By the end of August that summer however, so many were being brought down as they passed over the coast, either by guns or aircraft or by Henry's barrage balloons, that the things were beaten. Next month the V2 menace started instead, and although each of these was so huge and caused twice the damage of the V1, they were not nearly so upsetting because the explosion occurred out of the blue and without the psychological kindling of fear that made the V1s so intimidating. By April 1945 their launching sites around the Hague had been captured by the Allies and the threat ceased. Although they had landed in a widespread area over London, I felt I had done my bit in the very vulnerable spot on Erith marshes, and decided to move to another job in a less perilous position. Moreover, kind as everyone was in

117

Erith, I felt I needed a little uplift generally. The conversation there was confined to the most lowly topics, and was suffocating to someone like me who had a mind wide open for information and discussion. I badly needed a change of air.

There was a third reason also for me to move. I had been seeing Herbert now for nearly as long as I had been at Vickers, often under great difficulties, and always involving a long journey for one or both of us, which necessarily cut down our meetings. It would be far less tiring if I worked within a short range of where he lived to avoid the waste of time and energy. I started looking at advertisements in local papers and trade magazines, and soon found one for a school catering job at Harrow, which was the right side of London for Ealing and only about three miles away, with a good bus service between. It seemed very suitable, and I applied at once.

So it was that I eventually found myself cooking for a houseful of middle-class boys instead of a factory full of Eastenders, a very different exercise from what I had been used to, and very enlivening it was. These in fact were not Harrow boys but a 'House' from Malvern College who for some tangled reason had come to share Harrow buildings for the duration. This was of course Harrow-on-the-Hill, not its lowland neighbour, and the hill in question a steep little knob of an eminence like a cottage loaf perched on the flatter terrain round about. My room on the first floor of the house had a quite magnificent view south-east over London, and incidentally over the smoke and blast of the V2s. Harrow was leafy and pleasant, and did not feel at all like London, and the school had plenty of garden and playing fields round it. Although I blessed that steep road up from the station the many times I climbed it after my day off, I enjoyed the rise above the grime of the Thames Valley, and felt almost as if I was walking into the country.

The actual cookery was not very much different from Vickers' except that now I was only catering for a quarter of the numbers, but for all meals, including some 'specials' such as team-teas, and housemasters' parties. The food restrictions were no less, so it was a matter of appropriate juggling with the possible ingredients, and it still gave me a chance to use my initiative to produce something as special as humanly possible, though usually it had to be but a variation on a theme. If a boy was having a birthday, provided his mother sent the constituents necessary, I would make

118

a great effort to bake a celebration cake, and if he produced any icing-sugar (rarely) even if ersatz, I would try to decorate the top in keeping with his age and interests, for which I had to obtain ideas from the other boys. A number of the fathers were in Washington or Canada, or even South Africa or Australia, either in the Diplomatic Service or training with the forces, and they would sometimes bring home small parcels of sugar or dried fruit for an occasion. This made my job much more personal than the wholesale catering at Slade Green and I liked working with these boys. They were a pleasant group, well-mannered and thoughtful, and their jokes tickled me too. There was a good deal of laughter and jocularity, and it was strange to compare Harrow with the factory where the humour had been much earthier and more compromising. These were no little saints, but they had been brought up to be courteous, even if sometimes they sank well below what their mothers expected. They had already had a stream of inspiration, experience and mental stimulation both abstract and inventive, poured into their heads throughout their short lives, and as a result they had bright personalities and busy brains which exuded repartee and argument like a great tide, and which gave me plenty of food for thought. I found my mind had become sluggish, and just in time I was rescued from the cabbagey state into which I was falling, by these boys and their far-reaching ideas.

The other adults in the house consisted of Matron, with whom I became very friendly, and the housemaster and his wife, Mr. & Mrs. Cosgrave, who looked on me almost like their own daughter although they were barely ten years older. At any rate they were very kind, and did not interfere with my work or intrude into my private life. Gentle help and advice was always there for the asking, but rarely proffered spontaneously. My hours of work at Harrow were peculiar to fit in with the boys' meals, so now I normally slept at school except on my weekends off, when I went home to Gilberte, sometimes including Ebba in our arrangements. Harold had almost literally faded away since Richard's death, and last year, in 1944, he had had a mild chest infection, and seemed simply to lie down and die. One felt glad he was now out of his agony – or so one hoped – and poor Ebba certainly did not miss him except for mundane practical reasons, like painting the house or mending the plugs. It was all very pathetic.

119

It was on one of these visits home that there was a loud explosion, presumably a V2 landing somewhat off course. Gilberte and I were in the kitchen at the time, and we abruptly stopped what we were doing and froze, straining to listen for more thuds and crumps which often followed the first. I noticed her right hand was trembling, and I spoke to her sharply.

"Stop it, Gilberte. Pull yourself together." She looked at her hand resting on the table in front of her and shaking with a regular quiver. Then she looked at me.

"I can't stop it, Anne. It goes on all the time. I can even feel it in bed." Suddenly my eyes were opened, and I could indeed see that she was not able to help it, and that it was nothing to do with fear. Something told me to play the whole incident down before it became magnified.

"Oh, never mind," I said casually. "I thought you were scared. Couldn't think what had come over you after all these years in London. Lots of people have trembly hands. I shouldn't worry about it." And I turned back to the cabbage I was chopping up.

After that of course I frequently noticed the hand shaking, especially when she was reaching out to grasp something. It got so bad that in the end she used her left hand instead of her right for lifting or pouring, and she would hide the shaking one behind her when she could, placing it laboriously at the back of her waist as though her whole arm was stiff. I did not like the look of it, but it was only a trifle compared with what other people's nerves were doing with them after five or more years of bombing. I knew my own nerves were making me exceedingly jumpy or I would probably never have noticed Gilberte's hand.

I was seeing Herbert more often now I was in Harrow most of the week. We could go to a film together in the evenings if I arranged the boys' menu suitably, or I could bus over to his house for supper and a chat. It was pleasant to relax there, and feel completely at home, allowing him to fuss round preparing our meal whilst I sat back drinking the cup of tea he now knew I was badly in need of after my day's work. We talked endlessly on those evenings about everything under the sun which concerned us, and some which did not. I was astonished to discover how much alike we thought in spite of our age gap of seventeen years, which made him almost old enough to retire in the normal course of events. He did not seem to be very well off, and I rather doubted whether he would give up his little assessment business when he was sixty-five; was talking now of re-establishing it directly the war was over. There were only two of them in the firm, so they could please themselves, and anyway he thought his partner would not want to take it up again after such a long lapse.

I suppose most people would say Herbert was not a very exciting man, and I would agree with that. But it was this very ordinariness and predictability that appealed to me. My life had had too many uncertainties. All I wanted now was a firm friend to rely on, and I knew I had this in 'Uncle'. He was what Mother would have called 'steady'. But he also had an added attraction for me in his courtly old-world manners. Never before had I had my chair pushed in for me as I sat down to dinner. Never had I noticed the men stand when I entered a room, only sitting when I had done so. I was not used to having the menu passed to me first, or to having doors opened to let me pass through. Nobody previously had said 'Beg pardon' if they accidentally interrupted my flow of speech, or 'excuse me' if they stretched in front of me. One's own family did not bother with such niceties, nor did the students at the Pud School, or the men and women at Slades Green. The beginnings of it could be seen in the boys at Harrow – when they remembered – and the housemaster had comfortably refined manners. So of course had the old couple I had worked for at Barnsley, so I had seen such behaviour in action, and I thought it made life more civilised and gentle. Herbert's way of treating not only me, but everyone he met, elevated one automatically to being a lady, and a million dollar one at that. I did appreciate it after my years in the Styx.

Another thing I liked about him was his sense of humour, which was not unlike my own. If some little thing tickled him, he would laugh until he cried, the more absurd the circumstance the better. I think he could bring himself to see the funny side of anything, but that did not mean he would laugh inappropriately. His humour was always kind, and often against himself. Indeed his face was a mass of laugh-lines, from the corners of his eyes, and angles of his mouth, even his forehead and his neck, so constantly used were they to screwing up in restrained mirth. I found him an amazing person to be with, his fun somehow becoming exaggerated by the slow quiet London voice in which he expressed it.

I felt that in my turn I was able to help him, not only by companionship, but on the matter of opinion on everyday issues, when he needed someone else's approach to a problem to be sure he had seen it aright himself. May had been such a sensible down-to-earth person that he missed her sanguine view of things. I began to learn facts about the world of insurance and underwriting which were completely new to me. Lloyd's had been only a name, and I really did not understand its business ways. Nor had I ever thought about the openings for fraud it posed, and how people like Herbert had to be scrupulously careful with their reports on damaged goods, pointing to areas of doubt with solid facts about the case, and leaving the insurers to make decisions on the basis of them and individual circumstances. He had to be trusted by both sides, and no man could have filled that position better than he. He would sometimes furrow his forehead in doubt over his work, wondering if he had been given the whole truth of the case, and nothing would budge him from the narrow breadth of fact in order to fit in with uncomfortable evidence that might be brought to bear on his opinion.

"What do you think of this, Duckie?" he would say, handing me a claim form, and after I had considered it, would use whatever I answered to clear his own thoughts. I did not mind that he frequently disagreed, for good reason, with my opinion as I knew it served to make up his own mind for him one way or another.

As the months went by and the Allies followed up their landings in Normandy by a general advance towards the Seigfried Line, peace seemed to be a real possibility in the foreseeable future, rather than a tiny glimmer at the end of a dark tunnel. Like everyone else we followed the news on the wireless and the war maps in the daily paper eagerly, and as northern France was recaptured in August and the Rhone Valley in September, gradually we heard of the German First Army in south-west France giving itself up in the following weeks, and knew we must hear from Hilda soon if she was still alive. My heart gave a double bump as I realised that we should actually know one way or the other now. I both dreaded and welcomed the prospect, though the Occupation stories that managed to emerge from Europe gave one little confidence.

Poor France was in disarray, however, and we knew that civilian messages would be unlikely to come through for some time, and we must possess ourselves in patience. It was not until November that we received a short message from the Red Cross to say Hilda, Jeanne and Jacques were all alive and well (as they optimistically put it), but that Kiki had died in 1942. About the same time Gilberte received a note from her sister, Thérèse, in Paris to the same effect, so we knew now it was only a mater of time until proper letters arrived. We meanwhile wrote our own to them in anticipation, condensing four years' worth of family news into a squashed page as advised by the Red Cross, and feeling it would be a miracle if it ever arrived at its destination. Eventually, of course, we did receive a letter from Hilda, but never had her indifference to writing been more tiresome as the sum of information it gave us was minimal. Mainly she just sent 'love and kisses' which was her favourite expression. They were all alive, it was true, except that is for Jacques' very Jewish old parents and his aunt who had been taken away to Germany, heaven knew where, but presumably to a concentration camp. Jacques himself was safe, and busy helping on a farm, and because of this they had had more food than some town-dwellers. Jeanne had had a baby in 1943, her second and this time a girl. Then the letter finished with the ominous phrase "All rather thin. Food bad." Since our own rations were extremely short, we did not know how to take this, though as Lord Woolton had seen to it that British civilian rations were balanced if not lavish, we all seemed to be in good health, if a little more shapely than we were before the war.

The weekend after Hilda's letter came, my usual visit to Bromley coincided with John's. Bombs had been dropping on London again, and he had been kept busy, but was able to take a couple of days off to make up lost sleep and regain sanity. As I came down the path at the side of the house towards the back garden, he was carefully brushing out a canvas rucksack, cigarette as usual in one corner of his mouth.

"Now then, Anne. How are things on the Hill?" he wanted to know.

"Alright," I hedged, ignoring the veiled sneer. "Boys all fit and well. What are you doing?"

"Preparing to take off for Paris as soon as the way is open for non-combatants."

"Churchill was there last week. Don't you read your newspaper?"

"No time. They'll let people like me in as soon as pos. There'll be a lot of clearing-up to do."

In the event he was not allowed to travel there until after V.E. Day the following July, but he sent in travel application papers well in advance, and as a Paris resident normally, with property needing urgent repairs, and a job which would start up again as soon as normality began to exist, he was one of the first civilians to return. When the call came, one of his A.R.P. pals picked him and his rucksack and a case up from Bromley next morning, and he cheerfully waved 'au revoir' as they drove off, his feelings very mixed as he anticipated how he would find things in France. Gilberte saw the sense in his returning on his own at first, confident that he would send for her as soon as conditions were reasonable, and settled down with her usual compliant patience to wait for his summons.

It was soon obvious from John's letters that there was a long way to go before we reached that state of affairs. His pretty house at Le Vesinet had been used by Panzer Officers, who had not been over-careful about where they placed their booted feet. Several panes of glass were cracked or broken, and the beautiful polished woodwork of the staircase was now, alas, roughened and scratched. Doors had been labelled in paint, and the metalwork dented or removed. The whole place needed decorating, the plumbing renewing in parts, cracked basins replacing, and the kitchen completely renovating.

"How could officers and so-called gentlemen treat a nice house like this?" he complained in his letter. "The Third Reich doesn't appear to have expected a very high standard of behaviour from them." The garden also had been neglected, so some of his time had to be spent putting that to rights. Otherwise, when he was not occupied in his home, he busied himself in work with the British Legion, dealing with enquiries from British expatriots about their relatives or the state of their homes or business. There was an enormous amount of sorting out to do, and he was in the thick of it, and thoroughly enjoying himself, even if he would not admit it.

Whilst all this activity was going on all over France, I was trying to persuade Hilda to come and live with me in Bromley. Now that Kiki was no more, there was no reason to prevent her as long as she could visit her family with ease. Her son, Marc, had been working with the Resistance, but now released from that was temporarily with Jeanne, helping on the land until he could find a permanent job. My mind went back to 1915 when Hilda fled from France in the First War, half-starved and very frightened, and I thought that at least a few months in the rationed but easy-going atmosphere of England would do her no harm. Hilda's desultory way of corresponding, always a lack-lustre feature of her communications, had if possible become more vague and uninformative, but by dint of numbering the questions in my letter to her, and making each question unambiguous and simple, I at last received the answer I was seeking. Yes, she was very thin; yes, she was lonely without Kiki; yes, she could come to England; and even, yes, she would love to live with me. John had, by July 1946, already sent for Gilberte, and she was booked to leave England on August 4th, so without delay I wrote back to Hilda suggesting she come as soon as she could. I felt I needed moral support over these changes, so I asked Dick to come down for a few days from her northern fastness to cover Hilda's settling-in period and its unknown hazards. Eventually a telegram reached us to tell of her time of arrival, which turned out to be the afternoon of the day Gilberte was leaving, so Dick and I took Gilberte down to Victoria to catch her train, had our lunch in a cafe in Buckingham Palace Road, and were back on the station platform in time to meet Hilda's train. As we stood waiting for the train which was inevitably late, I felt my stomach turn over with nerves, and my breathing beginning to wheeze, and I could see that Dick felt the same, wondering if Hilda was going to look any different.

We were not, however, prepared for what we did see. I spotted her first, all in black except for a chic white collar – so French – carrying a bag in each hand and looking round to find us.

"There she is!" I shrieked in my excitement.

"Don't be absurd," said Dick, "it can't be. That person's far too old."

Then I myself felt uncertain, and hesitated, and just at that moment Hilda saw us and waved awkwardly.

"My goodness! It is." cried Dick, and we both rushed up to this little wizened old woman who was our sister. Then her smile broke, and we could see that beneath the lines of anxiety, the sorrow and starvation, it was indeed Hilda. Her appearance was enough evidence on its own without any words, to tell us what her war had been like. Her eyes, always large and dark, seemed bigger than ever in their hollows, and her voice more croaky. Her dentures, orange-gummed and huge, no longer fitted.

We took her back to Bromley, and the first thing she wanted was a 'good old cup of English tea'. That loosened her tongue, and she started to talk in a catarrhal manner, breaking into a loose phlegmy cough every now and then. She seemed very, very, weary; her skin was dry and wrinkled, her back rounded, her hands rough. I thought "The first thing I shall do with you tomorrow, my girl, is to give you breakfast in bed, and the next thing is to ask the doctor to give you a thorough going over." Just now though, I gave her a cheese omelette, using up all my cheese ration for the week and eggs for a fortnight. Then I took her up for a bath and bed.

"Shall I wash your back for you?" I asked her, interested to know how much her bones were sticking out under her clothes. She nodded, so I saw, to my horror, the exact tracing of her ribs and shoulder blades, the knobs of her spine, and her hips stretching her rough skin, and I knew we had done right to bring her home to England to recuperate.

Hilda was now both an English woman and at the same time a French rather like her little daughter had been when at three years old she interpreted between her English and French grandmothers in the last war. Her speech was a peculiar mixture of the two languages, with her grammar often gallicised, and frequently using a French word or idiom when she could not think of the English. At the same time her natural placidity did not prevent her gesticulating and exclaiming just like a true French woman, and "Oh, ma foi" and "Mon Dieu" often escaped her. Then, whilst she gradually settled down here, the French side of her receded as she regained her original nationality.

As far as her war experiences were concerned, we did not hurry her to tell us details, fearing what was to come, but hoping the telling when it occurred would exorcise the ghosts of the last few years. Their nightmare all along was the possibility that Jacques' Semitic appearance would bring trouble on them all, and with two small children in the household they feared the worst, and remained as unobtrusive as they could, which in the circumstances of Merignac was not difficult. Most of the local war news came to them second-hand, by word of mouth from the grocer as he was unloading their rations from his cart, and well away from buildings from where they might be overheard. German soldiers were of course in evidence in the towns, but not very much out in the country where they were, and although they heard rumours of harsh measures and of partisans being shot, they had no direct experience of this, and thought it safer to remain ignorant and as self contained as possible. "We dared not even talk to each other" she said, to my horror. "You trusted no-one".

The day the S.S. lorry came for Jacques' parents and his old Aunt Maria was the worst, but even that passed off without incident because the old people meekly did what they were ordered, being afraid that to do otherwise would threaten the whole family. No word had ever been heard of them subsequently. They just disappeared, and the family assumed they had all been herded into the gas chambers of a concentration camp and tried not to picture the scene.

Another bad time had been Kiki's death in 1942 from 'natural causes', if by natural one infers normal, but worry, overwork and under-feeding had surely been contributory to his fatal heart attack, and his end had come with terrifying suddenness. Even after four years Hilda was still visibly affected as she gave a bare outline of these events, and I felt a wheeze coming on as I listened, imagining myself in this position. She was remarkably sanguine about it all, but it was evident that the deep fear of the Gestapo was ever present, even if they witnessed little of it themselves. Just keeping their lives rolling along was as much as they could cope with, with shortages in every commodity, not just food which was near starvation levels, but soap, spare parts for all appliances, and tools for the farm. There was also shortage of male labour, so the women had taken over the heavy work as well as they could. The other lack was of anyone to confide in, or any social contacts, because they felt safer without, and had developed a dead-pan expression and attitude to anyone they did meet. Being naturally an introvert, Hilda had become withdrawn and outwardly unemotional, even apparently unresponsive, and although it would be abnormal for her to be exuberant, it was unnatural to have her so submissive and quiet.

127

"It's a good job you weren't with us, Anne," she observed with a smile, "you'd never have been able to stop chattering!" I agreed thankfully.

Fortunately Hilda had arrived early July, only a fortnight before the end of term, so before Dick returned home, I left her to keep an eye on Hilda one day and went over to Harrow to see Mr. Cosgrave, and to collect my things. Hilda was in such a poor way physically, and so withdrawn, I felt she ought not to be left on her own for any length of time, and certainly not the sort of hours that I would be out at school even if I slept at home. Mr. Cosgrave was kindness itself, and fully understood the implications, assuring me that his wife 'could manage' to the end of term. As I had already concocted the menus, and even done some preparatory work towards the leaving parties and other normal festivities at the end of the school year, I did not feel too guilty, but all the same was grateful for his attitude. I was genuinely sorry to leave Harrow, and also the independence which a full-time job gave me, but the few years I had been a wage-earner had taught me a great deal about people, and at that time I did not anticipate this was other than a temporary gap in my new career.

CHAPTER XII

1945

THE NEXT WEEKS and months Hilda and I lived very quietly. It was a good summer, and she spent much of the time sitting in the sun, often limply lying back in her deckchair with her eyes closed, but glad of a chat when I brought out the coffee or returned from shopping. I had never before seen anyone so fundamentally weary, in body and mind, and certainly also in emotions, as if she was completely worn out in every way, and had no reserve of energy for even the simplest task. I used my ingenuity to make meals as nourishing and appetising for her as I could, giving her small frequent feeds rather like a baby so as not to upset her insulted digestive system. For several weeks she was almost lifeless, and just sat mute with her hands on her lap. Visitors were discreetly warned not to stay too long, and being kindly souls took the hint, but in any case found it was hard work trying to converse with her as it was a one-sided affair and she was inclined to leave it all to them.

After a month or two, as I was deep in a novel one afternoon in the drawing-room, the clock struck, and on looking up, my eyes fell on Hilda who, as usual, was comatose. As I gazed at her sallow face, I realised that the hollows were beginning to fill out, the anxious expression to relax, and there was even the beginning of pinkness in her cheeks. She was still phenomenally thin, and looked as old as my grandmother would have done, but we had definitely made progress, and I was reminded of the hints of animation which she had produced in the last week or so. Gradually her wounded body was healing, and with this process, horrifyingly slow and probably never to be complete, she began to show interest in her surroundings and a flicker of exuberance in her actions.

"Right!" I said to myself. "Now we enter the second phase of recuperation. I'll draw you out of your lassitude if it kills me," and I resolved to give her little jobs about the house and garden each day, in an effort to bring back her regard for life.

"Will you shell the peas for lunch, Hilda? – I'm so rushed today," I lied, handing her the colander full of big ripe pods. She croakily assented, and over the next half-hour slowly shucked the small number of peas,stopping frequently to rest. My triumph was muted, but a week or two later when she spontaneously came to the kitchen where I was busy, and asked if she could dust the sitting-room "for you", I joyously replied "Of course, Hilda. It's as much yours as mine," and wondered what other little task I could gradually give her – all part of my special scheme for restoring her. Everything she attempted was done infuriatingly slowly, but she was at least willing to put a little effort into it, and able to achieve some success.

Now I was rather tied to the house and garden and Hilda, I took to phoning Herbert in the evening every week or so, and after she had begun to regain a spark of life again, suggested he came over one Saturday, which he seemed glad to do, saying he had been lonely without my visits. His gentle quiet manner was perfect for Hilda as she felt under no pressure in his presence, and both he and she were content to sit companionably, without speaking if they felt that way. The consequence of this, ironically, was that it induced her to tell him about her life in France, not just the recent episodes, but other matters from the past. He and she had been bereaved about the same time, so they had a fellow feeling. He would sit there with his long legs outstretched carelessly in front of him, listening with full attention and interposing a word here and there to encourage her to continue, until she seemed truly to think that he was chatting to her, and unaware how she was unloading herself onto him. I would take far longer than I really needed to prepare our meals on these days, for I could see how good he was for her in his subtle unhurried manner, and her recuperation leaped forward at an increased pace. It was a relief to me also to have Herbert to talk to myself. I had missed the soothing influence of my visits to Ealing, as much as he said he missed me. We seemed mutually to have a beneficial effect on each other, and now Hilda proved more of a catalyst to this understanding than an obstacle.

The time came when I felt I had to begin to live my own life once more, not least because it did not seem good for Hilda to remain totally dependent on me as she was at present. She needed to start using her own resources, such as they were, to give her freedom and power of decision – 'motivation' it is called nowadays. Herbert must have come to the same conclusion about the same time, as one lunch time he arrived unannounced, and suggested he and I went to the pictures that afternoon.

"What do you think about that, Hilda?" I enquired. "Do you mind if Herbert and I go to the flicks? We'll be back at five." She looked a bit startled, then quickly pulled herself together.

"Of course, Anne. You go and enjoy yourselves; I'll be alright here."

So we did. I remember it was 'Brief Encounter', which was a real tear-jerker and too apt for comfort, though he did not seem to have realised this previously.

After that we left her at least once a week to her own devices. Sometimes we went to a matinee at the theatre, other days Herbert had a round of visits to do in his car, which he was allowed to use strictly for work, and which was a pleasant outing for me. It enabled us to talk freely again, which we could not entirely do in front of Hilda, and it was a chance for me to learn more about his work. I think she missed me, but on the other hand realised that I must spend time with my own friends, and was quite cheerful always when I arrived back home.

I always took a thermos of coffee along on these jaunts, and on one occasion was in the process of pouring it out, still sitting in the car which was parked at Greenwich facing the old Cutty Sark, when, without a tremor, Herbert looked straight at me, and said

"You know, Anne, it's ridiculous us living at opposite ends of London." Then he paused before continuing. "Why don't we live together?" For a moment I was puzzled, and then the look in his kind eyes conveyed what he was driving at.

"You can't mean really together. You know - - - " I trailed off, lost in complete unreality and amazement.

"Yes, I do," he said firmly. "Why don't we get married?" and he put his hand on mine, and looked beseechingly at me. "Please, Hannah."

I watched the steam rising from his coffee cup as it balanced precariously where he had put it in the pigeon-hole.

"How can I?" I blurted out in a voice that did not sound like my own. "Hilda needs me."

"I've thought of that. The answer is easy. With just a few alterations we can make the house at Bromley into two self-contained flats, and Hilda can live upstairs, with her own little kitchen and mod cons, and we will live down. That will solve all the problems, and we can all live happily ever after!" he concluded triumphantly. Then he added that it might just give her the encouragement she needed to become an independent person again completely.

This idea took a good deal of swallowing whilst I imagined the result.

"I'll have to think about it, Herbert. I just can't pull my wits together now." He laughed and gave me a kiss.

"Don't worry. You can have as long as you want to think about it – as long as it's not too long. I shall get impatient."

I did think about it. In fact I thought of hardly anything else for days. I turned it this way and that in my mind, but every time it came back to Hilda. How could I suddenly uncover such plans to her? It seemed so cruel to take her home away from her when she had suffered so much; it was tantamount to telling her she was not wanted. And yet, I had my own life – I was only forty-five – and after all these years I had the chance of marriage. Then there was Herbert's point of view, and the yearning I had glimpsed in those eyes of his, and suddenly I knew it was inevitable. He was good and kind, and I realised with a jerk that I had grown to love him, almost you might say unwittingly, over these last years. In fact I found that I not only relied on him, but actually included him mentally in all my thoughts and plans.

Herbert and I talked and talked over ways and means after that, and in the end I told Hilda of our hopes whilst she and I were sitting over our coffee after lunch one day. For a minute she looked strained, and there was silence. My heart sank.

"That's alright, Anne," she said at last, and then just as if I'd told her Herbert and I were going to the pictures that afternoon, she added "You enjoy yourselves. I'll be alright." I went over and kissed her.

"Thank you, Hilda. It will be like gaining a new brother for you."

When Herbert came in later, I nodded and he went straight over to her and kissed her. "You're a brick!" was all he said, but later he brought her a big bunch of flowers out of the back of his car. The way she flushed with pleasure made me think no-one had thought of giving her a bouquet for a very long time, perhaps since the little knots of violets from the Paris flower-sellers when she and Kiki were engaged.

The next task was to tell the family, particularly Dick. I thought over my letter to her carefully, and suggested she came down to meet Herbert, as I knew she would immediately approve. I said how much Mother had liked him and May, and how kind he had been to me, and more recently to Hilda. I indicated that I had given up enough of my life to other people, and this might be my last chance of real happiness. It was not as if Hilda was necessarily going to stay in England the rest of her life (although I admitted it was likely), and if one really wanted to get down to brass tacks, the most likely thing was that I would outlive her by many years.

I read it over several times, and felt it gave a balanced picture, and that after the initial shock Dick would be pleased for me.

In fact her reply (which arrived only two days later) was more like a V2 landing. What on earth was I thinking of to tie myself to such an old man? I had looked after one old person up to relatively recently, and now I was going to saddle myself with another. Did I not realise that men died at an earlier age than women, so I was likely to have a short marriage and a long widowhood. As for her feelings about poor Hilda being cast off, it did not bear thinking about. How could I contemplate such a move? She was sure that Hilda and I would live happily in our ménage à deux without any man to bother about, especially an old one. This last was the aspect that obviously most concerned her, she who had been a mother to me once.

This missive was followed up the same evening by a trunk call.

"Is that you, Hannah?" shouted Dick in the distance, using the name she had used when I had been naughty as a child. "Can you hear me?"

"Yes, Dick. I hear you."

133

"Anne, you simply must not marry someone seventeen years older than yourself. You'll be worn out. Do you realise that when he is seventy, you'll only be in the prime of life. Do be realistic." Poor Dick! She was so anxious, almost tearful, for my happiness. "However nice he is, why don't you just be good friends?"

"We are that already. We want to make it permanent. A commitment. I love him." She knew she was battling against my Minska stubbornness, and she gave up.

"Well, I hope you will be very happy," she sighed. "I really mean it. I'll come and see him as soon as I can leave here for a few days." Then, she added hopefully, "James is coming to London on business next week. You could talk to him about it. Can he stay the night?"

"Of course. He's always welcome." And that was the truth. James and I always were close, perhaps because we had both lost our mothers early in life, and as neither of us lived with our fathers, we were a pair of orphans. I know he always felt some responsibility towards me, rather like an older brother, but I think he liked me as well, and respected the manner in which I had adjusted my life and started a new career after Mother died. For my part, I had the greatest affection for him because of his generosity of thought, and a regard also for his opinion on every matter on which he voiced it, knowing full well that if he was ignorant or doubtful about a subject, he would never commit himself.

Meanwhile Henry called in one morning unexpectedly. I recognised his cigarette smoke before I had even seen him.

"Anyone in the hanger?" he called from the hall. Then, as I emerged from the kitchen "Thought I'd do an emergency landing here to see how you are." He always talked R.A.F. jargon these days.

Immediately I realised it was him, I felt nervous about my news, and stupidly charged at it like a bull in a china shop without attempting to lead him into the subject more subtly.

"I'm going to get married, Henry," I blurted out, still in my apron, and before he'd even had time to sit down.

"Good God, Hannah! You don't mean it."

"Yes I do. To Herbert."

"Wizard prang!" he exclaimed. "So you've parachuted into love at last. Bang on!" I did not know whether to laugh or cry at his reaction.

When Estelle heard the news, she was ecstatic. "Darling! How super! When's the happy day? Absolutely wizzo!"

She fitted a Navy Cut into her black and gold cigarette holder, and lit it pensively. "Have a fag to celebrate, darling?"

"Not before lunch, thank you." I could see my marriage had limited interest for her, free as it was of scandal. "Why don't you go and chat to Hilda?" I said.

"She's so difficult, darling. Henry, go and talk to Hilda." Off they went into the garden, leaving me even less confident in my decision, and wondering what really was the right thing to do. In the perplexities of the First War and the years after Dad died, I used to go to St. Germaine's for comfort and strength. Now our nearest church was uncompromisingly modern and uninspiring. In any case, I was a hypocrite, and could not honestly pray 'If it be Thy Will". This time I very much wanted *my* will. Oh, dear heaven! How could I find comfort and peace?

Next day both came in the shape of James. He arrived from the City about 6 pm, and whilst his meal cooked itself, he and I walked round the garden, ostensibly admiring the plants.

"What am I to do, James? The whole family thinks I am neglecting Hilda by getting married."

"You're not a child, Hannah. And neither is Hilda. She knows what it's like to have the joy of marriage, and she would never wish you to forego it, especially for her. If you were rushing into it, that would be different, but you've thought out all the 'fors and againsts', and come to the conclusions it's a sound investment" (how like James!). "Go ahead, if that's what you want. Never mind anyone else's opinion."

Dear James! My big stand-by and comfort – certainly heaven-sent this time.

So Herbert and I were married, very quietly, at Bromley Registry Office, with only two clerks for witnesses. Everyone in my family, except James, had been less than enthusiastic over the match, and even Herbert's son and daughter, nice as they were, showed their suspicion that I was trying to take their mother's place, though accepting that I would look after their father very well.

I arranged for Edna to come and stay for a week, and slipped out of the house on my own early on the Monday morning, and walked down to the Registrar's, where Herbert was waiting for me. After the ceremony, we returned for breakfast. Hilda guessed what we were up to, and showed no surprise when I uncovered my ringed hand. She respected our wish for privacy, and said she would have done the same in our place. We felt it was our marriage, and no concern of anyone else. I knew that if I had asked one person to attend, then I should have had to ask everyone, and we did not want that. They would all come to know in time what a good thing it was. In addition, we decided it would be inappropriate to have a church wedding, as May was very much in our thoughts, and in any case I felt the actual place of our 'joining in matrimony' was irrelevant, and we would receive the same blessing wherever we were. Perhaps we were mistaken, but that is how it seemed at the time.

Edna stayed on for a few days with Hilda, and to supervise the minor building works that had to be completed to form the two flats. Herbert and I meanwhile went down to Christchurch, near Bournemouth, to rid ourselves of all the tensions of the past months, ready to start our new lives together.

The next year was not all roses. We tried very hard to be considerate towards Hilda, but also, as Dick would say, 'to start as we meant to go on'. We kept to our own territory at specified times, particularly evenings when I felt it would not have been fair to Herbert to have Hilda perpetually trailing in and out of our flat. In the event, our marriage did little to encourage her to broaden her life, other than to do her own shopping and housework, but she did not seem capable of making new friends. I viewed the future gloomily as it stretched inactively away into the distance for her.

"Do you think it's time you had a holiday, Hilda?" I suggested after about a year. "Why don't you pop down to Merignac to see Jeanne and Jacques?"

"Funny you should say that, Anne. They've just written to ask me to Marie's christening." Marie was the most recent baby, whom Hilda had so far not seen. "I should like to go to that. Evidently she's very dark like me, but with curly hair, not these awful straggles." She was pinning up her bun at the time, not very successfully, and wisps kept eluding her.

The idea of action seemed to wake her up, even produce some enthusiasm, as she gathered her packing together, collected little gifts to take, and sorted out her clothes. She smiled more, and hummed over her tasks. Could it be that she was homesick for France, and it was indeed time she went back. She became quite light-hearted the last week before she left, and gaily waved me goodbye as her boat-train pulled out of Victoria, still looking thin and old, but a little less gaunt, and certainly not the haggard creature who had arrived from France so many months ago. I wondered if she would ever look really robust again.

The christening was a week later. A few days after that we received a telegram from Jeanne. "Mummy very ill pneumonia. Love Kisses Jeanne." The next day we got another,"Mummy died yesterday. Funeral Friday."

I sat down heavily on the hall chair, feeling shocked and slightly sick, and as though my legs were turning to jelly. Hilda dead. I just could not believe it. And yet, that was no healthy person who set out happily for France, but someone who had been battered and bullied by life's trials. A victim of the war, although she had obstinately managed to survive it.

As I sat in the half-dark digesting the finality of the telegram's contents, feeling unreal and upset, and something akin to outrage that her life should be cut off in this heartless fashion, I began also to experience guilt. Ought I ever to have brought her to England? Was this last year so unbearable that she could not face life any more? Was I selfish, and Dick had been right after all?

By the time Herbert came home that evening, I was in a state of panic, and was sweating and wheezing and hopelessly overwrought. As usual, he quietly calmed me. Then he gave me a pill for my chest, and a cup of tea for my spirits.

"She was worn out, Anne," he consoled me. "No-one could have known how long she would last; it might have been a few years, but it turned out to be only a few months. You did your utmost for her, and it's good she died with her children. Don't fret, Duckie." He poured out another cup of tea and gave it to me. "Drink this. You'll buck up then and see it all clearly."

137

I did go to the funeral at Merignac. I felt that if I had not done so, I would never really believe she was dead, and the nightmare of incredulity would continue. The family thought my journey was out of respect for Hilda, and I let them think that. I knew I had a sanity to preserve as well, and Herbert understood this too. I took her few small personal belongings with me, one or two trinkets and photographs. A pathetic little collection it was and it somehow brought vividly back to me how much poor France had suffered in the two world wars, with invasion, occupation, starvation – all the awful words ending in -ion, I mused miserably.

I was right about my trip to Merignac. It did sort my mind out for me, and I came back more settled and happier than I had been for years, and determined that I would make a success of my life as a sort of memorial to Hilda, who had made who knew how much sacrifice for me.

It was not easy to settle down again after the funeral, I had become so used to having Hilda around. Even in the last months since my marriage I was conscious of her moving about upstairs, walking up and down the stairs, sitting in the garden, turning on her wireless. Most days she and I had had a snack lunch together, sometimes in her flat, sometimes in ours, and whenever possible outside. We had chatted about this and that triviality, compared our post from the family, discussed parochial items such as food, distinguishing between the French and English modes of eating, and of course (she was after all an adopted Parisian), clothes. In contrast, I was now on my own all day, unless I had a friend to lunch. Sometimes Herbert organised his work so that he was home mid-day for an hour. I did not mind being on my own, but I could not stop thinking of Hilda at every turn. The feeling of guilt, although fading, was still pricking me mercilessly, but as I mourned for her, gradually it subsided almost completely. I knew in my heart that I had done right by her, whatever my absurd conscience was trying to make me believe.

I worked hard in the garden that summer, almost as if it was a penance to absolve myself from blame for Hilda's death, throwing myself into the labour of brainless activity. The hard physical work dissolved the worries circling round and round in my mind, and I would come in for a bath about four o'clock satisfyingly tired, too exhausted to think, as though one more day could be added to my credit of absolution. Herbert understood my mixed emotions, and let me work them out in my own way. He never acknowledged the insult which he could have done, in my muddled thinking about our marriage. He knew that it was not the joining of myself with him that caused my doubts, but the sundering with Hilda, and he accepted the shock I had sustained with her death.

Little by little I recovered my equilibrium those summer months, and by the time the evenings were lengthening into the afternoons and my garden was being put to bed for the winter, I regained calm and tranquillity. My attention turned to indoor pursuits such as I had always enjoyed, now with Herbert as the sole object of my care. My brain started to function again. I began to read. I took up study of accountancy and insurance so that I could help him with his reports. I looked after the car and saw to its servicing, as far as possible carrying out the work myself, using the knowledge gained in the A.R.P. My days filled up with activity and achievement. There must have been no need for anyone to wonder whether I was happily married. They could tell it in my eyes.

Herbert's business became more onerous over the next few years after the war, as his partner finally decided to give up, and all the jobs came to him. Often they would range over a large area of the country, so that as well as having a lengthy journey, he would have to spend long hours measuring, surveying, noting down facts, and would arrive home worn out, and often very late. Now at last I was able to see that I could become a useful aid, and I enrolled as his chauffeur, his amanuensis, his typist and his accountant, as well as his cook general. He would come home announcing "Tomorrow it's Birmingham" or "They've lost a dozen cars over the wharf at Liverpool" or "Glasgow this week", whereupon I would go into action, gathering my equipment for the journey, cutting sandwiches, making ready large thermos flasks of coffee, baking pies, assembling clothes and stationery, and so on. We always left home in the early hours, often before sunrise, to catch as many daylight hours as we could, especially in the winter. Whilst I encouraged the cold cheerless car into action, Herbert would settle himself with his file into the passenger seat, and as we drove through the lamp-lit streets and the gathering dawn, he would work out his strategy for the day and re-read his instructions. Once at the site we were to visit, he would wander round with his tape-measure as if oblivious of my presence, whilst I followed, clipboard and pencil at the ready, taking notes as he dictated. Project completed, or if we were merely too cold to continue, we would adjourn to the car for coffee, and then either return to that job, or drive on to the next, usually managing to complete several visits in the one day. Eventually we would either put up at a local hotel, or drive home in the late evening, arriving home tired, but complete with material for the report, which he would compose next day, and I would thereafter type.

We toiled very hard indeed those years to earn our living, and our work took us all over England, and industrial Scotland as well. The journeys were full of interest as they meant us driving to parts of the country to which I had never been before, not to mention the nether quarters of the big cities which were a revelation, with their wharves, back-to-back houses, bomb-sites, and now newly-built blocks of high-rise flats which I thought the most inhuman of the lot. Often these places were approached through glorious countryside, such as Middlesbrough over the Yorkshire moors, Leeds through Wensleydale, Birmingham through Shropshire, depending on where else we had to go, and we endeavoured to drive to our destinations along pleasant routes if we could. The contrast between the industrial wastes and the untouched hills and valleys of rural England never failed to affect me, and I became navigator as well as driver in my efforts to include as many new places as time and energy permitted.

Hard as we worked, these turned out to be some of the happiest years of my life. The close companionship, such that we did not need even to speak to achieve a bond of warmth, was something I had never consistently experienced before, and it made me feel safe and was a type of belonging new to me. Added to this was the sense of achievement of a useful job well done, and of being needed and wanted; of something more profound than a partnership. Sometimes I felt idiotically euphoric like a teenager, almost drunk with the realisation of sheer happiness, of contentment too deep for credulity. As I collapsed into bed after a long day of surveying and travelling, amid the weariness of success, I wondered if I could be on a knife-edge; that such happiness surely could not continue.

CHAPTER XIII

1950

L IFE SEEMED PERFECT to me, though more sophisticated people would not have agreed. We worked hard, for relatively small remuneration, and yet we were rich in everything that made existence good. Herbert was energetic for a man of his age, reaching retirement age in 1949. But he had no intention of giving up his work. For one thing we could barely afford it, and the extra income, even though it diminished as he neared the seventies through the sheer lack of man-hours he was able to work, was a helpful addition to our small income. As I learnt the business, I was able to unload more and more of the routine framework of his labour from his shoulders onto mine, leaving him with the specialised and intricate professional aspects to deal with.

I supposed the only fly in the ointment was the house at Bromley. In many ways convenient and pleasantly familiar, it could never be 'our' house, having been used and then taken over almost by accident from my relatives. Herbert never felt it belonged to him, or even to 'us'. It was just a useful object which had been discarded by others when they no longer needed it, and being in any case quite an ordinary (though conveniently large) 'semi' with typical strip garden surrounded by similar neighbouring gardens, was difficult to give an identity of our own. It was not really home to him, but merely a building in which he and I lived. As the post-war years rolled along and affluence began to affect the south-east, we also discovered that the pleasant avenue in which it lay became a bypass for traffic, and lost the almost rural tranquillity it had had before the war. More and more of the inhabitants who had lived there for years and with whom (as typical Londoners) we had only ever become on nodding terms, were at least familiar faces who could be relied on in emergencies great and small, had moved further out into the country. Now nearly all our neighbours were newcomers, either with noisy children or out at work all day. Either way it contributed to lessening the sense of permanency and quiet which had been a characteristic of the road in the thirties.

Herbert's son, David, whom we visited when we could, lived in glorious wooded countryside on the south side of the Chilterns, and we envied his pastoral surroundings. His wife was an Irish woman called Mairagh, very doggy, always in breeches, and with a cigarette permanently hanging from her mouth. She kept two or three horses, and rode them around the lanes and fields encircling their cottage. She was a 'character' in the broadest sense, firm in her opinions and not one to shirk from expressing them in her broad Dublin brogue. Masculine though she was in many ways, she had a heart of gold like most of her countrymen, and she and David lived in perfect harmony in their isolated smallholding. With her typical Irish garrulousness, it was surprising she was so happy away from the crowds of a town, but she made up for lack of humans by continuous one-sided conversations with her dogs, which she much preferred to people, assuming that their opinions of affairs coincided with her own, and therefore never involving her in dissent.

Amongst the beech woods in this part of Oxfordshire one could travel many miles in narrow twisting lanes, closed in by banks and high hedges, every so often coming upon a clearing in the trees where a house would be partly hidden by the bushes and undergrowth. These were often former woodmen's cottages which had been added to and brought up-to-date, or sometimes replaced by a substantial dwelling and immaculate garden. A number of well-known names were connected with these beautiful hide-aways, and the people living here came for the quiet, many of them authors or actors who needed the peace of the countryside to recharge their batteries. One resident had even labelled his boundaries with small clear notices reading 'Beware of the snakes' to rid himself of human interlopers.

The peace of the place was therefore profound, and I envied David his seclusion, and was immediately interested when he rang up one morning to tell us about a cottage near him which was for sale, and what did we think about it. Our answer was immediate, and two hours later we were hanging over the gate of 'Little Orchard' savouring its stillness and isolation.

It was an odd little house, very idiosyncratic. It had started life as a peasant's bothy with two rooms downstairs and two up under the eaves. Then a small additional wing had been added, one up one down, at the east end, and then a further single storey room onto that. At some stage what was in fact merely a lean-to was built onto the west end, for a kitchen, and a bathroom had been squeezed into part of the landing and had a dubious and unreliable supply of hot water, or indeed any water at all. The whole house was now painted white, which was largely hidden by clematis and jasmine on the lane side as if it was pretending not to be there. A range of wooden outbuildings near the upper boundary gave the same effect of snuggling down in the jungle in an untidy but comfortable manner. Built on a considerable slope, we first saw Little Orchard as we looked down its steep little drive from the lane which ran along above it. Beyond the house we could see dense beech woods, and between the two, the sizeable garden quite obviously out of control. The house had a recently constructed terrace on its garden side, rounded like the poop of a ship, from where one could look out over one's property, but instead of the sea it was ringed around with rockery plants, and below it with colourful shrubs and perennials in abandoned confusion like great waves of the ocean. From there a large area of green – not dignifiable by the title of lawn – stretched down to the woodland, and through this patches of sky illuminated great areas of bluebells and anemones.

Ramshackle though it all was, and smelling stuffy and neglected when we entered through its squeaky front door, to us it was sheer delight, and we knew at once this must be our home. Prices in this part of the Home Counties, even in the early 1950s, were much higher than elsewhere, but though Bromley was now suburbia with a big 'S', the house there was a good one, and by dint of selling it well and cashing both our savings and most of our investments, we managed to accumulate sufficient capital to buy Little Orchard outright, leaving very little over besides our pensions to live on. But we did not care, and when we had moved in all our belongings and sold excess furniture too cumbersome to edge through the doors or up the curving staircase, this at last was home.

Now commenced years of physical labour, pleasant and creative, to set house and garden to rights. The entire cottage required decorating, and for weeks we slopped about with paint, papered literally over cracks, cemented broken corners, mended woodwork, fitted old curtains into these much smaller windows, and gradually made the house habitable. A labour of love if ever there was one, and never had I put so much thought and effort into an endeavour. The result was a dwelling of much charm and character, a delightful little corner we could really call our own, surrounded by our own knick-knacks.

While these great works were continuing, I gradually turned more and more of my attention to the garden to try to make sense and order out of the overgrown muddle, cutting out the undergrowth, throwing away the excessive foliage, and tidying up generally. As the summer progressed, I discovered many plants completely hidden away under or behind others, or inextricably intertwined with each other, and needing more air and light. I noted how many would required to be moved in the autumn, and how many thrown away altogether. Mowing the grass was no easy task, sloping as it did at a fair angle down from the base of the poop to the wood. Matters such as the clover and daisies with which it was infested seemed irrelevancies, and not to be tackled this first year. The rambler roses, however, which joyfully thrived round the house like the castle of the sleeping princess, must be dealt with as soon as possible, even if this involved cutting back flowers which peeped in at the windows in gay abandon. I discovered that once I had thrown open the casements to air the house, the bountiful collection of greenery which gathered over the cills prevented their reclosure, so that one of my first jobs was to clip round each window with sécateurs until they were all cleared. The same firm routine was demanded round the sheds before they were usable, and all summer we indulged in glorious bonfires in the drive, the only safe place, to get rid of the rubbish.

I had never really lived in the depths of the country before, and in the stillness of Little Orchard I learnt the sounds of the woods and fields. It was a paradise for birds, from the riotous chatter of the dawn chorus as the sun approached the eastern horizon, to the ugly screech of the pheasants in the wood and the rooks on high. The evenings were enlivened by the crows flying home at sunset, the leader squawking to his team to keep up, the squealing of the swifts as they wheeled exuberantly round the sky searching for food;

and after dusk the owls unseen, calling to their mates. The woods were full of life, and for the first time in my life I heard the barking of foxcubs wafted up from the spinneys, and the frogs' harsh croaking from the little pond down the hill. I had never before realised how busy nature is as it goes about its work, until the heat of a summer day subdues it all to the sleepy hum of bees and whirring of the wood-pigeons on the roof.

Shortly after we moved in, I was on one of my rare visits to the village to collect various necessities from the shop which doubled with post office, when I vaguely glanced on the advertisement board just inside the door to see if there were any interesting notices. There amongst the handwritten cards notifying sale of vegetables, old mowing machines, sides of bacon, jumble sales, and requests for 'morning help 2 hours reliable', I spied one with a sketch of a dog's head, and found it was advertising puppies for sale at a nearby house. I had done without a dog since mad Flash died before the war, after which I had never felt free to have one. Now we were settled in the country with plenty of space for a dog to roam and explore, and no hazards such as sheep, there was no reason for not acquiring his successor, and I went along to the address on the card to investigate. The owner was another doggy person like David's Mairagh, and she greeted me dressed in hair-bespattered old clothes, and with a puppy struggling under one arm.

"Only got three left," she said brusquely. "Come and see what you think."

The three were all about six weeks old, a mixture of hound and something more shaggy.

"Mother got out one day accidentally when she was on heat," said their owner with engaging frankness. "Mistakes, but they're nice healthy little beggers. One bitch and two males; which do you fancy?" I watched the three romping in their pen, and was attracted to the little female who was much the liveliest.

"I'll take her." I pointed, and bent down to tickle behind the tiny creature's ear as she rolled on her back with excitement.

"I've brought you a surprise!" I announced when I got back home, to find Herbert sitting on the poop with his coffee, and held the cardboard box containing my prize underneath his nose. He peered over the top and then laughed as the puppy curled round,

145

wriggling with joy at his face, and wagging her minute tail as she bit his proffered finger with her needle-sharp teeth.

"She's lovely. Let's call her Sally," he suggested.

"Whatever for? What a funny name for a dog."

"Well, she's sallied forth from her mother – just what we wanted," he argued rather illogically, and took her out of her box onto his knee where she promptly made a puddle in her exuberance. "Oh dear;" he added, "little so-and-so!", and put her on the ground.

So 'Sally' she became, and gave us great pleasure as we watched her grow and learn her way about, and attempted to teach her obedience. But she was a wild creature, uncontrolled and excitable, although affectionate in her rampageous way. Completely soft in temperament, her noisy barking and increasingly vast size made her a splendid guard dog, appearing far more fearsome than she actually was. In our diminutive cottage she could be a menace, her wildly waving tail sweeping everything off low tables, and her clumsy bounding activity sending her bumping into furniture and knocking movable objects flying. As she grew beyond belief, Herbert began to insist she slept out in the shed, and when I jibbed at this, my mind was soon changed for me when I happened to be lying down on my bed half asleep one afternoon and received the full weight of her hefty build as she jumped up on top of me.

"No, absolutely not," I said firmly, pushing her onto the floor. "I am not sharing my bed with you. There are limits to what I put up with, and this is one. Out you go." So poor Sally was despatched to the shed, where she cosily snuggled down on old rugs amongst the lumber we kept in there.

That summer brought me greater contentment than any other time, and if we had not had to lever ourselves out to work several days a week in order to earn our livings, we should happily have become hermits, seeing no-one but each other, and the milkman and greengrocer who called with their vans. The nearest village shop supplied most of our other wants, and anything outside its range must be bought on our 'visits' days, or if forgotten then done without. Life became very simple and free of frills, but infinitely worthwhile, and I learnt the aspects that are truly important, and the very few that are essential. My standards were turned upside-down, and many discarded, and the scent of the roses wafting

146

through the bedroom windows meant far more to me than a new dress or a visit to the theatre.

As I sat on the poop with my inevitable mug of tea, aching from a day's tussle with my jungle, and gazing with satisfaction at the scene around me, I could see that Herbert felt the same peace as I. The anxieties of former days had become sublimated, and we were content.

"You're putting on weight," I observed, thinking he was probably having a nap.

"Not surprising, Duckie," he said without opening his eyes. "You feed me too well. And anyhow," raising an eyebrow, "listen to who's talking!" Then he woke up completely and looked at me. "Happy?"

I nodded. There was no need for more.

By the early autumn the house was presentable and the garden more or less under control, and when Jeanne wrote to invite herself and her two little girls to stay before the warm weather finally passed into winter, I felt able to accept a full house for a week, and looked forward to showing off our home to someone appreciative. I knew the children also would revel in the garden with all its hidey-holes. They were then about ten and eight years old, and as they had had a simple upbringing with few excitements, they proved to be a pleasure in their enjoyment of unsophisticated games. The elder, Françoise was indeed my godchild, and for her I felt a special affinity. Dark haired and olive-skinned like her grandmother, she had a quiet observant manner, and stole my affections by her ability to find some kindly remark to make about every thing with which she had contact, a characteristic so reminiscent of her mother.

"Quel joli jardin!" she exclaimed when she arrived. "Oh Maman, regardez les fleurs et le bois. Comme ils sont beaux. Je vais là, toute suite." And off she ran to explore.

Françoise appreciated everything at Little Orchard. She loved her little bedroom, with the last roses clustering outside the window; she ran up and down the winding stairs for fun because they intrigued her, and the old Aga in the kitchen was her favourite place to sit beside, rather like a contented pussy, watching me prepare supper as the chill of evening spread from the woods after sundown. She picked great bunches of wild flowers, and arranged them in

147

vases around the cottage, and when she ran out of vases, fetched old jam jars from the pantry and filled them in turn. She explored the sheds, and had long involved conversations in French with Sally, who did not mind the difference in language, but was gentle and affectionate with her as if aware how easily she could knock down her little visitor.

On their last day at Little Orchard, Françoise put her skinny little arms round me, and her dark eyes looked earnestly into my face.

"Tante Anne, s'il vous plaît, puis-je viendrai ici – may-I-come-here – encore encore encore? It ees lov-er-ly!"

Her younger sister, Marie, was less effusive, less spontaneous, less affectionate, but she copied Françoise.

"Moi aussi, Tante Anne!" she shrilled, not to be outdone.

"You may indeed," I said, laughing, "whenever Mummy and Daddy can spare you."

It was several years before Françoise could travel on her own, but at fourteen she was sensible enough to fly over to Heathrow from Paris, from where I could easily meet her in the car. That summer she came for three weeks. Herbert was concerned when he heard of the arrangement, thinking it too long for the girl, and far too long for me to cope with a teenager in such a tiny house so far from a town. But I had been to France in the intervening years, leaving Herbert and Sally to look after each other at home, and I knew the character of this olive-faced girl with the dark eyes and black hair, and that the simple pleasures of the countryside were enough to make her happy.

"Don't worry," I reassured him, "she'll enjoy helping me around the house, and there'll be all the fruit picking by the time she comes. And, of course," I added as an after-thought, "we must concentrate on her English this time."

As I foretold, she was a quietly appreciative guest, finding her own amusements about the place, apparently content to work in the garden or take Sally for walks. The latter greeted her as an old friend, and forgot her former gentle approach, obviously remembering the little French girl who had cuddled her four year ago, and nearly knocking her over in her exuberance. Françoise was now an adolescent, with a slim developing figure, and true to her

148

origins, taking care over her clothes and her hair as a genuine French woman should. Quieter than her mother at the same age, she combined her thoughtfulness with a certain naivety which both entranced and delighted us.

"Don't worry, Auntie," was her favourite quip, "I'll do it for you." The three weeks passed pleasantly and quickly, and as I waved her through to the departure lounge at London Airport – just then becoming known as Heathrow – I felt as if a daughter of my own was departing from me, leaving a gap until she came next time.

Once we were settled into the cottage, and the bills involved were paid, I looked forward to a visit to John and Gilberte, still in their same house at Le Vesinet. I had managed a week or more with them most years and as the time unfolded, I felt that John needed my support as much as I needed his, as Gilberte now quite obviously was suffering from Parkinson's disease, the first signs of which I had noticed the day the V2 fell near Bromley. Since then she had gradually deteriorated, but John had settled back into Parisian life, and returned to his insurance work once the shock of the firm diagnosis had been met. He was an optimist by nature, and engaged himself even more with organising functions for the British Legion in France, and various other good works amongst the British expatriots there, especially those in trouble. I used to time my visits to coincide with the annual British Legion Dinner at the Embassy, which was The celebration for the British community in Paris. Very grand affairs they were, akin to the annual Lloyd's Dinners which Herbert used to take me to at the Mansion House in London, and John, who loved a bit of pomp and circumstance, especially if he was involved, thoroughly enjoyed them and wore all his medals from the two world wars with great panache.

It was very evident that Gilberte was becoming more and more disabled. I used to be terrified to watch her attempting to climb the stairs at Le Vesinet with their uncarpeted polished treads curving gracefully upwards. But she managed not to slip as she dragged herself up and down. Her tremor that I had observed in Bromley was now severe, but her doctor seemed avant garde in his trial of new drugs, and sometimes at the expense of her stiffness would control the shaking which caused her so much disability, or alternatively reduced the stiffness using other drugs which would leave her shaking so much that she spilt half her drinks.

Temperamentally the disease seemed to make her natural attitude of laissez-faire increase to frank lethargy, and it was difficult to be certain how much her lack of apparent effort to carry out tasks was due to disinclination, laziness or inability. Sometimes I found myself in a fury with the poor woman, shouting at her to apply herself, with the usual result that she managed to achieve what I ordered, but slowly and painfully. Left to her own devices she would make no effort, and would early have sunk into an inactive heap, so I was able to tell my conscience that my shouting was justified. John was patience itself with her, far more than could have been expected from his past form, when he was never one to treat fools with forbearance, but even he sometimes became hot under the collar and bawled at her to try harder. Normally he was not a tolerant man, but usually with Gilberte he showed a degree of restraint that astonished me, and these lapses were an understandable exception. Every year when I visited them she was a little more incapable, a little more bent, a little more inactive, and John was correspondingly doing more of the housework and shopping. It was this increasing shadow which drove him on in his work for the British Legion, as if to compensate for the horror of Gilberte's illness by making something worthwhile out of his shattered life.

He liked to come to England each year if he could, and he would bundle her into the back of the car, propped up by the luggage and a mass of rugs to prevent her toppling over, and drive like the wind for one of the channel ports, arriving at Little Orchard an unbelievably short time later. He loved speed, and now it seemed to be an antidote to the unconscionable slowness of her movements which so oppressed him. On these visits I was reminded of Hilda as Herbert treated this other French woman with the same courtly gentleness as he had exhibited when she was at Bromley, talking quietly to her and patiently waiting for her to collect her answer together, or walking with her in the garden to exercise her poor stiff body. As she deteriorated and her speech was accompanied by uncontrollable dribbling, he would unobtrusively wipe her chin as she struggled to express herself. She did not seem to resent his help; rather to welcome the understanding and humble way he offered it.

After a week with us at Little Orchard, John and Gilberte went off on a tour of the Lakes. I wondered that he found it worthwhile, considering all the effort it involved finding a suitable hotel to which he could take her, but he could not bear inactivity for long, and needed a goal in view. On her part she seemed without an opinion one way or the other, and was happy to be packed back into the car and do as she was told, which mainly required doing nothing until they reached their destination. Then he reversed the procedure by unpacking her and the luggage at the hotel entrance, and pushing and heaving until he got all his belongings including his wife into the lift. As he would not put up with second best, she could at least rely on a stupendous view from her bedroom window, and a comfortable chair to sit in. The necessity of moving downstairs for meals and to the bathroom at intervals, gave her some essential exercise, and him plenty of purposeful activity. So it suited both of them, and she was so used to his speed-hogging along the country roads en route, and as she was situated rather low in the car due to her bent back, was unaware of the hazards and near squeaks as he rushed round corners and through traffic, and was unruffled by the hair-raising journey. I had endured the same in the past, hurtling round the Place de La Concorde in Paris, with pedestrians jumping out of his way, taxi-men shouting obscenities, John yelling back, and everyone who had a hooter using it, that I wondered how he satisfied his ego in a quiet English country lane. I just hoped that he would remember there were other madmen on the road besides himself, some bound to be speeding round blind corners in the opposite direction from himself, and that the stone-lined banks of Lakeland lanes would be hard to crash into.

What with the physical effort of dealing with Gilberte, who could be very cussed, and like a sack of potatoes when she did not want to bother, and John who was quicksilver in temperament, I felt worn out when they departed to the Lakes. How I enjoyed the returned solitude, though it was only temporary. Our next visitors would be easier and require no effort on my part, either physical or mental. James and Dick arrived a week later, and it was a joy to have two people with whom conversation just flowed easily and naturally, and with whom stretches of silence were still companionable.

They arrived, surprisingly, in a large new car, a Ford Zephyr which was totally out of character, but I soon understood why James had substituted it for their previous small cars. Dick had developed various arthritic aches and pains, and soon became stiff and uncomfortable in a cramped space. With this affluent-looking vehicle, she could happily endure long journeys, and together they could enjoy returning to old haunts without her having to walk far. The Zephyr was reminiscent of Ma and Pop of H.E. Bates' fame, and had all sorts of gadgetry which amused especially James by their needlessness and extravagance. He was anything but a snob, and found it difficult to understand the waste involved in the multiplicity of knobs and handles in this car. Why anyone should want a cigarette lighter, a drinks cabinet, or a personal mirror, was quite beyond his simple world. The car's speed of acceleration and high class driving performance was, however, something he could appreciate, and he made the most of the fun he had with this acquisition. They had a happy few days with us, and then we saw them on their way.

Henry and Estelle were the next visitors curious to see our new ménage. They drove down from Chislehurst in their Jaguar to see how we were getting on.

"Darling!" she exclaimed as she emerged from the luxury of their limousine dressed elegantly in an unsuitable but characteristic black dress and heels of gargantuan height. "How divine living in the country!" Then, as she gazed around, puffing her cigarette in its black and gold holder, "Aren't you a teeny weeny bit lonely here?"

Not for her the quiet of the Oxfordshire woods, or the inconvenience of the rural plumbing arrangements, nor the distance to the village and the eccentricities of its only shop. After a couple of large gins, a fulsome meal, and a stroll round the garden, they returned with excuses to their car, and, revving noisily, blasted off back down the lane. We could hear them for fully a minute as they accelerated round corners, changed gear up the hills, and tooted at the crossroads near the village. As tranquillity descended once more on Little Orchard, we breathed a sigh of relief and appreciation of our isolation, and turned contentedly once more to our usual occupations, having satisfied for the time being the family's curiosity about ourselves and our doings.

CHAPTER XIV

1960

WE HAD MOVED TO Little Orchard in 1955, and the next five years were to me idyllic. I suppose that they passed in the way I had always yearned to spend my life, in the country, in rural and domestic pursuits, in garden and home, with flowers and trees and wild creatures. And a dog. Instead of this I had previously tasted town life daily, and then the upset of war and family troubles of one sort or another. Apart from mild bouts of asthma, I had been fit as a horse through all this, ever since my trip to Norway years ago. Herbert too had been well. In the early days of our marriage he had succumbed to an enlarged prostate – 'man's trouble' as it was politely known then – but an operation had put him right without any complications or difficulties, and now we were both healthy and energetic for our ages, and calm and happy in our surroundings and in each other. Life seemed to stretch ahead in an unruffled manner, and when we moved to Oxfordshire, we had already been married almost ten years, and were ready to settle down into contented old age when the time came. Meanwhile we busied ourselves at home, and gradually less and less on Lloyd's commissions, finding a decreasing income was sufficient for our simple needs.

Herbert of course was much older than me. He was seventy-one the year we arrived at Little Orchard, and was marvellously vigorous for a man of that age. But none-the-less, one could not get away from the fact that by the end of the nineteen-fifties he was an old man in reality, although I had not considered it, so happy was I in our relationship.

153

Then one day I asked him to move a cupboard for me. We were spring-cleaning the kitchen and I wanted to give the floor a good scrub, 'in the corners' as Dick would say.

"Just shove it along, can you, Herbert, while you're standing there", I directed as I continued on my knees rinsing the patch of tiles where I was. Silence. I looked up. He was standing there, bowed over the table, taking his weight on his outstretched arms which clasped the rim of the top of it.

"What's the matter?" I enquired casually, sitting back on my heels.

"I can't move," he gasped in pain.

"Can't move?" I echoed stupidly, as it dawned on me there was something badly wrong with him. I quickly got to my feet.

"Come and sit down," I said, taking much of his weight as he staggered to a chair, in evident pain and distress.

"Something has given in my back," he groaned. "Must be lumbago."

"You stay there," I said needlessly. "I'll phone the doctor." I had seen the haggard look on his face, and sensed his shock. Herbert was not one to complain without good cause, and I was scared as I went to the phone.

Together the doctor and I heaved him into bed, and gradually I undressed him, washed him and gave him a drink, doing the tasks in small stages because of the agony that movement gave him. He took the pain-killing tablets he was prescribed without demur, nor did he argue when it was suggested after a week's minor improvement, that an X-ray would clinch the diagnosis. He suddenly seemed to have become submissive, and even accepted an in-patient bed for a few days whilst tests were carried out.

My heart seemed frozen to my ribs with fear, but I was too busy to stop and think during the day. After dark, on my own for those few nights when Herbert was away at the hospital in Reading, I dared not think in case my mind came to dwell on the unthinkable. I read a novel throughout the nights when I could not sleep and was scared of dreaming, until in the small hours, my book still propped in front of me on the bed cover, I dropped off, half sitting up, into a confused sleep, restless and unrefreshing.

154

After three days Herbert came home. The complete rest in hospital had done him good, and he could walk with a stick if necessary, but he looked tired and ill.

"Hallo, Duckie. Here I am again," he said with a smile when he saw me in the ward doorway. "Good to be going home."

Next day our own doctor visited us, and brought some tablets for Herbert to take. Then I walked back up the drive with him to his car, and asked the question I hardly dared put, but knew that I must.

"Yes, it's the old problem back. The prostate. It must have shed some malignant cells, and these have slowly grown in his spine and his pelvis. The tablets will hold it at bay, even lessen it, but they will not cure it. It's in the lap of the gods for how long they'll be effective. Maybe months, maybe years."

Then he looked at me. "He knows – just intuition at first, then he asked me outright whilst you were out of the room."

I nodded. There was nothing to say. My world had collapsed. I felt too weak to respond, even to cry. My mouth was like dry leather and the skin of my face felt as if it was drawn tightly over my cheekbones.

"Ring me up if you're worried," he said.

Worried! I suppose in a way I felt nothing at all. Not worried. Not confused. Not even sad. Just blank and numb as if hypnotised.

I looked at the rooks whirling round the tops of the trees as the doctor sped away down the lane to his next case, revving round the corners as Henry had done, tooting at the crossroads near the village, accelerating up the hills. Why did the rooks have such a free and easy life, without the battering and assault that we humans endured. How wonderful to be flying freely around above the trees and above the sadness and blackness of human experience.

I turned to go into the house.

"Are you there, Duckie?" said Herbert's tired voice. "Think I'll have a nap before lunch." I shook up his pillow, tucked him in, and half drew the curtains.

"I'll bring your lunch in an hour," I said as I kissed him, and went downstairs and out onto the poop to think. But thoughts would not come; at least, coherent ones would not, so I went into the kitchen instead and did some jobs there while Herbert rested, and while I tried to sort out my mind.

The tablets did help a good deal. He improved considerably until he was up all day, could walk round the garden, and even do a few light jobs in it. We did not discuss his illness. We both knew the other understood the nature of it, and we did not want the time left to be spoilt. From then on we lived very quietly, even contentedly, and if it had not been for the knowledge of the future, happily. I came to think of time as an irrelevant quality. Whether one lives for a long time or for a short time does not in the end matter. Either way it ends in the same manner, and all that is in the past, whether it is great or small, long or short, important or trivial, is sublimated in death. Whether one lives to forty or sixty or eighty does not signify in the long run after we have all gone on our way and the past merges into infinity. Time is unimportant and finite, and quite beside the point of life. What matters, if anything at all matters, is how we pass that time, and I was determined that such future as we had together should be tranquil, unravaged by fear or upheaval; companionable. What happened after that was a closed book and one into which I did not care at the moment to peer. My whole energy and purpose was in the present. We were all small people and in a hundred years it would make no difference at what moment we ended our lives; only the manner of our going would add its tiny influence to the way the world progressed. Individually we made little effect, but in total we held the future in our hands. The present is all-important because of what is beyond.

Thus my thoughts muddled along, ever more pessimistically, trying to grasp the loose ends of life and what it means, and often missing their connection with my ensuing idea, so that there was a slightly mad quality about their disorder. I had never before considered in terms of infinity. My upbringing and my continuous clinging to the Church only made the future more of an unknown quantity. If I were a humanist it would be easy, and death would be the uncompromising end. Blank. Nothing. But everything within me argued otherwise, and thus I had to come to terms with the fact that people throughout the ages have coped with the reality of death, as I was now attempting to do. I found this comforting. If all the population now dead had managed to face this unknown, so surely could I. And so on and so on I would wend my way round the maze of uncertainty, trying to find peace, or even order in my thoughts.

We spent a cheerful Christmas on our own. I gathered holly from the woods, and arranged it in vases and draped it over the pictures. I picked a large bunch of Christmas roses, searching under their large finger-like leaves to find the white buds, cutting the stalks as long as I could, and putting the vases near to the Aga so that the heat would open the flowers for Christmas morning. I even blew up some balloons to hang from the banisters to brighten up the hall, and I dug up a tiny fir tree from the garden where it had seeded itself, and planted it in an old Victorian jardiniére, decorating it with red ribbon and tinsel, and a few candles over from Christmases past. I cooked a duck for our dinner, with my best stuffing and apple sauce, sprouts and potatoes, and lashings of thick gravy such as Herbert loved. Then we finished off with lemon souffle instead of the curranty fare which I hated. We listened to the Queen on the radio, and then we watched the circus on television. And finally we had quiet, and I read aloud from Pickwick Papers until supper-time. Next day David and Mairagh came to lunch as if nothing had happened. That was the way Herbert wanted it, and instinctively I knew that David had grasped the situation when he held my hand in his as he left, and looked into my eyes.

"Give me a ring if you want me," was all he said.

Troubles never come singly. A week later one of Dick's children phoned to say she was desperately ill and was unconscious. Heart failure. I began to feel very old and forlorn. Next day a telegram arrived to say she had died without gaining consciousness. What next? I thought as I composed a reply calculated to sustain and comfort. I could not contemplate travelling up to Yorkshire just now although my dearest friend had died. I knew the emptiness which faced James in spite of his three daughters. It had been a wonderful marriage, over forty-six years' duration of grace both to themselves and to everyone around them. How hard it is that dire sadness comes to one in old age when one is most vulnerable. And yet this is not quite true. Vulnerable physically, maybe, but very strong and full of wisdom when it comes to character, at least for people like James. He would be entirely in control of the situation, and able to contemplate his future wisely. I wished I felt as confident.

That year passed in an extraordinarily contented manner in spite of the storm clouds on the horizon. Just as James was learning to do, so I began to come to terms with my own circumstances gradually, though I still could not completely accept them. One welcome piece of help came from an unexpected quarter. James acquired a new little granddaughter that autumn, who of course was my great-niece, and seemed like a symbol of hope amidst the anxieties. They named her Victoria, and I thought of her as nature's way of replacing old tired life with youthful vigour. When we received a phone call announcing her safe arrival, I felt genuine happiness for the new life that had evolved in the family. I could see that Herbert shared my thoughts. Victoria represented the world's source of light and optimism. Being a down-to-earth person, a practical individual, I had never thought like this before, and it suddenly occurred to me that being always so pragmatic I had missed something of the spice of life. Now Herbert's illness had taught me a little of other approaches to existence, and in the process I had grown, and perhaps gained something worthwhile.

"Dear me!" I laughed to myself. "How philosophical I am getting in my old age," and went into the garden to do some weeding, feeling almost light-hearted for a while.

Eighteen months after Dick died, Herbert gradually sank into a coma. He had kept well until nearly the end, and when it was inevitable and almost upon us, he smilingly faced his Maker calmly and without fear. Pain was not quite controlled, but I was thankful that I could look after him at home; ("quite the best hospice" he said) surrounded by the woodlands and garden he loved, with the last rambling roses peeping in at the window, and the pigeons' whirring coming from the eaves.

"It's been a good life, Duckie," he said as he drifted away, and just then, looking at his peaceful face, I thought so too.

James and his son-in-law came down for the funeral, and John flew over from Paris, and strangely, we four had quite a jolly evening together, once the service and obsequies were over. It had an unreal sensation about it, and yet these three men were alike in the confidence they gave me. John stayed on a further week to help me sort things out, and then I found myself alone with Sally, and memories in every corner. Winter was just round the corner.

It was eerie at first, especially indoors. From pure habit I kept finding myself turning to tell Herbert something or ask his advice, only then realising with pain the truth that he was not there. I did not dare let myself think, or I would start imagining ghosts. Part of me would say what nonsense this was, and part that Herbert would never be so unkind as to haunt me. I could hardly believe that I, the practical Hannah, should have this fear, but there it was. I had been so completely one with him that he was part of myself even though he had departed. I was not really sure of myself or my fancies, and if I stopped to work things out, I was scared I should see him in a sort of unearthly revelation. In the calm light of day it was easier. I had plenty to do to keep me and my mind busy. After dark it was difficult not to be fanciful, and I firmly put my nose in a novel and made myself read until I fell asleep from exhaustion. Sally was my mainstay. Without her I think I would have gone mad. Perhaps I did become a little bit unhinged, but no ghost would come near when she was around, and from now on she slept in my bedroom, keeping all evil thoughts and hobgoblins at bay. Never have I so depended on my dog. She kept me sane that long dark winter, as I struggled to adjust myself, and face my life again. She was solid and real, protective in her canine affection. Without her I would have run away in panic. With her I gained Dutch courage, and forced myself to pooh-pooh any notion of ghosts.

The past sixteen years seemed like a dream, but they were true enough, and now I felt weak and vulnerable, and on top of that, guilty that I had let Herbert slip away. I wondered if I could have spotted earlier that there was something wrong with him, so that he could have been treated whilst it was still possible to save him. Where had I gone wrong? Had I been too concerned with my own affairs, neglected what I should have done for him, been criminally unobservant of his welfare? How could it have occurred?

I wore myself out by turning the rigmarole of the last two years over and over in my mind, coming to no conclusion, no answer to the puzzle. Finally, fury with my own stupidity and obliqueness turned to anger at the fates for grasping Herbert away from me; the unfairness and cruelty of breaking into our happiness, into our lives, when we had done no harm or hurt to anyone else. I kicked hard against the inevitable, the demons of unkindness, and longed for peace as I stormed in my mind night and day, and turned my raging into frenetic activity in house and garden, completely wearing myself out in the process.

For months this went on, ceasing only when someone visited me, or when I was forced into the open by the necessity of shopping. Then anyone who saw me did not suspect the truth about me, thought I looked a 'bit peeky', but that was 'natural in the circumstances'. I dared not think of God or prayers or church or heaven, or any of the other things which should have calmed me. The slightest approach of any of these into my mind started up the fountain of tears which for months had lain dormant within me, raging in the deep of my soul like a black whirlpool. Now at last they came as a blessed relief, a catharsis, like the belching forth of the accumulated filth of a volcano. And after the storm of my tears came quietness and cleanliness and utter submission. Then, gradually but surely, the sun came shining weakly through the retreating clouds, and fair weather on the horizon increased and grew into my soul. I knew then that the tempest had subsided, and I had grown and would continue to grow, and life would become good again one day.

I went into the garden, and for the first time for months picked a huge bunch of flowers for the house. Next I opened all the cottage windows to let the fresh clean air into the stuffy rooms, and then, whistling to Sally who immediately bounced to my side, strode off into the woods in my new emancipated self.

These phases of recovery, which only took me a few pages to describe, actually lasted twice as many months to work through, and by the time I had reached the first beams of light, the darkness and clouds of winter had come and gone, matching the blackness of my soul. Now at last spring was just round the corner, the days were beginning to lengthen, the air becoming fresher, and the clarity of the light to shine through the trees whose branches were already swelling with leaf buds. In the garden the plants were starting to stir, and the birds were busying themselves with first thoughts of their new families. There was a cheerful atmosphere in the woodlands where the aconites were bursting into golden glory, taking the place of the carpets of snowdrops already fading.

That evening I rang up Jeanne in France, and asked if Françoise would like to come over to stay with me for a couple of weeks during her Easter holidays.

160

"Are you sure you can do with her?" she enquired anxiously.

"Of course. As long as she won't be bored. If it's sunny we could go out in the car – Windsor, Runnymede, and so on. She'd like that, wouldn't she?"

"Oh oui! That she would adore!" returned Jeanne, breaking into her French-English in her exuberance.

So it was settled, and a fortnight later found me near the arrival gate at Heathrow awaiting the flight from Paris, and searching along the emerging crowd for the familiar face. Suddenly a hand waved, and I saw the olive complexion and broad grin I knew so well, but which now was growing into that of a beautiful young woman. The kind expression which had so impressed Herbert and me when she had stayed with us before, was still dominant, but now more mature. The dark hair had streaks of henna, and the cheeks were skillfully concealed by make-up. Every inch a French girl and yet so much a part of me, this lovable elfin figure came running out to greet me, dumped her luggage unceremoniously at my feet, and gave me a typical French double kiss, one on each cheek, before she shouted in her excitement, "Tante Anne! 'Ow har you?"

If there had been any prior nervousness at our meeting after such sad events, it was dispelled immediately in the flood of warmth and pleasure between us. Françoise chattered all the way back to Little Orchard, half in English but lapsing into French when the pressure was too great, recounting family news, her own enjoyment of her lycée, baccalaureate coming up next term; tennis, swimming, walking in Savoy, and all her other interests. She was like a breath of fresh air, bubbling with life and vitality and cheer. When we arrived at the cottage, I stopped for her to open the gate while I drove in, and after she had shut it behind me, instead of following me down the steep little drive, she ran to the shed where Sally used to sleep.

"She sleeps in the house now, Françoise," I called after her, and she turned to come racing down to the back door.

"Oh, that 'ees nice company for you," she said unselfconsciously, and gave me an English kiss to show she appreciated the reason for Sally's elevation. Immediately I had unlocked the door, she threw herself at the dog who was frantic to welcome us, yapping and rolling over on her back in wriggling excitement, whilst Françoise hugged and kissed her.

Françoise was a sensitive girl, and knew instinctively that I was unable to cope with this level of emotion for long these days. Once Sally had quietened down, she left me whilst I made a pot of tea, and lugged her case up the winding staircase that always amused her, to the little room she used to share with her sister Marie. The roses were not yet out, but a spike of forsythia just tipped the window cill, and she breathed deeply with pleasure as she took in the view over the wood, alive as it was with birds and wild creatures. After we had had our tea, she excused herself, and quietly went off round the garden, searching for old hidey-holes she had loved as a child, looking along the plants for their flower buds, studying each bush and climbing shrub, peeping into birds' nests. Sally discreetly followed her, and every now and then pushed her cold wet nose into Françoise' hand as much as to welcome her once again. Finally they disappeared together into the wood, and I knew she would have gone down to look at the pond.

That week and the next were joys. Françoise was an entirely easy visitor, happy to read to herself or write letters, take Sally for walks, work on her embroidery, or just chat the afternoons away. Whatever she did, was achieved in her pleasant relaxed fashion, so that I, who had hardly spoken to a soul all winter and was out of practice in the art of conversation found it without strain to talk unselfconsciously with her, even discuss myself to some extent. She had an uncanny knack of drawing one out of one's protective skin, unburdening oneself of sentiments, opinions, even anxieties. How does she do it, I asked myself after an evening when I had found myself telling her, quite unplanned, all my concerns about the house, especially my finances which were on a very rocky base. She seemed instinctively to understand my worries, even the most trivial; in fact the more obscure and lowly, the further she appreciated their personal significance for me. We were more like sisters or cousins than aunt and niece, and had a firm bond between us, which remained in place even if not a word was passed.

Content to live simply as she was, and to enjoy the countryside, after a few days my conscience pricked me, and I realised we were nearly half-way through her visit and she had been nowhere further than the village. Next day I packed up sandwiches and two thermoses of coffee, and announced that we were going out for the day. We drove over to Windsor first, and I managed to park the car in a little square off the High Street at the back of the Royal Mews very near the castle, so that we walked, appropriately through an ancient street to reach the outer gate of the huge complex, thus setting the scene for what we were about to see. Most French people, like Americans, are envious of our British pomp and circumstance, if the truth be told, although often the French will not admit it as the tourists from the States do. Françoise was more naive and less inhibited than her countrymen, and was hypnotised by the Guards in their bearskins and scarlet uniforms standing motionless at the entrance to the outer bailey of the castle.

"Are they real?" she whispered in awe, and almost jumped when they came to attention and started to march. The Grace and Favour dwellings in their Mediaeval courtyard entranced her, as did the view of the Round Tower up the hill, and the panorama of Eton from the terrace. Perhaps the sight that thrilled her most was the peep she had through the railings to the Royal apartments which she long gazed upon, hoping for a glimpse of the Queen. It delighted me to show round a visitor who was so genuinely thrilled with the place. History was one of her favourite baccalaureate subjects, and she was able to fit Windsor into the picture she had in her mind of several episodes in the past.

On emerging from the castle precincts, we felt almost breathless with the pleasure of it all. It was a lovely spring day, and Windsor looked at its best, with the trees in the park coming into leaf, and the early sunshine gracing us. There was an appetising smell of newly baked bread coming from a cafe nearby, so we retired into the tiny front room to recover ourselves, and settled down to tea and scones straight from the oven. When the waitress gave me the bill, I hardly gave it a thought as I opened my purse, and then, horror-stricken, realised that it contained only a few coppers. No silver and no notes. I quickly did some mental arithmetic without letting Françoise know my predicament. It was quite right. My week's pension had gone into the purse when I called at the village post office on Tuesday, and with extra groceries, petrol, a bill at the joiners' and another at the butchers', and now entry fees to the castle, there was nothing left. I was stunned to think that immediately I had any extras, even an inexpensive guest like Françoise, my income would not stretch far enough.

"What's the matter, Auntie?" she enquired at last, sensing that I was having problems. "Shall I pay for this? Do let me."

I felt tears pricking my eyes in sheer frustration and humiliation. Here was I, having economised to the hilt, and not even able to pay for tea and a bun for two as a treat.

"I'm afraid I'll have to let you," I said. "I've left my proper purse at home." The lie came glibly, but I could see she understood.

"Don't worry," she replied. "It's my treat for the holiday."

I felt shaken that my finances were so vulnerable, and when we went to bed that night, I lay awake turning over and over in my mind how I could spend less. Hardly anywhere in my budget could I reduce expenditure; a little here, a little there, but that was all. I seldom ate meat. I did all my own baking for the week, and grew practically all my own vegetables. Only enough fruit to keep healthy. No help in garden or house, even for painting and odd jobs, unless I was forced. The fact was that almost all my capital was tied up in the house, which, in that part of the Home Counties, was appreciating rapidly, but not increasing my income. If I lived somewhere cheaper, investing part of the money the house would bring at auction, and buy a smaller place with less land, I could manage. But how could I leave Little Orchard, which was part of my soul and where I had been so happy. It was unthinkable. I must struggle on somehow.

We spent the rest of Françoise' visit quietly and contentedly in the environs of the cottage. We went for picnics near the Thames, and visited Marlow and Henley and Wallingford. The weather was good, and Françoise' English had improved, so I felt that we had achieved at least that. In addition, it had been a real change for her away from her lycée, and I myself felt much better and able to cope with life. As always, I suffered a pang as I waved her into the departure lounge at Heathrow the day she left. The elfin form with the dark hair streaked with henna waved as she made for the passport control desk.

"Can I come again soon?" she called. "England is so loverlee." Everyone near her in the queue turned round and smiled at me, and then followed her into the cavernous interior of the airport.

The cottage seemed very empty when I returned. Usually after a visitor had left, I found it a relief to be on my own again, to think my own thoughts uninterrupted, and get on with jobs in the garden which had been neglected. With Françoise it was different. She only added warmth to my recovery, and I indeed hoped she would continue to want to repeat the visit before long.

Meanwhile I had James booked to stay for a week in a few days' time, so, once I had washed them, Françoise' sheets went back on the spare bed ready for him, and the room was dusted and filled with fresh flowers for his arrival. I met him off the train at Reading, and immediately experienced a different but equally welcome companionship as with Françoise, as if now some of the responsibility of being on my own was temporarily lifted from my shoulders. He travelled very light, bringing only a hand 'grip' with but one change of clothes, and having donned his 'garden' trousers, remained in those for the rest of the week, enjoying the quiet of the place, and peace to work out his stocks and shares. At home he now lived (since Dick's death) in a purpose-built flat attached to his youngest daughter's house. He had his own front door and all his own facilities, so that he was independent but yet not isolated, and could enjoy the children in small doses. This perhaps was the ideal arrangement for someone in his seventies, and I envied him the solid base of his domestic affairs.

"It's very nice here," he observed thoughtfully as he made himself comfortable in a deckchair on the poop, crossed his legs and reached for his pipe, filling the bowl contentedly and squashing the tobacco down with his little finger.

I started to cough. "Sorry, James," I spluttered. "Can't stand your smoke. Would you mind going down the garden with your pipe." His face dropped, and obviously concerned and distressed to have cause this hubbub, he tottered down to the wood, where he wandered about puffing his nauseous weed and considering matters. Every now and then he looked up at the house and I knew he was thinking about my sojourn there and the practicalities of my remaining now that I was on my own. After ten minutes, I could see him knock out his pipe on a tree trunk, scrape the ash from the bowl with his penknife (the implement "for horses' hooves") and put everything in his long-suffering pocket, before returning to the poop. But he did not sit down immediately. Instead of this he slowly and deliberately meandered all round the outside of the house (James never walked fast) continually studying the details of the cottage and garden, finally coming back to rest in his chair, and crossing his legs again.

After a few minutes during which he said nothing, I was longing to hear what he thought about the place.

"Well?" I said. "What would you do?" I knew he would refuse to be hurried into an opinion. There was a pause.

"Very nice," he said thoughtfully at last. Another pause. "But what about the winter? And what about ten years' time, or if you had asthma in the night? It's a long way to your neighbours."

I knew he was right, of course, and I was getting older. I knew the time would come when I should be forced to move to somewhere more civilised where help could be summoned if needed, and there would be someone to notice if I did not appear for a day or two.

"I've got a phone," I said lamely. James was not one to argue, or to force his point. It was clear what he thought, and by doing only this, he had made me think seriously about my future. I knew, as he had quickly grasped, that this was no place for an elderly woman to live and grow old on her own, and the sooner I moved away, the more chance I would have of making a real home for myself elsewhere.

"I simply don't know where to go," I said, answering his unasked question. "Anywhere round here is far too expensive." But as I admitted this, I knew my real reason for hedging was not the difficulty of finding an alternative house, or even the awfulness of turning out our accumulated belongings from the cottage, and compressing everything into a smaller space; nor even putting up with the intrusion of neighbours, and returning to a conventional existence. It was all these things, but it was more, much more.

Once again, like the night I had lain awake worrying over my finances when Françoise was staying, I found it impossible to settle to sleep, trying to imagine where on earth I could move. The idea of leaving these woods, my previous independence and sweet isolation, and all the memories was impossible for me to accept. Everything in the cottage had a story behind it, every inch of the garden Herbert and I had tended together. The flowers, the trees, the grass, the shrubs all had some connection with our love. Old jokes came to mind, old habits raised their heads, early morning departures in ice and snow, fog and rain, sometimes in the promise of a sunny day. Always we had returned thankfully to the peace of Little Orchard from that other world of industry, confusion, noise, rivalry, and human idiocy. Back here to the rambler roses, the yellow irises round the pond, the pigeons whirring on the eaves, the smell of autumn dampness and summer tea on the poop. All my recollections jumbled in confusion as I grew more and more sleepy. An owl whoo-whooed in the wood, and its very calmness made me recognise that Little Orchard was a part, a very dear part of my life, but that part was over now, and I must go.

But where? I had not many relatives left, and did not want to go back to Yorkshire where I had never felt a native. I was too old to go to live in France near John or Jeanne. I had Ida, one of my oldest friends, in Truro, but no-one else in Cornwall. Edna was in Wilmington, but she was the only person I knew in that part of Sussex, and I was aware that I must not depend on friends and relations for my future social contacts. So I continued to turn the problem round and round in my mind, without finding an answer, until finally, still with the owl's hooting in my ears, I fell sleep.

Next day I felt blotto. I must have looked it too, but James was never at his best in the morning, so we ate our cornflakes in silence. An hour later, when he had smoked his first pipe of the day wandering round the garden, he sat down near where I was sewing on the poop.

"Hannah," he began, "I have been doing some calculations, and I have come to the conclusion you cannot possibly manage on your present income."

"But you don't know what it is – exactly," I protested.

"No, and I don't want to pry. But it is very clear to me that it is difficult for you. What I have decided is, that I shall help a little. But it won't be regular, and it won't be by cheque, as I don't propose to line the tax man's pocket on money that has already paid a high rate of tax. So, every now and then I shall send you cash, notes that is, several at a time. I shall keep a record of it in my 'Children's file', so I know exactly what it adds up to, and I don't want you to bank it regularly, but use it for household expenses. Do you see?" His hand stole to his pocket in search of his pipe, his comforter, but he thought better of it and the hand went back on his knee.

167

Had anyone else in the whole world said this to me, I should have burst out in fury at their interference in my affairs, not to mention the effect it would have had on my pride and self-respect. From James it came like a comforting balm from someone who was truly concerned, kind and perceptive. Most other people would have done it as charity, much of which anyhow is given to salve the donors' conscience and make them feel good. James was entirely unselfish, in the true sense of the word, and in his unegotistical manner wanted only to help me. It was a gift I could accept gratefully from him without losing face. And in any case, only he and I would know about it.

"James, that is generous." He was an undemonstrative person, but I could see by his slow quiet smile how pleased he was when I went across and kissed him lightly on his forehead. "You're a dear," I said.

He was as good as his word. Every few weeks several envelopes would arrive from Yorkshire with just his address on a bit of paper inside, wrapped round anything from five to twenty pound notes, always different amounts, but adding up to about seventy pounds or thereabouts each month. This made all the difference between penury and solvency for me, and was the end of my fight against an overdraft.

So the year rolled on, the warm months full of activity in the garden, the physical work giving me pleasure in itself by helping me to continue the process of revival. By the time the autumn clearances of dead annuals and pruning of the shrubs were due, I once more felt fit and energetic, and enjoyed the bonfires I had to stoke into action to rid myself of all the rubbish. It was almost as if throwing with my loaded fork the old dead branches onto the pyre and watching them burn and crackle to nothing but ash, was another catharsis in readiness for the new growth next year. The very sting of the smoke in my eyes was a welcome penance and the lingering smell on my clothes like incense, to remind me of the sacrifice.

I began to leave the cottage and go out a little more, and not just when essential. Mairagh's mother lived a few miles away through the woods. She was a dynamic Irish woman called Shona, of considerable mental calibre and a great heart, whose kindness was often hidden beneath her awe-inspiring exterior. A lady who held firm opinions on most aspects of life, and voiced them in no uncertain way in her rich fruity southern brogue, she was a pillar of the Protestant Community, and thus differing from the majority of her compatriots, she none the less remained at the Anglo-Catholic end of the church spectrum, enjoying the colourful ritual which indeed matched her character. Now into the eighties, her days were filled with charitable acts, but in no sense demeaning the recipients of her largesse. The wealthy widow of a shipbroker, she was willing to put herself to any amount of trouble if it would help someone, but so great was her sensibility, drawn no doubt from her many years sitting on the local Bench, that she would refrain from offering succour where it might be resented or give offence.

I had seen little of Shona since Herbert's death, I think by mutual recognition that our characters were too much alike, not to say fiery, to mould happily together. Herbert himself had always steered clear of David's mother-in-law if he could do so unobtrusively, as he found a little of her went a long way. She was a very positive person, very rich, very well dressed, a serious bridge player, and wore bangles and necklaces, make-up and nail varnish both tastefully applied in moderation, but none of which was my own mode of living. And yet I had to admit she always looked the height of elegance, which was more than could be said of her daughter, who constantly clung to trousers, jersey, and her cigarette dangling from the corner of her mouth. I also acknowledged Shona's polished and aristocratic facility in the social world of Henley as a conversationalist and a hostess, and envied her ease with people of all classes. In my present frame of mind I had found that her very self-confidence and drive grated on my own complete lack of stability and purpose, and her Irish loquacity clashed with my need for quiet. However, now that I was coming up to the surface once more, I felt that her indomitable spirit, even her masterful enterprise, might act as a catalyst to my return to normality. I climbed into the car and went to visit her.

"Well, to be sure, good it is to see you again," she greeted me. "Will ye have a seat now and tell me all about yourself."

I sat down on her deep luxurious sofa, and found myself remarkably at peace.

"I thought I might begin to go out a bit more now I am gardened up for the autumn," I began. "Shall we go to tea in Henley tomorrow?"

"Well now," she responded brightly, and as completely flexible as a much younger woman. "That's an idea that's splendid, so it is." The Irishness of her did not now irritate me. Rather it offered warmth and comradeship.

And thus it was that Shona helped me to complete the process of renewal and recovery that winter, and accompanied me back into the full life that I liked, guided me towards finding purpose in my being by drawing me into her sociable activities, and last but not least, welcomed me back to the church I had not dared to enter since Herbert's death because of the disastrous affect it had had on my emotional equilibrium.

This is not to say that everything went smoothly from now on, but when there were ripples in the sea I was able to cope with them, and when adverse waves swept my course I could now dive through them and come out, breathless but unscathed, the other side. I did not feel I was helplessly drowning as I had done before, but that there were people within my grasp who would pull me back onto dry land.

CHAPTER XV

1960-1972

THE SIXTIES WERE A time of change and upheaval in the Western world, and no less so in England than elsewhere. It seemed to me as if every time I picked up a newspaper some new exploit was being mooted, some new method or trend introduced. Everything old was bad and must be superseded. Anything new must, per se, be better. The world, or at any rate our part of it, seemed to have gone mad, throwing away all that was comfortable and familiar, and often substituting something at odds with what we had been used to. I suppose this process had started at the Festival of Britain in 1951, already ten years ago, when the dreary image of the thirties and the destruction and desolation of the war, were forcibly and consciously being replaced by a bright new world. New buildings being speedily and enthusiastically run up, which were urgently needed to erase the sea of bomb sites and to house the growing population, were big and square and, to many eyes including mine, exceedingly brash. This was the era of tower blocks, with their tidy filing away of families into pigeon-holes of uniform size. Factories and office premises followed suit, then schools and hospitals, often novel, practical and well-lit within, had faces that were inhuman because they were large and blank and hard, window after window of the same rectangular dimension devoid of decoration. The picture window, the flat roof, the unhidden fallpipe, the featureless wall and above all the omnipresent concrete became popular, and with them a new vocabulary to describe these 'in-things'.

Not unexpectedly colour raised its head, not subtle and subdued, but primary and positive and intrusive. Panels of bright green, garish yellow, vivid red and deep blue appeared on new building, youthful and exuberant, but unrestful and portentous as if insisting on making their point. With this uncompromising design came sculpture to adorn open spaces between the new blocks, and enigmatic paintings of strangely-shaped creatures, vaguely anthropomorphic, with flat cheeks and straight bodies, staring eyes and accentuated features. Modern offices such as banks and even churches would hang these works of art on their walls to show they were aware of the new world in which we lived, and I began to find such pictures in the corridors of hospitals where I visited old friends, and on the landings of the stores in Reading. Youthful and virile as they were, they succeeded in producing the shock which they intended. They certainly brightened up the place. The only trouble was that I did not want to be shocked or brightened up. I needed reassurance and stability after the years of war and change.

By the time I was again living on my own the media were daily bringing reports onto the T.V. screen or into the newspapers of the burgeoning youth cultures. Like the developing traits in art and construction which the most unobservant could not ignore, even such as myself who only occasionally drove into the big wide world of progress, youth seemed to become more and more of primary importance, whilst those of us past middle-age were counted for less and less. It was young people and their cults which caught the headlines. Colour, strange dress, screaming pop groups highly amplified, strange new instruments, ear-rings, nose rings, rings on every finger and several on each wrist, and the whole vision surmounted by hair of shocking pink or brilliant lime green. Boots, mini-skirts, purposefully frayed trousers, coloured tattooing on just about any part of the anatomy, all this combined in what was known as 'flower-power', the flower children, and LOVE with a big L. In order to enhance their perceptions, so they thought, the young then took to drugs which they were persuaded all too easily would deepen self-knowledge, but which often instead quickly hooked them onto exotic 'trips' from which the real world receded, leaving the colourful light-headed dream fantasy where control of self was exchanged for indulgence in every weakness to which man is prone. Peculiar pseudo-eastern mysticism thrived, but without the discipline of the real thing, super-sexual in content, holding its disciples in thrall from which they often could not extricate themselves. Pop festivals became the vortex of all these activities, and were fed by the decreasing influence of home life, school discipline, church direction, and sadly declining social mores generally. I even heard one independent headmaster friend of Shona's grumbling that he had been forced by parents to relax school rules because they complained he was too strict and they would withdraw their sons if he persisted in disallowing long hair, mocassin shoes and earrings, not to mention visits to pop concerts in term time, and possession of crude long-playing records of shrieking groups who had replaced the crooners of old. He had even been censured for banning the burning of joss sticks in school, which, as everyone knew, camouflaged the smell of cannabis smoking.

I vividly recall these features of the sixties in some detail because to someone like me, then elderly, living alone in my woodland retreat, they were foreign and confusing and really quite frightening. Their very familiarity now indicates how pervasive and insidious the pop culture was that it not only managed to reach me, but to have this effect on someone who was normally staid and not easily moved. This made me wonder about its effect on individuals more impressionable than myself, perhaps young, but of whatever age easily influenced or nervous. When I went into town for shopping I felt I was in a new atmosphere of the crazy imaginative Animal Farm variety, with bands of leather-clad, pink-haired, flower-wreathed youth of both sexes striding down the footpaths so that we lesser folk were pushed onto the road as they passed. This, it seemed to me, was a parable in itself, and I wondered how far this pushing process would continue, and whether we – 'the rest' – would cease to exist, so important were these young people with their love-ins, their psychedelic clothes, outrageous ideas, and their idealistic aspirations and unreal demands. Particularly I, who had laboured so hard to maintain my independence, heartily disliked their selfish attitude to work, and their grasping of social benefits of all kinds without contributing to their own upkeep.

"You don't understand, Auntie," said one of my great-nephews, who had roared along on his motorbike to see me on his way to his hippie friends in Wales.

"Just thought I'd drop in instead of dropping out!" he grinned when he spied me in the garden.

"Flower people contribute to world happiness by their colour, love and music, so they deserve to have the State pay them."

"At whose expense, I'd like to know?" I said self-righteously.

"No-one's. They don't cost anything."

"Yes, they do. I'm helping to pay for their dole in my taxes."

"You'd have had to pay taxes anyhow. It makes no difference to you."

"Well, their parents then. They must be helping them to keep alive."

"They wouldn't help if they couldn't afford it, and most of them can. So it's only fair they should use some of their ill-gotten gains to clothe and feed those less well off. In our new co-operatives everyone will be looked after because we'll pool our money."

"What if it runs out?"

"Oh, it won't run out because we'll farm and keep ourselves with what we produce."

"But farming is very hard work - - -"

"Not if everyone joins in."

"What about the know-how? You can't pick up farming when you're not used to it."

"Auntie," pityingly, as if to an uncomprehending fool, "lots of us know about farming, and there *are* instruction books."

I felt quite dizzy by the illogicality of all this and changed the subject abruptly, as I felt we were getting nowhere. "Would you like me to mend your trousers?" I ventured.

"God, no, Auntie," he returned, scandalised. "But you could put a nice bright patch on the knee if you like."

"But it doesn't need a patch there."

"No, but wouldn't it look great?"

I declined, feeling exhausted by this whole conversation, endearing though I found his cheerful dottiness. I think he felt the same way about me, and he happily tucked into a huge plate of ham and salad before kissing me heartily and joyfully booming off to his psychedelic friends, hooting continuously as he revved round the corners to the village.

Paul was an intelligent youth, and although this light-hearted attitude had its pleasant side, on the whole it infuriated me for its irresponsibility, and for once I was thankful I did not have teenagers of my own to contend with. I could see how difficult it must be for parents to be wise. Instead, I shrank back into my comfortable old-fashioned existence which Paul found so deplorable and dull. The thought of ever leaving this Shangri-la for a new housing estate with its uniform semis and no doubt its amplified 'Muzak' was something I could not contemplate. I stuffed the whole idea to the back of my mind.

At the time I was very well, and once the period of depression following Herbert's death had lifted, my energy returned, and providing I kept my activities within reasonable control, I felt I could go on for ever at Little Orchard. I ventured out of my retreat quite often now, either locally to one of Shona's charity functions, helping her organise fund-raising events, or visiting my nearby friends. Some of them would 'drop in' on me like Paul had done, or, bringing a sharp knife with them, would beg plant cuttings from the garden, or contributions for some sale of work. I knitted, embroidered and crocheted hard to fulfil these requests, and relished the creative energy they required.

The car was my one expense. I did not count it a luxury but a necessity without which I could not have carried on, as also was Sally, who by her affection and her splendid facility for frightening strangers with her fearsome bark and large size, made me feel safe. When I went away for a few nights, she was used to staying at kennels in the village where she was subdued but content, greeting me with tumultuous excitement on my return.

Each year at least once, I travelled over to France, always for a week in Paris with John and Gilberte, and sometimes if funds would stretch (God bless James) also to stay with Jeanne. France had been utterly shattered by the war, not only physically, but in her self-respect, and took much longer to recover than Great Britain. General poverty remained visible, as was the big divide between rich and poor. It took longer to repair and repaint its buildings, and student unrest, so much a part of the youth culture of the sixties everywhere, was correspondingly greater. I loved France and was saddened to see her struggling to regain poise and respect.

Gilberte was gradually declining in activity, and becoming more and more bent and stiff. She could only walk now with the upper half of her body doubled right over so that her face was completely hidden from view. She dribbled constantly, and her speech was difficult to understand. So stiff were her arms and shaky her

175

movements that she could barely feed herself unless it was some solid food which she could eat with her fingers. She used a baby's cup with a lip and a lid, and with this could manage to give herself a drink slowly and erratically. Thank heaven she was not incontinent, and so John still took her out for rides in his Renault. Not that she saw much of the passing scenery, but it at least gave him an outing himself for he dared not leave her alone for long at home. My presence at Le Vesinet gave him an opportunity to visit his own friends by himself, and see to his own affairs whilst I kept an eye on Gilberte at home. I tried to make up my mind how much she understood of what was happening to her. She was so slow in her reactions now, and her speech so poor, that her natural disinclination to exert herself which had been a feature of her character as long as I had known her, was now completely overlaid with a physical inability to respond. As I sat in her drawing-room with its long Victorian lace curtains, its polished wood-block floor, and its multiplicity of framed photographs and old fashioned prints, and chatted to her whilst I continued with my embroidery, I discovered gradually how very small was her present world. Any animation she might previously have shown was now buried by years of inactivity and lack of mental stimulation. I felt as though her brain was slowly winding to a halt, and her emotions were flattening out to a straight line. "How merciful," I thought, "is nature in its working." Mute, uncomprehending and unemotional, this was one way of passing out of life without shadow or strife. I honestly did not think that she now was suffering.

One evening John and I left Gilberte to her sister, Therese's care, and went off to the British Legion Dinner at some grand hotel on the Champs Elysée. I had resurrected my full-length pre-war dance dress for the occasion, and given it a new look by stitching a huge artificial flower to the low V-neck, covering my arms, which embarrassed me by their loose, floppy skin, by my old fur cape. John was wearing dinner jacket and black tie, and in fine form, determined to enjoy himself amongst his cronies. "My sister from Henley," he grandly introduced me as we shook hands all round, full of bonhomie and British joviality. From being children John and I had always got on well together, mainly because I treated him as my revered older brother, and he regarded me as someone weak and needing care. I laughed to myself when I thought of how I had looked after myself very well throughout the bombing in London

176

and now in my isolated cottage in the middle of nowhere at home, but if it did his self-confidence good to pretend he was looking after me, I did not mind, and found how much I was enjoying once more the experience of being taken out for the evening with a male to see to my comforts. It was reminiscent of the old Mansion House Dinners in the City to which Herbert and I used to go together. Equally dazzling were all the silver ornaments, the cutlery and glassware, the flowers and the white starched napery on the tables, as well as the jewellery and insignia glittering around guests, and I realised how, unperceived, I had actually missed this side of life that I had not tasted for years. Even the usual problem of acquiring a plain glass of water from the shocked waiter ("Water, Madame?" he queried quizzically, and brought it in a wine glass – "A jug, man," ordered John) was a reminder of past dinners.

We ate, we drank, we danced (sedately), and we talked – how the French can talk – and at last we returned to the car, and drove twice round the Place de la Concorde before making our way at high speed and somewhat erratically back to Le Vesinet. For a few hours both John and I had wallowed in a fantasy of make-believe, pretending that the real world of decrepit Gilberte and dead Herbert were not facts. It had been a lovely dream though, and I did not regret it, for it floated us above reality into a rainbow, from which we brought back sweet memories of true comradeship and fun. As John returned to his committed care of poor Gilberte I realised how fortunate I indeed was that Herbert had not declined over many years, nor suffered the gradual destruction of his body and intellect like her. Is this the last phase of grieving, I thought to myself. Now at last I have come to terms with Herbert's loss and can even feel thankful for the way it occurred.

It had taken over eight years to reach this stage, but I had now achieved an equilibrium. I was in control. Perhaps after all, the beatniks held a truth when they said one must acquire self-awareness. I had found mine over many vicissitudes and much stumbling, but completed it unexpectedly and appropriately during a fun evening in Paris.

Coming back to Little Orchard after being away always held mixed feelings for me, but this time I was relieved to snuggle into my comfortable rut in spite of having enjoyed being in Paris. It was always exciting to pass from room to room, each so familiar, to see them through the eyes of an outsider, and glean the impression a new visitor might be given by them. One becomes so used to one's own home that one forgets what a newcomer's first thoughts may be. My own first, on returning this time, were how deliciously welcoming and familiar it all was. My second was how tiny. My third, how stuffy. I threw open every window and let in the fresh air and country sounds, and looked around happily to handle, note, and appreciate all my possessions. I realised how much I loved this home. Its distinctive muddled design suited my character, blending its own with mine, its very eccentricity suiting my need to be myself. In most ways I was a very ordinary person and I just wanted to be left alone to enjoy my own life as I felt. I could not agree to follow all the newfangled fads that the world directed I must. My fastidiousness extended to more than food. I wanted to mould my own life for as long as I could, however long or short a time that might be.

These high-minded thoughts flowed through my mind during a period of contentment, when I was physically able to contend with the potential difficulties, and the sensible part of me admitted to this. Just as John had adapted his life to Gilberte's increasing helplessness by creating his own distractions, so I would alter my ways to fit in with the demands of Little Orchard as long as I could.

It was not many weeks until I heard from John again, accompanied this time by two photographs from a Paris newspaper reporter. To my astonishment, they portrayed my big brother lighting the Flame of Remembrance at the Arc de Triomphe on November 11th, and afterwards signing the Golden Book of Remembrance, surrounded by British Legion characters in their uniform berets, and other obvious V.I.Ps. Whatever next, I thought. It was a great compliment for an Englishman to perform this Ceremony, and recognition for all his work for other ex-servicemen over nearly fifty years. He had become in effect an honorary Frenchman in spite of tenaciously retaining British citizenship, of which he was very proud. I too was very proud – of him. I took out old photographs of us from a tatty envelope in my desk in which they were kept, and soon came across the one for which I was searching. It was of John and me in 1938, taken of us sitting on a low wall at Le Vesinet during my last visit there before war broke out. I was pictured gazing with unfeigned admiration at him, both of us remarkably youthful, but I had now just that same feeling of awe. Others might say he was a 'big head', conceited, talked only of himself. I knew better. He was enterprising, courageous and selfless, and I swelled with pride as I thought of this mark of French appreciation for his prowess.

Within a year, and perhaps connected behind the scenes with this event, came the announcement that John had been awarded the O.B.E. in the Queen's Birthday Honours List. I was quite bowled over by this piece of news, to me entirely unexpected, and wanted to shriek it all the way through the village. "Hey, do you realise my brother is in the Honours List! Hi there! My John is going to Buckingham Palace!"

In fact he did not go to Buckingham Palace, but received the insignia from the British Ambassador at the Embassy in Paris, in a very select gathering and with much pomp, which he hugely enjoyed. Once again his photograph appeared in the Paris newspapers. They even reproduced an old one taken in the early years of the Queen's reign when she visited Paris for the first time as Monarch. There she is in her New Look dress with its full, calf-length skirt, the familiar handbag over her left arm, and a floral toque on her head, with the Ambassador, Sir Gladwyn Jebb, on one side, and John with the British Legion colours, about to be 'inspected', on the other, and the Embassy gardens full of admiring onlookers.

I felt myself growing in stature by these disclosures, and when he rang from Paris and suggested he and Gilberte pick me up on their way to a holiday in Scotland at the end of September, my joy was complete.

They duly arrived on September 20th. I remember the date particularly as it coincided with the thirtieth anniversary of Mother's death in 1940, and so my mind was abuzz with family memories. As usual they stayed at Little Orchard for two or three days, and then John was fidgety to be on the move again. Gilberte was not only no better, but by now completely submissive, and unable to think or care for herself. "This is her last trip to England," John muttered, and as I took my place beside her in the back of the car so that I could prevent her toppling over, I sadly agreed.

To sit at the back when John was driving was actually a more soothing experience by far than sitting at the front beside him with full view of the road, although it meant that conversation had to be shouted. However, it prevented me from witnessing all the potential hazards as we sped along, and as usual when being driven by him, I mentally shut my eyes to threatening disaster as we hurtled round corners or past farmyards, with squawking hens scattering in all directions, and cows mooing passively at this madman disturbing their peace. It was an invigorating ride in spite of the jitters it gave me, as I had such confidence in his skill, I knew he would always manage to avoid disaster. With Gilberte huddled impassively beside me, alternately dribbling and grating her teeth, I managed to remain calm.

We tore through England, taking the nearest route to the border, and found ourselves up over Carter Bar by sunset and into Edinburgh soon afterwards, where John had booked us into an hotel in the New Town. Next morning, after a brief walk along Prince's Street whilst Gilberte was coming alive to the day, hunched safely into the depths of an armchair in their bedroom, we set off again for Blair Atholl for a couple of nights. Then on to Inverness, where we branched eastwards to see the Field of Culloden, so sadly evocative with its simple little gravestones to fallen Highlanders, but though I felt a lump in my throat, John remained unmoved. After that we turned north-west through Strath Oykell to Inchnadamph and Unapool, his aim being to circumnavigate the northern part of Scotland where he had not previously been. On and on we drove, goaded by his fidgety impatience constantly to be on the move. It was as if he could not bear to be inactive at one place for any length of time, but he must be on to the next. Seldom he stopped to stretch his legs, accept the coffee I offered from the thermos, admire the spectacular views, or just to relax and rest on the soft turf of blueberries and heather. As we progressed, I realised that this was a man under intense strain accumulated over the years, controlled and ruled by his own assertive self-confidence which was threatened by events outside himself. His outward assurance which was responsible for his apparent conceit, was in reality his defiance of this intimidation. Unknowingly, Gilberte was the foundation of this facade. I understood now the reason for his restlessness.

As we drove into Sutherland, traffic became more and more scarce, just as we correspondingly left trees and habitations behind. Occasionally there were crofts to be seen, cowering behind hedges to protect themselves from high winds. More often there were rocky outcrops surrounded by closely trimmed grass and the ever present sheep. The road bucked up and down in an uncontrolled manner, first north, then south, then north again, with glimpses of water sparkling in the northern sun, alternately the sea, then the kyles breaking inland between the headlands. I felt on top of the world as we span along, the fresh breezy sunshine lifting my spirits as high as they had ever been. John was singing jauntily, part English, part French, as we raced eastwards away from the setting sun, every now and then punctuating his song with a swearword of universal connotations as the road unexpectedly changed direction.

Suddenly, coming towards us round a corner bounded on both sides by high rocks, and with scant grass verge, unexpectedly loomed a Land Rover travelling at high speed in the middle of the road. The brilliant setting sun behind us illuminated the driver's face and his screwed up eyes, and whilst John did not suffer the hazard of dazzle, he had not passed another vehicle for many miles and was carefree of traffic.

He had no chance to avoid catastrophe. There was horrific screeching of brakes and squealing of tyres, sickening revolution of the car as it thumped from one rock to the next, and we span and tipped chaotically, finally steaming to an abrupt halt whilst the windscreen shattered all about us, adding its own tumult to the cacophony of metal crunching and tearing, clattering and collapsing.

My main memory is then of complete silence, broken only by the car's frame creaking as it strained to regain its previous shape. Then came the sound of water running gently from the engine – or perhaps it was a nearby burn. Too shaken to move at first, I wondered vaguely if I was still alive, finding myself half out of the front window, my feet hanging over what had once been the passenger seat. I gingerly moved one limb after another, then my head, and finally flexed my spine before deciding I was in one piece, but still dazed and disorientated.

A whimper came from the direction of my feet.

"Anne, qu'est ce que c'est?"

I dragged myself back to where Gilberte was wedged between front and back seats, half on her side and immovable, and thanked God there was no fire. Then I heard a man's voice which was not John's, and realised we were being rescued. Someone, rather optimistically, I thought, said "Stay where you are. We'll soon have you out," and I felt like giggling idiotically at the inappropriateness of the remark as there was no possibility of extricating myself from the wreckage, much less Gilberte and John.

John! Where was he? I had been so concerned with my own predicament, I had assumed he would, as always, be nonchalantly unscathed. Then I saw him. At least, I saw what I presumed was he; a ragged contorted heap of humanity pinned down by the steering wheel which had stove into his chest, and the twisted ruins of the front section of the car, inextricably wedged, part under, part within the bonnet of the Land Rover. His head was at a peculiar angle, his eyes staring. Then I began to comprehend. He was dead.

I turned to Gilberte who was lying now on the side of the road where they had put her, a little way round the corner on a small island of grass between the rocks.

"What 'as 'appened, Anne? John – Ou est il?"

I looked again at the mangled confusion blocking the road, to try and bring home to myself the truth which I could not, dared not, believe. There were two men bending over his body now, still entombed in the remains of the car. One turned round, and seeing me staring at him, shook his head.

"He's gone, I'm afraid," he said briefly.

I turned back to Gilberte, lying so defencelessly on the ground. "He's been killed," I heard myself whispering. All she said was, very quietly, "Oh, mon Dieu," and a tear rolled down her poor, inert, expressionless face. It was followed by another and another. Even crying was almost beyond her. "Oh, Anne," she moaned.

The fact that Gilberte's tragedy was greater than my own, and that she needed every piece of help and comfort I could give her, took my mind off my own numb loss. All my energy was centred on making her as comfortable as possible, trying to soothe her and ease her pain. Terribly shocked and bruised as we both were, my own thoughts were centred on her, and I had no time or spare emotion to dwell on John. I felt muddled and dazed, and could not think clearly. Only I knew I must look after Gilberte. Time ceased to exist. The world bounced around me in a light-hearted fashion. My words were coming out of someone else's mind. I could not think constructively or even clearly. Notions danced madly about my brain. I felt heavy, unutterably tired, slightly light-headed, dotty. My emotions jumbled themselves together so that I wanted to giggle, then scream, but finally with an effort, pulled myself together, answering the simple questions the ambulance man asked me, with peculiar intonation and goodness knows what actual words.

"Parkinsonism," I kept repeating. "She's got Parkinsonism." They heard and understood, and off they drove us to Thurso hospital. There the nurses recognised my inarticulate shock, and gently put us both to bed in a double room, were kindness and patience personified, and cared for us in capable Scottish fashion for two or three days. We were tactfully left to rest and gather ourselves as far as maybe, and were only faced with questions necessary to our welfare. Neither of us cried very much, Gilberte because she remained dazed and impotent, me because I knew that if I lost control of myself, I should go mad. We slept a good deal through sheer exhaustion, and on the third day Sister announced we were going to fly back to London next morning. Still I felt responsible for Gilberte and dared not give way, so I just mumbled thanks to the nurses as well as I could for the frog in my throat, picked up my handbag which had been recovered from the crash, and trotted obediently along beside Gilberte's wheelchair which had been borrowed from the hospital. I hardly noticed the drive to the airport, or the flight south.

At Heathrow they gently and almost affectionately transferred Gilberte to the Paris flight, and I was helped to a car with remains of my luggage, and driven the short distance home to David's house, where I stayed for, I think, a week. Confused impressions still blurred my recollections as I tried to regain my equilibrium and realise the enormity of what had happened.

This was the most horrific thing that had ever smitten me. Worse than my father's death, when I had been left an orphan, more lonely than when Herbert died because that had been expected, and worse even than the repeated sadnesses of both world wars. I was near desperation and lost the will to live. I just did not care what happened to me and I could not bear to think about the terror of having to go on living. This time there was no guilt, no fury, no blaming, and no acceptance. I just wanted to be left alone to die. I was limp, completely exhausted, mentally and physically.

Emotionally I approached breaking point. I did not know that life could be so black, like a great, dark, enveloping, frightening cavern. Nothing I did or thought gave me comfort, let alone hope. I could not reason. I could not plan. I just existed through each day, and fell exhausted into nightmarish sleep in the evenings when I eventually dragged myself to bed. All my good intentions, all my affections, all my interests, all light and colour, air and warmth had gone. I had no thoughts because my mind was empty. Or else my thoughts came scrambling madly one after the other in uncontrolled chaos. I hauled myself from one job to another, neglecting those that I imagined could wait another day. I let the house gather dust, the garden its entangled weeds. I failed to answer letters, or wash my hair. I ran out of bread and milk or Sally's food. I forgot to lock up at night, and if I remembered, did not care. Although there were in reality plenty of people who were concerned for me, I felt utterly alone.

If this was not hell itself, the ultimate was unimaginable. Day by day passed without a glimmer of light. Friends called, and I pretended to be pleased, but I felt lifeless, and I think they noticed and came less often. Fortunately old Sally's needs kept me from complete inactivity, and once again she rescued me from despair, took me for walks, forced me to get her meals ready even if I neglected my own, placed her soft muzzle on my knee and gazed at me with consoling eyes. She even helped me to dig snow from the path round the house, and to fetch logs from the shed.

That winter of 1971 was the worst of my life. I knew now that I could no longer exist at Little Orchard.

CHAPTER XVI

1972

"HALLO ANNE. IS that you?"

It was Rose at the other end of the phone, Herbert's daughter who had lived and taught in Sussex all her married life. She was now widowed, but had stayed on in the same bungalow where she had been housed happily for thirty years, teaching in a local junior school and with a finger in all the local pies. 'Happily' is a relative term, as Rose was the world's most intense worrier, and every day she anticipated all the things that could possibly go wrong during the next week or two.

"Good gracious, girl," I would say (she was ten years younger than me) "life has got enough problems without you looking for them. It may never happen." But my remarks made no difference, and only confirmed her view that I was far too happy-go-lucky and careless for my own good.

Not least of her worries were those regarding her health. My own robust opinion was that ills are made worse by dwelling on them, even caused in the first place by thinking of their possibility. Rose's interpretation of this philosophy was that I was foolhardy, but she assumed that as my health had always been good, I just 'did not understand'. I horrified her by what I ate, the meat, the cream, the sugar, and even the occasional bread-and-dripping which I so enjoyed. I, on my side, was nauseated by the vegetarian messes she made for herself – 'muck' I called them to myself – though whenever I joined her for lunch she compromised with a boiled chicken rendered tasteless by being denuded of its skin, and denied all added salt and herbs. Having constantly studied the medical columns in newspapers and magazines, and an avid viewer of medical programmes on television, she was full of good advice on current cures and medical theories, and stocked all the latest medicines which could be bought without a doctor's prescription, and some that ought not. Being a teacher born and bred, she expected some notice to be taken of her advice, but had to be content with my ignorant pooh-poohing of her health warnings, and held up her hands in despair at my wilful neglect of her help.

Rose hated housework, surprising in one so tidy and meticulous in other matters, and the thick dust adorning her furniture contrasted with her fussiness over food. She was very clever with her hands, and produced all sorts of beautiful embroidery and knitting, which put my own efforts to shame, but she preferred to engage in these pursuits rather than dusting and sweeping her tiny bungalow. She adored animals, and had always had a dog herself until recently, but now felt it was 'too much for her', and she borrowed other people's instead when they wanted to go out without them. She had never had children of her own, and lavished much of her pent-up affections on these animals, reading up all the articles in magazines about their care, and constantly producing items to be sold in aid of the local Dogs Home. Having taught junior children all her working life, she expected the same obedience both from her dogs and from their owners, and recently I suspected from me too, now I was on my own. I was suspended between gratitude for her kindly concern for me, and annoyance at what my less tolerant self felt was interfering in my affairs.

"Just like a school marm," grumbled my horrid persona, whilst my honest self recognised her thoughtfulness – "Just like her father," it whispered.

As well as extreme kindness, she had also inherited from him her anxious personality, and the lingering illness and death of her husband and her lack of children on whom to transfer her worries, were reason enough for her now to target all her anxieties on her own health, and on mine when she could get a word in edgeways. Ever since Herbert's death, she had recognised my aloneness, and had phoned me at least once a week to make sure I was alright, and just to have a chat. This was sheer kindness on her part, never put off by my frequent abruptness, and even brash rudeness when I felt that way. Her forgiving nature accepted this as part of my grieving

186

and continued to care for me in a deeply concerned and unselfish manner. Since John's death, her contact had increased, and was both a blessing on which I knew I could rely, and an annoyance which I dreaded as I was obliged to reply in a like manner which I often did not feel. Sometimes I could have screamed at her down the wretched phone, for her very tolerance which infuriated me.

This particular morning I was receptive to her overtures. It was March, and the days were getting lighter, the evenings shorter, and the woodlands were beginning to bristle with activity.

"Anne," she repeated, "there's a bungalow in this road just been put up for sale. Why don't you come over and have a look at it?"

My first impulse was to squash her, and aver that I would never leave Little Orchard, but I knew now that I could not face another winter like the last, and perhaps Tufton, where Rose lived, would serve as well as anywhere for me to drag out my last years. At least there were shops and taxis and civilisation within easy reach, and not any steep slippery slopes to drive up in winter. So I thanked her and got out the car in a sort of numb duty.

Tufton was a product of the Brighton railway, its oldest houses having served the local station as workers' cottages, a few shops, and a typical Victorian 'commercial hotel'. Commuters to London or Brighton could alight here in the countryside, which they liked so much that they soon converted it into suburbia by spreading their new lookalike houses out from the station in typical Pooter terraces, and later into huge semi-detached housing estates, trim and well-looked-after but conventional and unexciting.

Rose, appropriately, lived in Violet Grove, some way from the station where land was already built on by earlier immigrants from the big cities. Her house had been erected in the thirties at the same time and with the same aura as thousands of other little dwellings all over England to accommodate the increasing population, at last able to possess their own homes once the shortages and unemployment after the First War had been stemmed. In this case a builder named Mr. Grove had designed and constructed a small cul-de-sac of two-bedroomed bungalows, and named the road after his wife, Violet. Mr. Grove had had elderly people like his Violet in mind, and his houses were compact and easy to run, and if their materials were not of high quality, and their facades were all the same, over the years the inhabitants had gradually transferred their own personalities to the properties, producing en route a comfortable, trim atmosphere where everyone proceeded with their own lives without reference to each other, but where, if there was trouble or sadness, neighbours rallied round to help. Thus, if the small front gardens echoed their owner's character in their variety of baubles, gnomes, windmills, troughs and polythene-lined ponds, or even merely concreted over the lot in a mixture of remarkable colours, gossiping was at a minimum and confined mainly to next door. As the inhabitants of Violet Grove had nearly all lived there since its first inception, they were aware of all their neighbours' vagueries, and were mainly now in their seventies or eighties. From many years' experience they had learnt self-reliance, albeit in a somewhat inflexible and conservative manner, knowing that everyone else there had been brought up in a similarly ordered background to their own, and disliked innovation as much as they themselves.

Violet Grove lay on the south-facing slope of a gentle hill with a splendid view of the South Downs. At least, the bungalows at the top of the road, the blind end of the cul-de-sac, had that view; those at the bottom had it obscured by further housing, and so only saw each other. Rose, being one of the first residents, and incidentally, now at sixty, one of the youngest, lived at the top of the road facing down it, with a big roundabout in front of her gate where traffic could turn, and on which the residents clubbed together to keep a large rose bed in trim. From her front window she could see right down Violet Grove and the various comings and goings at all the lower houses. Straight out ahead she had uninterrupted prospect of the Downs surmounted in majestic isolation by two windmills silhouetted against the sky. Named Jack and Jill because of their appearance of falling down the huge hill, they added an uncanny exhilaration to the conventional pretensions of Tufton, where the main road was pompously called 'Grand Avenue' in an effort to upgrade its social standing. Jack and Jill on their lofty green eminence, were both more natural and more ethereal than the modern erections at Tufton, mysterious in contrast to the predictable suburbia spreading beneath them.

As I visited Rose frequently over the years, I knew exactly what to expect in the lower bungalow we now inspected, and it was merely a matter of assuring myself of its condition inside and out, and making up my mind whether I really wanted to live there. House and garden both proved to be in good order, and as I did not want to live anywhere at all just then, the second question was hypothetical. However, I knew it made sense to grab this opportunity, and so I submitted, my own stipulation both to Rose and to myself being that I must be allowed to create my own life here, and not depend on her or her many friends to provide social interrelations for me. Rose, who was as sensible as her brogues, her twin set and her tweed skirt, agreed – with reservations. To do her credit, she had not tried to persuade me to buy, merely presented the possibility to me, as a good teacher should, and waited without comment while I made up my own mind. Perhaps she had already learnt of my cantankerousness and knew from bitter experience that if I suspected that someone was making decisions for me, I would be likely to do the complete opposite just for obstinacy's sake.

So, eleven years after Herbert died, eleven years of learning to live on my own, to face people again, resurrect all my old self-reliance, I left Little Orchard for the suburbia at which I had often sneered. The hard physical work involved in cleaning up the cottage, throwing away the remains of Herbert's belongings, discarding some of his larger furniture, and resolving what to retain, was nothing to the strain of constant decision-making and parting firmly with the past. The bodily stamina it needed to lug cases, loads of books and papers, odd bits of furniture and pictures, into different sections of the house depending on their ultimate disposal, was actually the greatest blessing as it prevented me from thinking too deeply, or even regretting my resolve to move. Every day I had a bonfire of the articles that either were worthless (worn-out chair covers, towels, files and magazines for instance) or personal and private and now no longer relevant to anyone, least of all to me. Stoking and forking and adding more rubbish to the flames, gave me a respite from the never-ending job of sorting out, and once again was cathartic to me in its destruction of the past and the finality of its result, so that the ash which it left was a comfort in its unequivocal permanency and privacy, and assured me that no outsider could pry into the memories that died with them.

Energetic though I was, I collapsed into bed each night exhausted, the physical weariness accentuated by the emotional strain, little though I was able to find the time to ponder on my activities. As always, Sally was my companion, but now so slow and old and decrepit, hardly able to find strength to follow me down to the bonfire with each load, or raise spirit enough for a slow wag of her tail. Poor old thing would hardly last the move, I thought, and wondered if it was time I took her on her last journey to the vet, finding that the reality of that prospect was too great for me to tolerate on top of all the upset of leaving Little Orchard.

Selling the cottage had been easy, even to obtaining the price the estate agent advised. Inflation was whirling up, and Oxfordshire was sought after more than ever by wealthy people willing to pay incredible prices for a pied-à-terre there. The result for me was a pleasantly solid residual piece of capital left to see me through to the end of my life, even after buying the much cheaper property in Tufton. This was a bonus with which I had not reckoned, and so, for the first time in my entire life I had no need to worry about finances, which was an extraordinary state of affairs to which it took me some time to accustom myself. It did not make me any less thrifty – I was too old to change my habits – but at last I had no pecuniary anxieties. It should have had no effect on my outlook on my fellow beings, but in fact I was surprised to discover how much it boosted my morale. For once I felt as good as them, not any more an orphan dependent on others. Except for my years of paid employment this had never happened before, and even then I had been grateful for the help from Dick and James, particularly in these last years. I had now a great feeling of emancipation, and set off for Tufton with a heart lighter than it had been since Herbert died, even finding some optimism in thoughts of my future.

Rose was waiting for me, sitting at her front window from which it was impossible to escape her notice, as I soon learned. She was dressed in her latest jersey suit, and beckoned to me to come up the hill.

"Got the kettle on," she called as I walked through her gateway.

"Oh heavens!" I growled to myself. "Here we go! The school marm!" Then "I will NOT be managed." But I enjoyed the tea – she knew my weakness for it – and insisted that it would be simpler if I directed the moving men on my own so that my belongings would be set down where I had planned. She saw the sense in that, and in her understanding way realised the trauma that leaving my old home was for me, and that I wanted to be left alone.

The next few weeks went smoothly enough, and as I took up residence at Tufton, the whole atmosphere of the place was so entirely contrary to Little Orchard that it almost eased the change. There were no comparisons possible. The prosaic suburbia I had always loathed and sneered at, had now provided me with a sanctuary for all my needs, and was to be my home. I disliked its unenterprising predictability no less, but had to learn to accept its solid assets however much it hurt my pride to admit this and that the 'Good Life' of the cottage at last had defeated me.

Rose visited or phoned me every day at first, but even she had her ardour cooled by my attitude. I was a fish out of water in Violet Grove, and I knew it. I was the new girl, whom everyone greeted politely, but seemed to them self-sufficient and in no need of sociability beyond that. I cringed at the thought of making close friends with this narrow community, thinking myself so much more superior. Which of them had ever travelled outside the confines of the country as I had done many times? Which of them flipped over to France every year? Who had had relations in the French Resistance, a brother with an O.B.E., a brother-in-law in a high position in industry, read books on all sorts of subjects, and a newspaper without a 'page 3'? They were little people, Pooter people, people without enterprise, people of no account, whose opinions simply did not matter. Old, gossipy, provincial, and that most debasing of characteristics, boring.

I could and would exist here at Tufton because I had to, but never would I become 'one of them'.

Rose recognised this great trough of depression into which I had fallen and in her quiet capable voice, tried to help by introducing me to her friends, asking me up the hill to coffee with her and Sylvia, inviting me to help with her Dogs Home bazaar. But I was not ready for all this. It was foreign to my past life, and I did not want to be dependent on her or her friends. I wanted my own kind, and yet I was too old or too obstinate to seek them out. I chatted to strangers at the shops, the bank, the library, and even passers-by in the street. They were kindly folk, but I was so desperately lonely I could cry, though I instinctively warded off approaches of friendship because my intense obstinacy yearned to

191

prove my independence. I felt deeply isolated in my misery, far more so than in my woodlands at Little Orchard where the flowers and the wild animals and the birds were my friends.

Poor Rose stuck to me, however much I shouted at her, argued, contradicted. She continued to call, and quietly withdrew after passing the time of day and perhaps commenting on local events, the price of tomatoes, or some national happening. She had been through depression herself and knew the twin feelings of wanting comfort yet shunning approach. She would gently stroke Sally's silky head as she talked, and I knew she was in effect stroking mine, and I was at once grateful and infuriated, like a naughty child.

The garden was my saviour. At seventy I was still full of energy, and I genuinely loved growing green things, watching them develop, and planning the future of my small plot. I now entirely fed myself with vegetables from it, and loved to pick and arrange the flowers from the tiny borders, and chew at the apples from the miniature fruit trees. The soil was dense clay, but it was fertile and well-drained being on a slope and sunny in aspect. I spent hours in that garden, Sally stumbling over to watch me or lying out on the tiny terrace sleeping the hours away. On Sundays I left her at home, and walked the mile or so to the nearest church, where I found balm for my soul in the sincere words and beautiful music of the familiar prayer book cadences. It was a church of middle-of-the-road persuasion, with a restrained personal welcome but without the intrusive camaraderie of the evangelical kind. I found it dignified and genuine and the services helped me as much as anything in my confused state. Very gradually I discovered a kind of peace that I had lost, different from anything I had known before in its quality, but appropriate to my present life. I felt calmer.

I was soon to be thankful that this degree of control returned to me when it did, as I was badly to need it. One morning early I was awakened by peculiar snortings and blowings from the direction of Sally's bed, a low home-made affair like a box on legs without a lid. I switched on my bedside light and hurried over to her. The poor creature looked as if she was having a heart attack, with irregular puffing and convulsive movements as she tried to breathe. I stroked her head and talked quietly to calm her, and then suddenly realised she had collapsed, the movements had ceased, the kind eyes were fixed, and she had gone.

My own heart gave a great bump, as I collected my wits. Dear Sally! I had had so many blows that I was familiar with the old tumult of grieving, and whilst part of me accepted that the old dog had to die sooner or later, yet the reality still hurt in its finality. Sally had been a good friend through many of my troubles, but it was time for her to go to her doggy rest, and I could accept that. She belonged really to the past, not to my Tufton present. Her departure now was only one more facet of my new empty existence.

I could not live without a dog, and I soon acquired her successor – never could it be called Sally's replacement. I was tired of having articles swept off low tables by Sally's waving tail, of being nearly knocked over by her big bulk, not to mention her huge appetite when she was younger, so this time I went for a smaller breed more compatible with my present diminutive house and garden. The vet suggested a beagle puppy that had recently been born prematurely to one of his client's bitches, warning me that the tiny animal would need a considerable amount of extra care.

I thought about it, and quickly decided that as time was no object, and I dearly loved dogs, I should enjoy the challenge now I had no-one else to look after.

A day or two later the vet drew up in his car and emerged with a box in one hand and an envelope in the other. Inside the former, cringing terrified in one corner and pretending to be hidden by the straw, was a minute puppy. In the latter – much larger than its subject – was the puppy's pedigree.

I lifted the tiny creature out onto a newspaper spread on the kitchen table, a warm writhing bundle of movement, his whole trunk weakly reverberating with apology for tail-wagging, squirming his head and back into curves and coils, licking my hand limply, trying to roll over but only succeeding in falling onto his side, then struggling onto his front again, but not onto his feet. Smooth-haired, long-eared, white, with patches of autumn bronze on head and tail, he had the typical beagle's long nose and short stumpy legs. Then the truth came to me with a shock, that his tail and hind legs were almost useless, flaccid, and beyond his control. Not entirely paralysed, as every now and then he moved them purposefully and raised his tail momentarily before collapsing again and dragging them along behind him. He was weak and thin and fragile. A runt.

I looked at the vet with my eyebrows raised and a question-mark in my expression.

"I'd no idea he was like this," I said. "Is he fit to go on in this condition?"

"It's only temporary, like a shock to his system because of his pre-maturity. If you can give him every care, he will gradually recover, though he may always be rather weak on his legs. In the wild he would not survive, but in a domestic situation where he doesn't have to chase after his food, he'll be a good pet for you, and a marvellous house-dog. He will be very valuable if you succeed," he added enticingly.

"I don't care about his money value," I rejoined, "as long as I'm not letting myself in for more than I can cope with. He looks very delicate."

"He is. But I'd put him down if he was hopeless. You'll find a list of his needs, food and so on in the envelope. Keep him warm, plenty of fluid, and I'll call in next week to see how you're getting on." And he hurried off, leaving the puppy and me to get used to each other.

At first the little dog continued his affectionate but weakly writhing, but very soon he tired and came to a halt cuddled into the straw, and immediately settled down to sleep. It was as if his small strength was rapidly exhausted, and most of those early days were spent by him rounded under the cover of his bedding quietly slumbering. Every two or three hours I offered him diluted milk from a dropper, and he soon learnt to suck the fluid down before collapsing back into his nest worn out. Even through the night, whenever I heard a rustle from his box, I offered him a drink, setting my alarm three hourly so that he did not go too long without its nourishment. Far from finding this a chore, I discovered meaning and purpose in the labour, and was rewarded as he imperceptibly grew stronger, moving his back legs with greater control as the weeks went by.

"What are you going to call him?" asked Rose, who watched his progress with deep interest.

"Toby," I replied without hesitation, "just like the jugs – no hind legs." She laughed, glad no doubt to see me happily engaged in something I enthused over at last.

194

Toby remained in his little box for some weeks. It seemed the best place for him while he was so tiny and frail, protecting him from draughts and interference. He had little inclination to move around it and I sometimes wondered if we were doing right to try to rear him. The vet was as good as his word, and called in every few days at first. He never charged for this, and I think he was sincerely interested to watch the dog's progress, and perhaps a mite conscience-stricken that he had landed me with such a formidable task.

After I had completed six weeks of this programme, though feeling very tired, I was rewarded. One morning Toby not only lifted his tiny head to greet me, but his tail gave a definite thump and a wag. I felt that all the broken nights were showing results at last and were worthwhile, anxious though they had been. Over the next few weeks he very gradually gained some strength in his hind legs, still mainly dragging them, but showing slow improvement. There were signs of positive movement.

"Time to get you out of your box, my lad," I told him, and the spiky tail gave a single voluntary flap in reply.

The weather was fairly mild and dry now, so every day I lifted him out onto the lawn, and watched his efforts to progress towards where I had put his food bowl, at first only a foot or two away from him, but gradually further and further, seeing with pride his puny efforts increase as the weeks went by.

Meanwhile his skin, so loose and baggy when I first had him, began to fill out, his fur became thicker and more silky, and his eyes brighter, his head movements quicker. It was fascinating to watch him come alive, and though still without the energetic romping of a normal puppy, at least narrowing the gap between his own lethargy and a healthy youngster.

It was not until six or seven months later that one day Rose came running in from the back garden.

"Anne, look! Come at once! He's standing!" I rushed to the back door, and there in the middle of the lawn was Toby proudly up on all four legs, tail at half mast, head up in the beagle fashion.

"He's standing! He's actually standing," she crooned. It was a revelation to me, not only to see Toby up on his legs, but Rose

195

beside herself with excitement, a state completely foreign to her demure nature, and which I had never witnessed before.

"Oh, good dog," I cried, infected by her enthusiasm. "Good boy! Come to Missus." And he turned my way with, I could swear, a smile of achievement on his doggy face, as much as to say "See how clever I am, Folks! Just watch me!"

Suddenly he moved his head away so that he pointed up-wind. His nostrils quivered, his tail stretched out to the full extent of its length. Then, slowly raising his face to the sky, he rent the still air with a moan which became a call and then higher and higher, in roll upon roll of increased sound until it became a prolonged howl. Over and over again he filled the garden with his strange unearthly wail, the view halloo of the true beagle about to chase his quarry; his hunting cry. Round the hill it travelled, echoing on walls, back and fro, bouncing down the streets as if he had been far out in the wilds; pretending to be a big grown-up hunting dog, emancipated from the nursery stable, ready for the field. Exciting, unnerving, ghostly – but Toby.

We knew now we had been right to let him live. Now it was clear that he was going to grow up a healthy, happy hound, and from that day he quickly gained ground, every week making a difference to his strength.

Very soon I started the habit of walking him round the roads near Violet Grove twice a day, at first just stop-and-carry-one strolls whilst he nosed the grass verges and met his friends.

"'allo dear" would come a cheerful Cockney voice from a nearby garden. "Nice to see your little daug getting better." And then I realised that all these silent houses were in reality alive and their inmates aware of what was going on outside their own territory. It gave me an opportunity to talk to other dog owners traversing the same round also, and although it did not create deep friendships for me, at least I did not go through a day without talking to a soul. I should not have minded becoming a hermit, but common-sense declared that it would be 'good for me' to make the effort to converse in a civilised manner, and indeed I began to know quite a number of doggy neighbours as we all passed the time of day on the grass verges standing around as our dogs did their business. It is certainly one way to become acquainted with people, and as we waited, we discussed the finer points of our pets and their peculiarities and fads, which, I discovered, were often much as their owners' characteristics. I wondered if these people had the same sort of impressions of me and how most I resembled Toby. Probably my wobbly legs and loud voice. Thus Toby served as my Go-Between, and taught me the value of at least minimal sociability.

My next lesson was much more acute and frightening, and made me eternally grateful that I had left Little Orchard when I did and was now in the midst of all these kindly people, even if they were not very exciting; perhaps that was their great asset.

I think it must all have been due to a pent-up anxiety that had been hidden from my consciousness by blind determination to carry on, and also to an insidious weariness from months of broken nights caring for Toby. Now that he was improving and the pressure on me was released, my own will to remain unscathed was brought to naught by forces stronger than my own, and I soon succumbed.

Once again I was awoken early morning before it was light. This time by a nightmare in which someone had tied a tight band around my chest, preventing me from breathing. I was sweating and heaving and gasping, trying vainly to catch my breath; choking, suffocating, fighting. The more air I took in, the tighter my chest, expanded already to extreme limits and yet unable to push the old air out. My lungs felt immovable, huge yet inflexible; useless, great inflated drums that were dragging the life out of me. My shoulders were hunched, working hard to release me from the vice-like grip of the spasm; my mouth hung open, gasping and drooling, puffing and battling for breath in a frenzy of fear, my nostrils dilated with each fresh effort. Oh heavens! How terrifying! Shall I ever get my breath, I wondered vaguely as my head span and my heart-beat banged like a hammer in my brain, my ears, my whole body; thudding, reverberating, thumping. I was already sitting up – that had occurred before I had woken to this devilry. Now I struggled to turn sideways with my legs over the side of the bed to give myself more air, more room to breathe – breathe – breathe. Is this the way I'm going to die, I heaved through the mist? I needed air, air, air, more air. The noises of my frantic efforts to exhale were weird even to myself – perhaps it was not myself but that poor soul sitting on the side of the bed – a great groan from deep down in my chest and rushing in my throat. My mouth was leather-dry, my eyes onion-streaming. I staggered to the window and hung out over the cill to absorb the cool dry night air, clinging to the frame to steady my exertions, yearning for help yet anxious about the fright I would give anyone spotting me. No, don't be silly. I'm going to die. I must have help. Phone the doctor. No. Can't get him out of bed this time of night. 'Course you can. You'll die if you don't. Number? Hands dithering; eyes bleary; puff, blow, puff. Shoulders helping to push the old air out; puff, dizzy, fighting, swirling. Number by heart; can't dial; try again. Only four digits. "Hallo?" "Mrs – twenty-five puff – Violet puff – quick – please." "OK" said the calm competent voice at the other end. "Be there in ten minutes." Thank God! But no let up in the fighting. Sat on straight-backed chair in the hall; grandfather clock ticking, head reverberating, chest wheezing; need to cough; no air to do so; fight, sweat, exhausted, then – sound of car, injection, near oblivion, face mask, fighting it, couldn't bear anything over mouth. Firm voice "Breathe into it, it will help you." Tried. Perhaps it did. Too weak to care. Fear defeated by exhaustion. Funny word – must mean breathing out, which I can't. Must stay sitting up; can't lie down, no breath, half-dead; pillows, ambulance, long corridor hollow sound, puff, hospital smell, mask, white paint, starched apron, cool hands, capable, puff, very far off, Where's John, out of focus, thumping in head less, but puff, mask helping. Can't bear blanket – too heavy. Help Gilberte. Air. Sip water – sister's arm to support – spilt down neck – cold. Lovely cold water. Like the burn by the roadside. Wheeze, blank, dazzle, nurses, clatter of tin cans. John's wrecked car. Mask. Injection. Puff. Shoulders. Refreshing wash. Sweat. Weary beyond description. Sleep.

When I awoke, the battling of breath had stopped. Only the wheezing in my chest with every movement, like the basketwork of the old easy chair in the Rookery kitchen, reminded me of the last frightening twenty-four hours. I found myself propped up in bed amongst the semi-circle of pillows, supported by a bedrest. A cage over my legs took the weight of the blanket. An oxygen cylinder stood beside me, with its tubing and a mask ready for use. I felt like a wet, floppy piece of sponge, something that Toby had been shaking about between his teeth and then dropped in disdain. I reached towards a glass of water on the side-table, and then discovered I was so dithery I could not grip it, and that even the effort needed for that sent the basketwork creaking louder and more rapidly than if John and George had been swinging on it. I sank back and waited for other people to deal with me. I did not really care if they did.

This, I discovered, was Cuckfield Hospital, and here I was cared for with gentle understanding, encouragement and kindness. The white starched apron reappeared at intervals, the cool hands did what was necessary to make me comfortable, a different uniform arrived bearing nourishment, and yet another with tablets on a spoon. Injections were efficiently repeated. Stethoscopes, blood samples, occasional oxygen. Sleep.

And then Rose, sitting by my bed, not chivvying with questions, but softly imparting news of home and of Toby whom she had brought up to her own house, and relaying good wishes from everyone at Violet Grove. She filled the locker with clean nighties and slippers, nice perfumed talc and lavender water, things I would never normally use but which she wanted me to enjoy although secretly I wondered if they would set me off coughing again. I felt completely indulged and pampered, and indeed quite overcome by all the thoughtfulness. My eyes pricked with tears, so I must have been ill. Other people visited, a niece from Yorkshire came all that way on a day trip, another from Northampton, then Rose again with more nighties. I slept and slept for a week or more, and then I began to improve and walk round the ward to try to get myself back into training. The wheezing had almost ceased, but the cough and the breathlessness remained whenever I made any effort, reminding me of my fragile state.

And soon it was time to go home, and to my silent concern about how on earth I was going to manage, the answer came in little acts of kindness from all sorts of unlikely people, neighbours who had hardly seemed to notice me before, but now came round with their offerings. One did my shopping; another brought in my coal; someone delivered a pie; my grass automatically was mowed whenever someone did their own. Rose walked Toby twice a day, and changed my sheets when necessary. And so it went on. Sheer thoughtfulness and quiet relief. As any conversation set off my cough – a fruity graveyard one – no-one stayed to gossip, so I was shielded from that hurdle.

Thus it was that I emerged through that dark tunnel of creaking, scaring basketwork, and reasserted my natural independence. The day I shouted at Rose, she knew I was better. Poor, kind, long-suffering Rose merely murmured that she would pop in tomorrow for Toby and shopping list, closed the back door behind her and left me feeling a worm. But I was not ungrateful in reality. Far from it. I was actually terrified that I was losing my independence, which was breath of life to me, as much so as the fresh dry air I needed for my lungs. To be hemmed in by other people's decisions was to me death, something with which I could not exist. If I could not be free, I might as well not continue. If other people took over my care, I would die. In no way could I face being an invalid and doing what I was told. As with John who had died a straight, clean death with no ragged ends left untied, so did I want my end to be. Not to deteriorate gradually like poor Gilberte, a dependent, a parasite, a thing of pity. That I could not stand. However imperfect ('hack-handed,' Dick used to call it), if I could not look after myself, that must be the time to go. Rose must learn this, even if I had to shriek it out word by word to her.

Poor Rose. Kind, quiet, unselfish. Her zenith of life was to care for other people; as a born teacher, to see that they did what was best for them. It was quite against her nature to accept that someone who had been as desperately ill as I had been, was fit to look after themselves. Of course I still needed help, with Toby, with shopping, with some cleaning jobs. But how and when these were to be achieved I must decide for myself in my own dog-in-the-manger way, and if they didn't get done, it really didn't matter. I preferred independence to cleanliness, I am sorry to say. She dimly understood – against her better nature but achieved a magnificent compromise as she knew that the one thing I could not do was to take Toby for his twice daily run. The shops would deliver goods, my old neighbour would run errands. Even the cleaning would get done eventually. But Toby was my Waterloo, and I would not allow him to be neglected. So, each morning at 7.30 Rose appeared briefly to fetch him for his jaunt, and after tea she would pop in again for the same task, and this arrangement just nicely gave her the opportunity to make sure I was alright. So, I was defeated after all, and I knew by how much.

As I improved, I came to terms with my position however, and perhaps my understanding of myself was more complete. Whilst never becoming a confidant of my neighbours up and down Violet

Grove, I was mellowing, and as long as they did not intrude into my thoughts or my home, I was able to accept them as mutual well-wishers. Starved of intimate friendships I still had old acquaintances of my previous life who visited and even came to stay; James (who now automatically walked down the garden to smoke his pipe); Lila from the Isle of Dogs with her cockney commonsense; 'Matron' from Harrow days with reminiscences to amuse me; Ida from Cornwall; nephews and nieces in plenty to discuss their worries. And my two favourites, Françoise who came over from Paris several times a year to see me, and Edna from nearby Wilmington and shades of Blackheath High, with whom immediately she set foot in the door, I was engaged in companionable banter which rocked the house with noise and laughter.

Thus from a quiet solitary existence, sewing, crocheting, knitting, writing letters of great length, I was suddenly flung into activity and chatter with one or other of these good people, ultimately exhausted but happy when they departed, to sort out the chaos they left behind in both my house and my mind. Rose never really entered into these encounters. She paid her respects, passed the time of day, and withdrew, pleased that I had a compatible friend to exchange my wild ways, but puzzled over our outrageous hilarity.

The sad side of life raised its head, as it must do in the nature of things. Gilberte's sister, Therese, wrote to report that she had faded very rapidly after her return to Paris from the disaster of John's death, and within a year was herself dead. I could only breathe "Thank God", knowing she had nothing left for which to live. James, too, died a year or two later, quickly and quietly and competently as he did everything. He had reached eighty-two, a goodly age, and had completed a life blessed with children and grandchildren, and had the satisfaction of having combated all the anxieties of two world wars and the intervening social concerns which surrounded him. I would miss his sane judgement and wise advice, but I was glad that he was now at rest with Dick. Other relatives and old friends departed, but I found that I grieved less and less because this was merely a normal pattern in which we all naturally participated. I was used to death and it was ceasing to hold me in thrall. Instead I welcomed the new members of the younger generation who were taking their place, and tried to keep up-to-date with them and their new-fangled ways. I liked young people and thought they had a tough universe with which to deal nowadays. I found they appreciated clear plain speaking which is what I had always been noted for, and we got on well together. I was amazed how every one of my young relations took the trouble to come to see me – and it was not merely the good meal which I prepared for them. We had some hearty discussions on topical items, and always parted friends in spite of often agreeing to differ.

So I built up for myself a world made-to-measure for my requirements. A world I could cope with, where anything that defeated me was discarded, much as my old car was dumped when it no longer paid for its keep. Having jettisoned the unattainable, I found a sort of contentment, and a satisfaction in discovering ways round the obstacles that ever continued to cross my path. As I entered my eighties, I had my problems; my eyes were dim, my neck ached, my knees sometimes felt as if a needle was being jabbed into them, my brain didn't seem to work properly. But still, by hook or by crook I managed to remain independent in my own little house.

1989

A NUMBER OF YEARS passed peacefully by, and to my amazement I found myself celebrating my 87th birthday. 'Enduring' would perhaps be a better word sometimes, when the needle in my knee jabbed deeper than usual, and my neck ached so much that I knew it was time to pay a visit to my friend the osteopath in Grand Avenue, to be clicked back into working order. My health was better than my temper on occasion, and some of John's French swear-words which he had shouted with vigour in the traffic jams of the Champs Elysée, came in useful in relieving my frustrations at these times. Otherwise a short sharp 'damn and blast' sufficed to clear the air and set me on my way again. I wondered afterwards what my old neighbours must have thought of my language, but it probably merely compounded their previous puzzlement at my goings on.

When I was eighty-five, I succumbed to Françoise' badgering, and found myself a 'help'. Up to that time I could not face having a stranger in the house who would relay all the gossip out to other people, and spend her time here chattering over coffee, whilst only dabbing at the surface of the cleaning. Eventually I capitulated, realising that the place was getting increasingly grubby, and probably even worse than I thought because of my gathering near-blindness. Through a series of acquaintances, I discovered Mrs. Brown who lived far enough away to have no interest in local gossip, and being recently widowed, wanted some occupation to fill her time as much as the pin-money it provided. Mrs. Brown was no oil-painting, but as well as steel plates in her hip, so she told me, she soon displayed her heart of gold. Moreover she was a hard worker, and thoroughly 'did' for me once a week.

In the garden I had to compromise between no less than four men, who each came for short periods of time when required to keep it tidy. One even brought his own motor mower which he preferred to my old push-me-pull-you, in spite of the handkerchief size of the lawns. Privately I thought it was more trouble than it was worth when I saw him struggling to unload it from his trailer. In fact, by the time he had paid for his car, there must have been precious little profit for him in his wages from me, but he seemed happy with the arrangement, so I did not quibble. Another man came with his electric hedge-cutter (how ridiculous – why not the old-fashioned kind for my minuscule privet?), a third attended to my vegetable patch, and his son came every now and then to hoe the side beds. In addition, I had a lady decorator called Flora and her girl friend Karen, who arrived with their ladders and paint pots several times a year to deal with the grubbiest corners of the house, inside or out, as their turn came round.

I was feeling very ancient and stiff by this time, no less so than Toby. Each day we sallied forth together, unless the winds off the Downs were too strong for my breathing, in which case Rose would come to take Toby round the houses. Failing her – it was usually her migraine – I would simply push him into the storm of the back garden, much against his will, for a few minutes. He did not like the wind any more than I did, and was soon yapping to be let in again. Poor old thing was very slow and dilapidated – just like his Missus. We made a good pair, tottering about together.

It was a matter of some astonishment to me that the motherless baby of 1902 had managed to survive to this extreme old age, and still going strong. I think I was born tough, and what was not inherited as familial obstinacy, was developed insidiously to counteract all the trials of my life. To realise at an early age that one's father does not want one is a shattering experience which I never found easy to absorb, especially as my elder brother, without any effort on his part, was the apple of his eye. It was probably the most hurtful thing that can happen to a child, and taught me my independence from that moment of enlightenment. If my father did not want me, so equally I could do without him, and in the end I had to do just that as he died so early in my life.

The other lesson I learnt early was due to my split existence between two households, which soon taught me not to gossip from one to the other. This was the lesson that stayed with me all my life, so that now I have become the repository of all the family secrets, because each member knows he or she can communicate their confidence without the slightest fear of betrayal. This has been something they have appreciated, and so lifted burdens of secrecy from their shoulders, but for me a fascination with their lives as well as a certain humility that they honour me with their concerns. Just as I depended on Dick with whom to share my girlhood fantasies, so in later years they found comfort in my interest.

Because my father was such a disappointment to me, I magnified the character of my brother, placing him on a pedestal far beyond his desserts. I told myself that I recognised his faults, but they were far exceeded by his achievements in my estimation. Having virtually no parents, I had to have someone of my very own to admire and show off, whom no-one else could steal from me. When John married I could have felt deprived, but fortunately Gilberte was so very different from me that I found no rival in her. She was a much more malleable character than me, though kind and tolerant, which was just what John needed to maintain his ego once the glories of war were past. She and I served different purposes in his life, Gilberte a willing cushion for his self-possession, me a strong foil for his own rock-solid personality. The three of us made a companionable triangle, equi-dependent on each other. There was deep affection too, inherited from our mother, whose portraits show a bubbling, vivacious quality under her curly fly-away hair and her wasp-waisted gowns. From her too came my indestructible perseverance – how else could she have put up with my father's pomposity for those few years of their marriage? I wished so much during my early years that I still had her by me, and later this unfulfilled yearning turned to inquisitiveness to know the roots from which I come.

Dick had gone far, in spite of her youth, towards supplying the mothering I had lost, but she had her own life to live. 'Mother' gave me a home and an upbringing, and then when she showed a will of steel to face events after 'Dad' died, I developed an enduring respect for her. Thus my role as her companion, and later her housekeeper, was wished upon me as a natural throwback to pre-war English custom. Marriage was forfeited as a result, but the strong moral pressure on me, both directly from her but also from my own conscience, to stay with her, was too strong to resist. I was a reversion to the Victorian and Edwardian order of domestic arrangements despite my longing for a wider world.

The Second World War was my saviour, as no relatively young single woman was left unemployed, but it coincided with Mother's death, so there was no question of my staying at home by then.

Now I was able to make up for lost time, and I was fortunate in that Herbert appeared at just that moment to share with me the happiest period of my life.

Those years in which I had him passed unimaginably fast, like a dream, and then I was on my own again. But not back to cold spinsterhood. The experience had enriched my being, broadened my sympathies, taught me a different, warmer sort of patience, given me love and forbearance. Made me a complete person, I like to think. Certainly they prepared me for this last portion of my life which might have soured me, recreating the Old Maid image which I had barely skimmed when Mother was alive, but now was utterly foreign to me. I was obstinate, persevering, independent; pig-headed, some would say. I created my own life, counter-acted the sorrows with tenacity tinged with irrepressible sense of humour, common sense aided by determination. Where I found I could not make close friends, I discovered serenity in tending green plants which I thought more dependable, filling my house with colour and variety. Where I needed human contact, I turned on my radio for the daily service or a talk. Somewhere around me I knew there was a Power who cared for me and would strengthen me. Unsentimental and practical, I still missed my life-long habit of church-going, but replaced it by quiet times at home with my thoughts.

The madcap irrepressible laughter of my mother re-surfaced in the long extrovert letters I wrote to all the family, putting down my thoughts just as they came tumbling out, exactly as I spoke, chattering away with colourful familiarity, in companionable exchange and picturesque language. They formed an image of my present, the result of the crucible of my experience; I hope an encouragement to my loved ones. They summed up my attitudes in their lively refusal to bow to difficulties and their disregard of the cynics by blossoming into sunny optimism.

I remember when I was at school being taught that a sacrament is an outward and visible sign of an inward and spiritual meaning. This is an apt description of my letters. My position of honorary parent has filled the void of childlessness which had so hurt me, but which had had to be stifled by activity. Now my family – 'my children' – expands annually unto the third and fourth generation, and I am well content. Life has, in the end, been filled with meaning.

POSTSCRIPT

1998

HANNAH DID NOT die for nearly a decade after she wrote this Epilogue. It was a slowly down-hill path after that, with increasing deafness, and surgery for a cataract in one eye when she was nearly ninety, which gave her a few more years of independence. She could not face the other eye being similarly dealt with, and was fortunate to receive for the rest of her life, the affectionate attentions of a near neighbour who was also a working nurse. She concentrated on "clearing her desk", quite literally, sending all her photos for safe keeping to one niece, and discussing the disposal of her goods and chattels with another who lived nearer. She made a new Will, and when she was almost ninety-five underwent gynaecological surgery for a malignancy. When she emerged from hospital she was taken into a local nursing home as a permanent resident, and was visited daily by her nurse friend as a labour of love. Rose too, who by this time was halfway through her eighties, was driven by a friend to the nursing home to see her most weeks.

One day Hannah fell, and thereafter suffered severe pain in her thigh, which was kept in check with morphia. Those of her nephews and nieces who were still able to, visited her right up to the last weeks, and several regularly wrote short chatty letters which had to be read to her as now she was almost blind and very deaf. True to character, she retained her sense of humour, and still managed to see the "funny" side of things; she only took to her bed two days before the end.

Hannah died in her ninety-seventh year. Her funeral at Brighton Crematorium was attended by her dear Françoise, who came over from Paris with her husband and her daughter on the shuttle especially. Two nieces were present, one with a daughter,

207

the other with her husband and a son. Her step-daughter, Rose, was too unwell to come, but was represented by a friend, and several other faithful friends were present including "Matron" from Harrow days. Hannah had herself chosen the hymns. One was "Rock of Ages", surely a joke on her own longevity; the other was "Abide with me" which Edith Cavell had repeated over and over again as she awaited execution in the Belgium of 1917 – a vivid memory of courage amongst many others for Hannah during the horrors of the First World War.